M000289721

The
Handbook
of
Pairs
Trading

Founded in 1807, John Wiley & Sons is the oldest independent publishing company in the United States. With offices in North America, Europe, Australia, and Asia, Wiley is globally committed to developing and marketing print and electronic products and services for our customers' professional and personal knowledge and understanding.

The Wiley Trading series features books by traders who have survived the market's ever changing temperament and have prospered—some by reinventing systems, others by getting back to basics. Whether a novice trader, professional, or somewhere in-between, these books will provide the advice and strategies needed to prosper today and well into the future.

For a list of available titles, please visit our Web site at www.Wiley Finance.com.

The Handbook of Pairs Trading

Strategies Using Equities, Options, and Futures

DOUGLAS S. EHRMAN

WILEY

John Wiley & Sons, Inc.

Copyright © 2006 by Douglas S. Ehrman. All rights reserved.

Published by John Wiley & Sons, Inc., Hoboken, New Jersey.
Published simultaneously in Canada.

No part of this publication may be reproduced, stored in a retrieval system, or transmitted
in any form or by any means, electronic, mechanical, photocopying, recording, scanning,
or otherwise, except as permitted under Section 107 or 108 of the 1976 United States
Copyright Act, without either the prior written permission of the Publisher, or authorization
through payment of the appropriate per-copy fee to the Copyright Clearance Center, Inc.,
222 Rosewood Drive, Danvers, MA 01923, (978) 750-8400, fax (978) 646-8600, or on the web
at www.copyright.com. Requests to the Publisher for permission should be addressed to the
Permissions Department, John Wiley & Sons, Inc., 111 River Street, Hoboken, NJ 07030,
(201) 748-6011, fax (201) 748-6008, or online at http://www.wiley.com/go/permissions.

Limit of Liability/Disclaimer of Warranty: While the publisher and author have used their
best efforts in preparing this book, they make no representations or warranties with respect
to the accuracy or completeness of the contents of this book and specifically disclaim any
implied warranties of merchantability or fitness for a particular purpose. No warranty may
be created or extended by sales representatives or written sales materials. The advice and
strategies contained herein may not be suitable for your situation. You should consult with a
professional where appropriate. Neither the publisher nor author shall be liable for any loss
of profit or any other commercial damages, including but not limited to special, incidental,
consequential, or other damages.

For general information on our other products and services or for technical support, please
contact our Customer Care Department within the United States at (800) 762-2974, outside
the United States at (317) 572-3993 or fax (317) 572-4002.

Wiley also publishes its books in a variety of electronic formats. Some content that appears
in print may not be available in electronic books. For more information about Wiley
products, visit our web site at www.wiley.com.

Library of Congress Cataloging-in-Publication Data:
Ehrman, Douglas S., 1976–
    The handbook of pairs trading : strategies using equities, options, and futures
/ Douglas S. Ehrman.
        p.   cm. — (Wiley trading series)
    ISBN-13 978-0-471-72707-1 (cloth)
    ISBN-10 0-471-72707-5 (cloth)
    1. Pairs trading.   2. Stocks.   I. Title.   II. Series.
    HG4661.E37   2006
    332.64'5—dc22

                                                          2005016417

Printed in the United States of America.

10 9 8 7 6 5 4 3 2 1

For the women in my life . . .

my daughter, Victoria, the answer to any father's prayers;
my wife, Veronica, without whom I would be lost; and
my mom, one of the true unsung heroes, who always keeps me going.

Contents

The Handbook of Pairs Trading

Introduction

In today's atmosphere of market uncertainty, geopolitical unrest, and a weak economic landscape, many investors find themselves still feeling the sting that was created when the bull market reversed in early 2000. The days of triple digit returns are long gone and, for many, so is a substantial percentage of the personal wealth that was created in the late 1990s. It is no wonder, therefore, that many of these same investors have sought shelter in fixed income securities, cash instruments, or in increasingly popular market-neutral strategies.

Broad exploration of one particular market-neutral strategy that has not been widely publicized but which has endured for years as a successful approach among many institutional money managers and hedge fund experts is the focus of the following pages. The strategy is called pairs trading. In simple terms, pairs trading consists of buying one stock in an industry and selling short another stock (with which it has been paired via standards to be explained later), usually in the same industry. This approach has become something of a lost or rarefied skill, but currently it is resurfacing rapidly in the mainstream.

This work is divided into five distinct parts. The first four explore the elements that make up the trading of equity pairs and the requisite skills that accompany that endeavor. The final part introduces alternative applications of the theory to alternate security types including options, futures, and currencies. This part also takes the reader step-by-step through a series of trade examples across the various asset classes to both highlight the nuances of each and solidify the reader's understanding of the theory. The discussion of each topic, equities and advanced strategies, is designed to serve a specific purpose and, in a sense, be able to stand alone. Collectively, however, this work should serve the reader as a comprehensive resource for all of the various types of pairs trading.

EQUITIES

The first four parts of this book explore pairs trading from a variety of angles, each with the goal of both illustrating the general tenets of the strategy and presenting one particular approach that the author believes to be superior to others. Toward that end, each section consists of two approaches. The first outlines the general principles that govern the strategy; this will allow those readers who wish to develop their own systems to apply the concepts as appropriate to their ultimate end. The second provides specific instructions about how to trade pairs of equities following the guidelines that the author believes are critical to portfolio optimization. It is important to acknowledge that no two traders will ever agree fully on the best way to manage a portfolio, and no one is suggesting that the methods favored in this book are final or foolproof words on the subject. What can be said with confidence is that when readers come to the end of these pages, they will not only be familiar with the concepts behind pairs trading but will also have a concrete approach from which to build their individual methodology.

Another issue that should be addressed early on is that of security type. The majority of this book focuses on trading equity pairs. The strategy can be employed with derivative instruments as well and made more complex with various detailed options strategies. These are not the focus of this work because some of the central ideas that drive pairs trading are easily lost under the vagaries of various complex derivative theories. Remaining focused on equities will provide a foundation necessary to understanding the strategy. Options theory will be added later.

A first perspective for our exploration will be a more formal definition of pairs trading:

Pairs trading: a nondirectional, relative-value investment strategy that seeks to identify two companies with similar characteristics whose equity securities are currently trading at a price relationship that is outside their historical trading range. This investment strategy entails buying the undervalued security while short-selling the overvalued security, thereby maintaining market neutrality.

This definition lays out three main areas of focus which play out as subtexts to the overall idea of pairs trading and must be considered and understood before the unified strategy will make sense: market neutrality, relative value or statistical arbitrage, and technical analysis. While there are certainly smaller topics that flow from these three main subjects, those are addressed later as each is explored individually.

In this section, a brief and topical overview of each of these focal points is considered so that the advanced reader may consider which topics he may wish to skip. The reader should keep in mind that this text is not attempting to replace other books written on market-neutral strategies, arbitrage theory, or technical analysis. The aim is to set forth simply the building blocks that go into understanding pairs trading. Many sections may be redundant for experienced traders; anyone who already understands the underlying topic of discussion may wish to skip ahead and focus on only the second part of each section where specific theory and application are discussed. Others may feel that too much of a knowledge base is assumed on the part of the author as they approach pairs trading. These readers are urged to explore other sources to expand their understanding of the underlying subject matter. The goal here is to find a middle ground that will prevent the beginner from getting lost and the experienced trader from becoming bored. As this investigation proceeds, each concept builds upon the last, with the assumption that the preceding principles have been well understood.

Market Neutrality

Market neutrality is the first of the three major features of pairs trading selected for investigation. The term *market-neutral* has come to be a quite appealing label in the past several years because many investors mistakenly take the term to mean risk free. The marketing community has fixated on the term and applied it, often inappropriately, to any methodology that could be loosely construed to reduce risk. The label does, in fact, cover a broad range of trading and investment strategies. The proliferation of so-called market-neutral products makes it important to understand the key features of market neutrality, the different ways in which they can be applied, and how they relate to pairs trading.

There are three key features to a market-neutral strategy: the combination of long and short investing, the ability to use leverage, and the inclusion of an arbitrage situation. Arbitrage is a central element of pairs trading and will be discussed in detail in Part Two, but it is important to take note of its presence. Furthermore, as leverage is not a necessary feature of either market-neutral investing or pairs trading, it will not be discussed in great detail, but should again be noted. The long/short relationship is key to pairs trading and is therefore the focus of the market-neutral discussion in Part One.

While this definition will be repeated and refined, it will be useful to state a working definition of market-neutrality that can be applied to any type of market-neutral strategy:

Market-neutral strategy: A trading strategy that derives its returns from the relationship between the performance of its long position and the performance of its short positions, regardless of whether this relationship is done on the security or portfolio level.

This definition speaks to the central idea of market neutrality: that portfolio performance is achieved through relative performance rather than through the absolute performance one would expect to find in a traditional portfolio. In a market-neutral strategy, the return on the portfolio is a function of the return differential between the securities that are held long and those that are held short. In a perfectly market-neutral portfolio, holding all other factors constant, the performance of the long portfolio and the performance of the short portfolio are perfectly explained by fluctuation in the general market. Net performance for the overall portfolio will be near zero because for every move up or down in the long portfolio, there will be an offsetting move in the opposite direction for the short portfolio. In such a case, the investor would expect to earn roughly the risk-free rate. In a managed market-neutral portfolio, however, if the manager is skilled, the investor expects the long portfolio to outperform the short portfolio in rising markets and the short to outperform the long in falling markets, thus creating a consistently positive return regardless of market conditions.

In more traditional long only strategies, managers are constrained by the client-specified benchmark, and are not permitted to maintain short positions. This long only constraint reduces managers' ability to efficiently utilize their forecasts of the relative attractiveness of all the securities in their investment universe. A typical forecasting model ranks stocks based on their expected relative return within the universe under consideration; a stock that receives a high rank is expected to outperform one that receives a lower rank. A traditional portfolio makes the assumption that this outperformance must be positive and constrains the manager based on this assumption. If the outperformance is negative, however (both stocks decline, but the higher-ranked stock declines by less), the return is still negative because the manager failed to capture the complete predictive value contained in the model. A market-neutral strategy is designed to bridge this gap and take more complete advantage of the information available. This ability to transfer this information to the portfolio enhances the return for a given level of risk. Simply put, the ability to use more information translates into a higher information ratio for market-neutral strategies.

There are several types of market neutrality, all of which will be discussed later in more detail: share neutrality, dollar neutrality, sector neutrality, and beta neutrality. Each of these has a different impact on the portfolio and relates differently to pairs trading. Understanding each and how to apply it appropriately will directly impact the portfolio construction process.

Market neutrality is perhaps the most important feature of pairs trading, and the one on which all others must be built. It is important to have a solid understanding of this concept before continuing to subsequent chapters.

Relative Value or Statistical Arbitrage

At the most basic level, arbitrage seeks to exploit an inefficiency in the market by buying a security and simultaneously selling it for a profit. While the existence of such opportunities seems somewhat fantastic in the information age, it was once possible for a select group of individuals with superior resources to capitalize on just such situations. Today, however, with a nearly unlimited level of computing power available on any desktop, simple arbitrage is mostly a thing of the past.

While certain market inefficiencies do still exist, the majority of arbitrage activity today is based on perceived or implied pricing flaws rather than on real ones. These pricing flaws are not the result of faulty or slow information, but are the result of an individual's perception that the relationship between two securities has deviated from its historical average in a statistically significant way. Relative value arbitrage, therefore, is the activity of taking offsetting positions in securities that are historically or mathematically related, but where the relationship is temporarily distorted. Over time, these relationships fluctuate around an average, moving away and then back to a mathematically determined midpoint. In terms of pairs trading, then, the most important feature of arbitrage is the convergence of these fluctuations back to their expected values.

Understanding statistical arbitrage is important to understanding pairs trading because it is essentially the same thing, or should at least be considered a form of pairs trading. Where pairs trading may be driven by either fundamental or technical information and may have almost any time horizon, statistical arbitrage is based purely on historical, statistical data that is utilized in the very short term for numerous small positions. The most significant point of differentiation is that statistical arbitrage is almost purely model and computer driven, with very little human analysis affecting any single trade. Once a statistical arbitrage model is constructed and accepted, it is fed into a computer that makes all trading decisions based on the pre-screened criteria. This often involves hundreds of trades a day, each trying to capture a very small positive price movement. This kind of trading obviously requires both very sophisticated modeling capabilities and a fairly extensive technology infrastructure.

Pairs trading has elements of both relative value and statistical arbitrage. While every pairs trader uses different criteria when selecting his stocks, all are centered around the concept of mean reversion. These managers operate under the assumption that anomalies among stock valuations may occur in the short term, but that over time these anomalies will correct or mean-revert. When one stock's price anomaly reverts back to the mean price of its group, this is known as mean reversion. Thus, within a group of stocks that trade similarly, such as within a specific industry, despite the fact that some of these stocks may underperform the group during certain periods while others will outperform, over time virtually every stock in the group will follow the average performance of the whole industry. The strategy seeks to take advantage of this phenomenon by capturing the move in stock price as a give stock moves back toward the group average. Traders seek groups of stocks with a sector, industry, or specific risk factor that are positively correlated. Over longer periods of time, these groups have relatively smooth trend lines. In the short term, however, the trend lines for the individual stocks within the group fluctuate significantly; these fluctuations can be exploited with a relative arbitrage structure.

The pairs system is essentially an arbitrage system where the trader is able to capture profits from the divergence of two correlated stocks. The market as a whole is broken into indexes, which are divided into sectors, which are made up of individual equities. The retail stocks make up the retail sector, and the trucking stocks make up the trucking sector, and so on. Obviously, the retail stocks must then follow one another in price movement. Can these stocks trade in perfect tandem with one another? The answer is no; there has to be divergence, as no two equities can trade with a perfect correlation coefficient of 1. They cannot be identical twins. They can trade very closely though, veering away occasionally to come back together once again. This divergence and convergence produces opportunities of which pairs traders may take advantage.

Pairs trading contains elements of both relative value and statistical arbitrage in that it often uses a statistical model as the initial screen for creating a relative value trade. A careful pairs trader will perform several layers of analysis on top of the model output before any pairs trades are actually executed. Clearly arbitrage theory plays a fairly central role in understanding pairs trading; it therefore receives very careful consideration later in the book.

Technical Analysis

The third central element to pairs trading that will be discussed is technical analysis. While it is possible to use fundamentals as the primary basis on which to base a pairs trading approach, the methodology favored through this book relies more heavily on a technical approach and reserves fundamental analysis as an overlay to check the logic of the original positions. It should be made quite clear to readers that this is not another book on technical analysis and that the explanations and discussions contained in these pages are offered for the sole purpose of advancing the exploration of pairs trading. Countless books have been written on technical analysis for those readers who wish to delve more deeply into the subject. While it will be necessary to cover a number of technical indicators, and relevant terms and formulas will be used when appropriate, no final authority on the subject is suggested and readers are encouraged to bring some of their own expertise to bear when considering the methods described herein.

While a fundamental analyst considers a huge amount of very subjective data, the technical analyst deals with only three pieces of data: price, trading volume, and sentiment. These are evaluated to form an opinion on the likely direction of prices over a shorter period of time. The complete analyst looks at the fundamentals to decide whether a significant movement is likely or to compare two or more companies on a longer-term scale, and employs technical analysis to determine the most propitious time to enter the market. From a pairs trading standpoint, and especially a short-term statistical arbitrage standpoint, technical analysis plays a much more important role, and, in a majority of cases, is the driving force behind trades.

Technical analysts use computers to reconstruct past market activity in an attempt to predict the likely behavior of a stock or group of stocks in the future. The underlying assumption of this technique is that patterns that can be identified in the past are likely to repeat themselves in the future. System traders seek to identify a group of quantifiable indicators that, when used together, have a high predictive value for stock behavior. The process of analyzing which indicators are most effective when used in tandem is called *optimization*. This process seeks to build a model that has the greatest ability to both predict profits and avoid losses. The inherent difficulty, however, with such an approach, is that there is not guarantee that past behavior will be repeated. This is a significant risk that faces the pairs trader and is know as *model risk*; a major flaw in a trading model can result in a complete breakdown in the system and have significant negative results.

Delving more deeply into technical analysis later in this book requires covering some of the major indicators that are most helpful in analyzing pairs of stocks. Some of the very basic principles that are used when building a trading model are covered. It is important to note that the vast majority of these "black box" models, whether they are being used as preliminary screening tools or feeding complex statistical arbitrage systems, are proprietary. How some of these models are constructed is briefly explored, but since specific construction usually requires the assistance of both a mathematician and a skilled programmer, no model is endorsed as most successful, nor are exact details presented for building one.

There are, however, ways in which an individual can benefit from the use of proprietary models. By opening a managed account with a skilled manager, an investor can get the benefits not only of that manager's model but also of his experience. In other cases, it is possible to receive the output of a model, along with a detailed explanation of what the model does, without needing to receive the actual proprietary structure of the model's construction. While this may seem inadequate to some readers, many of the most successful traders on the street use the services of other traders and managers as a part of their investment process.

Unified Pairs Trading Theory

After exploring each of the three major components of pairs trading, it is necessary to spend a little time putting these components together. Most of the interrelations between each section will be fairly clear, but only after each has been explored will some of the big picture issues that affect pairs trading become clear. Part Four examines the risks involved with the strategy and how to manage them, various approaches to pairs trading that can be taken, and finally the methodology the author believes to be superior to the rest.

When readers come to the end of this book, they should understand the major components of the strategy, various approaches to trading pairs, the methodology that is being recommended, and, most importantly, how to integrate pairs trading into their investment or trading style.

ADVANCED STRATEGIES

The final part of this book explores the application of the Unified Pairs Trading Theory to alternate asset classes and securities types. While pairs trading is easiest to understand when considering equities, the addition of options, futures, and currencies gives a trader an expanded collection of tools by which to manage his portfolio. Readers are again cautioned to keep in mind that this book is not attempting to be a comprehensive tool for understanding option theory, futures trading or the currency markets. The aim is to set forth simply the building blocks that go into understanding pairs trading. Many sections may be redundant for experienced traders; anyone who understands the underlying topic of discussion may wish to skip ahead and focus on only the second part of each section where specific theory and application are discussed. Others may feel that too much of a knowledge base is assumed on the part of the author as they approach pairs trading. These readers are urged to explore other sources of reference to expand their understanding of the underlying subject matter. The goal here, again, is to find a middle ground that will prevent the beginner from getting lost and the experienced trader from becoming bored. As this investigation proceeds, each concept builds upon the last with the assumption that the preceding principles have been well understood. It is assumed that the reader has a working understanding of equity pairs trading as each new security type is introduced.

Options

Through the use of options, a pairs, trader is able to greatly expand both the number of approaches and the tools available in the construction of a trade or an entire portfolio. In some cases, the trader may wish to substitute options for equities when doing so provides a distinct advantage, while in other cases, options may be used as an overlay to manage risk or adjust the complexion of a particular trade. The addition of an options strategy will be more or less complex and thus difficult, depending on the approach employed, but will always involve greater skill, experience, and care than a straight equity trade.

As a basis to begin our exploration of options theory as it applies to pairs trading, it will be helpful to begin with a working definition of an options contract:

Option: The right, but not the obligation, to buy or sell a stock (or other security) for a specified price, on or before a specific date. Intrinsic value and time value are two of the main determinants of an option's price and are driven by both the price and volatility of the underlying stock or security.

From this definition, it should become immediately evident that when constructing a matched equity pair using options, one must consider the factors that drive the associated options as well as the elements of the underlying pair. There are four key factors when considering an option, each of which must be assessed prior to executing a trade: relative value, timing, volatility, and changes in the relationship between the option and the underlying stock. Each of these affects how the option is priced as well as how the option is likely to react to various changes in the underlying stock and in the general market.

While all of these four key factors are explored in detail, it is helpful to begin with a basic understanding of each before proceeding. It should be noted that in aiming for clarity, some of the formal jargon of the options markets has been purposely omitted. This language is introduced in Part Five but would do little to advance this preliminary discussion and can be confusing to the uninitiated.

Relative Value   While this term has many meanings that appear throughout this book, in the case of options it refers to the strike price of the option contract relative to the price of the underlying stock. Options are classified into three groups of relative value that carry the following definitions:

At-the-money (ATM): At-the-money means that the strike price of the option is the same as the market price of the underlying stock. In the case of ATM options, the price of the options contract represents time premium only and is neutral relative to the underlying stock.

In-the-money (ITM): In-the-money means that the option is carrying a degree of intrinsic value. For call options, this means that the strike price of the option is below the current market price of the underlying stock. If the option were to be exercised (the stock called and purchased at the strike price), an automatic profit could be generated by immediately selling the newly purchased shares at the higher market price. For put options, ITM options carry a strike price that is above the current market value of the underlying stock. If the option were to be exercised (the stock put and sold at the strike price), an automatic profit could be generated by purchasing shares at the lower market price and reselling them at the higher strike price.

Out-of-the-money (OTM): Out-of-the-money means that the option is carrying no intrinsic value (time premium only) and would result in an immediate loss if exercised. For call options, this means that the strike price of the option is above the current market price of the underlying stock. If the option were exercised (the stock called and purchased at the strike price), an automatic loss would be generated because the stock was purchased at a price above that which is now available in the market. The reverse mechanics apply to put options.

Timing   Timing, when referring to an options-based pairs trade, refers to both the appropriate expiration date of the option and the time premium built into the price of the option. Traders must consider the expected time horizon of the trade and select their options carefully. Options that carry a lower time premium, that is less likely to be eroded during the life of the trade, are likely to produce greater returns than those with higher time premiums if all other factors are held constant. While time premium serves as an indication of the underlying volatility of the options being considered (higher time premium indicates higher volatility), the net effect of time premium must be considered.

Selecting the appropriate expiration month is equally important and directly tied to time premium. Options contracts that have shorter time until expiration will always carry a lower time premium than those with longer expirations. It is important to allow sufficient time for the expected mean reversion to occur, but a trader does not want to overpay for additional time premium that is not needed. If an option expires too quickly, the desired mean reversion process may not be complete. If an option's expiration is too distant, however, the added expense may significantly affect the return the trade generates. It should be evident that of the two choices, selecting options that carry unneeded time until expiration is preferable, as this choice still allows the trade to successfully run its course, but careful analysis should be performed to determine what duration is reasonable.

Volatility   Volatility is central to all types of options trading and is of particular importance in the context of options-based pairs trading. The volatility of an underlying security is one of the critical factors in determining an options price; generally, the lower the volatility of the underlying stock, the lower the time premium that will be built into the price of any associated options contracts. This relationship exists because a lower volatility underlying the stock provides less return potential and thus a lower price. In another sense, options are priced so that return potential is similar; an option based on a stock that is likely to move only a few percentage points before expiration is priced lower so that the return, based on the price of the option, is similar to that of a more expensive option on a stock expected to move more significantly.

When constructing a pairs trade, a trader not only must consider the volatility of each of the stocks being analyzed for pairing, as this will affect time premium and options price, but also must consider the relative volatilities of the two stocks. Similar to beta neutrality, this can have a significant impact on the degree to which systematic risk is controlled in a given trade. In certain cases, as will be discussed later, pairing the options of securities with mismatched volatilities can yield successful results. In either case, prudent traders do well to be aware of the volatilities of the stocks they are analyzing in order to avoid taking on unwanted risk.

Changes in the Option-to-Stock Relationship   In addition to considering the relationship of an options contract to its underlying security, a trader must also consider how that relationship changes. Over the expected duration of a given trade, changes in this relationship can have a significant impact on the success of the trade. For example, if during the duration of a given trade the volatilities of the two stocks decrease significantly, this will likely cause the relationship between an option's price and the price of the underlying stock to change. In this case, one would expect the option to decrease in price more rapidly than initially expected because the market will no longer require the buyer of the option to pay as much time premium for a contract on the now less volatile underlying stock; the relationship between an option and its underlying stock changes over time and must be factored in when considering initiating a trade.

The rate at which this relationship changes is quantified in options theory and referred to as gamma, one of three relationships labeled with Greek letters; along with vega, these four statistics are commonly referred to as "the Greeks." Gamma is the first derivative, or the rate of change of delta, the relationship between the price of an option and the price of its underlying security. The definitions are:

Theta: The rate of time decay of a given option.

Delta: The degree of change in an option's price based on a change in the price of the underlying security.

Gamma: The rate of change of delta.

Vega: The relationship between the price of an option and the implied volatility of that option.

The Greeks are formally defined and discussed in the options chapters in Part Five, as is their relationship to pairs trading. While they are considered some of the most subtle and complex material in options theory, they are very useful in pairs trading and need to be adequately addressed.

Futures and Currencies

Futures contracts are similar to options contracts but, much as the name implies, there is no option feature; upon expiration, a futures contract is executed either for cash or for physical delivery. Futures contracts are most commonly associated with commodities, but the futures markets for financial indexes, bonds, and currencies are among the most liquid in the United States. Much of this discussion is focused on commodity futures, although the differences are explored later. There are a few unique attributes that distinguish futures pairs trades from those is the equity or option markets, but most of the mechanics are very similar. There are three major features that distinguish a futures pairs trade: Their dependence of extrinsic events, the inclusion of natural correlations, and the speed with which they change.

Extrinsic Events Climatic, geopolitical, and government forces tend to have a more direct and therefore significant impact on the prices of commodities. As a result, futures prices are highly dependent on the same factors: A drought may send corn prices soaring, a war in Iraq may drive up gasoline prices, and a new protective tariff on cotton may change the demand structure and therefore the price of the associated futures contract. In each of these cases, an outside force is responsible for pushing the price of a commodity in a much more direct and uncontrollable way than a news event in the stock market. While the announcement that Intel is releasing a new, faster processor can be predicted and planned for, a drought that cuts soy output is much more difficult to predict.

The effect of these outside forces on pairs trading in the commodity markets is critical because it violates many of the principles already discussed. When a trader observes a significant divergence in two correlated commodities that are statistically likely to mean-revert, an understanding of the external factors affecting the trade is critical. The divergence may be caused by an extrinsic event that will not sway under the pressure of statistical analysis; a two standard deviation divergence implying a 97 percent chance of mean reversion cannot make it rain. Furthermore, there are often conflicting forces, the effects of which are difficult to determine. For example, while a war may push gas prices up, consumer preference for hybrid or diesel engines may help to keep prices down. Predicting the power of these individual trends and how they interact can be a serious challenge.

Natural Correlation   Throughout the commodity universe there are many natural correlations that can affect how a pairs trader approaches the market. Soybeans relative to soy meal relative to soy oil is one such example, known as the "soy crush." Many of these spreads have been traded by futures traders forever, which aids in the probability that they can continue to be successful (the difference between spread trading and pairs trading will be discussed later). While it can be argued that two retailers share a type of natural correlation and both are affected by general trends in consumer spending, their products are neither interchangeable nor dependent on the other. A rise in soybean prices must result in an increase in soy oil prices, as one is derived from the other. While paradigm shifts may occasionally occur (such as the development of a cheaper refining process), these will only serve to adjust rather sever the relationship. In the example of the retailers, by contrast, one may miss earnings or go out of business without destroying the other.

The effect of natural correlation on pairs trading is that while in many cases the trader may be more confident that a particular trade will ultimately mean-revert, the corresponding moves may be very small and difficult to capture. A relative-value strategy is dependent on the trader's ability not only to identify but also to capture the divergence and mean-reversion movement. In stable markets, certain opportunities may be lost because there is insufficient volatility in the relationship between the two related commodities to make a trade profitable.

Speed   The final significant difference between a commodity futures pairs trade and one in the equity or options markets is that of speed. This can also be expressed as a difference in the expected duration of any given trade. The futures markets employ large degrees of margin. The result of highly leveraged positions is that small moves in a trade result in very significant changes in the dollar value of the trade. While options are also built on margin, the denominations tend to be smaller and the delta measure, rarely 1, ensures that small moves do not impact the dollar value of a trade as quickly. A single point move in certain futures trades can result in tens of thousands of dollars gained or lost very quickly. The result is that a commodity futures pairs trader may be in and out of the market very quickly, picking up and losing fractional points in each trade toward the end of net profit. This often means that analysis must be purely techni-cal and that execution becomes of supreme importance.

Currencies   Currencies are a specialized form of futures contract that trade globally and are highly liquid. These are the only pairs relationships that are tracked and reported as pairs (exchange rates). The result of such high visibility is that these pairs tend to offer a plethora of resources and opinions as to their likely behavior. They are more deeply influenced by macroeconomic events than any other security type and, as such, require a degree of awareness that may be troubling to beginning traders. They are presented here in an effort to be thorough, but the combination of the depth of information available and the nuance associated with successful trade execution makes it unlikely that significant advantage can be gained from their exploration in this context.

Trade Examples

The final chapter of this book examines a number of trades spanning se-curity type, approach (technical, fundamental, and blended), and success from start to finish. This chapter can serve as a layman's step-by-step guide on how to initiate a pairs trade from a variety of perspectives, how to manage the trade, and how to exit the trade. It is intended to reinforce the principles that have been explored before it and to allow the reader a glimpse into the daily activity of a pairs trader. From this material the reader will be able to get a feel for which style of pairs trading is most ap-propriate for his own level of experience, time availability, and dedication.

PART ONE

The Market-Neutral Element

When you bet on a sure thing—hedge!
—Robert Half

CHAPTER 1

Pairs Trading: A Brief History

B efore beginning a formal investigation into pairs trading, putting the strategy into a historical context may be of some interest to the reader. Pairs trading and market-neutral strategies alike are not new. They have been around in one form or another since the beginning of listed markets and have been studied and used by some of history's most notable traders. The hedge fund industry, however, has given a new face to these strategies as well as the specific vehicle needed to demonstrate their successes and failures. Prior to the hedge fund boom, these strategies were found folded into the portfolios of high-net-worth individuals and institutional traders who had the ability and resources needed to make them work. They were rarely differentiated by their specific characteristics, but rather represented collections of trades within a larger framework.

The explosion in the hedge fund industry meant that these strategies now had a place to stand alone. This produced two distinct results. First, as each strategy formed the foundation of a given fund, that strategy could be analyzed without the background noise of other trading techniques. The result of this shift was that fundamental analysts, technicians, and statisticians could each apply their own style of reasoning to determine whether a given strategy was sound and repeatable. In other words, for the first time, the scientific method could be applied to these methodologies and the results standardized in a format that was widely understood. Standardization is often the precursor of proliferation and, as more traders became interested in these new strategies, an increasing number of them began to appear.

The second result of the hedge fund boom was that as more traders began to study these strategies, using more advanced tools and technologies, the strategies themselves began to be improved and refined. Strategies that began as a collection of "back-of-the-envelope" analyses evolved into comprehensive, computer-driven systems capable of accounting for the results of millions of calculations per second. In addition to the funds themselves, various ancillary services became increasingly advanced. Charting, price and fundamental data, and trade execution systems all evolved to meet the changing needs of hedge fund managers. The investment industry was experiencing huge growth and inflows of capital; hedge funds were equal participants.

THE GROWTH OF HEDGE FUND INVESTING

If one disregards the specific strategy employed within the market-neutral and hedge fund universe, it is evident that during the past decade or so assets have flooded into the hedge fund market and created a significant market segment. In 1990, there were approximately 200 hedge funds in existence that managed roughly $20 billion. By 1999, those figures had risen to include almost 3,500 different hedge funds managing in excess of $500 billion. By 2005, the estimate has again risen to include approximately 8,000 different hedge funds managing in excess of $1 trillion. While it does not further our understanding of market-neutral strategies generally, there are some important insights that can be drawn by considering some of the reasons for this explosive proliferation.

The first reason, and probably most significant in terms of the last several years, is that hedge funds provide an alternative source of investment return. The fact that market-neutral strategies in particular have a very low correlation to traditional investment portfolios makes them particularly attractive as a diversification tool. Through diversification, investors are able to improve their overall risk-adjusted return profile.

In addition to the diversification benefit, there have been huge opportunities within the hedge fund market in a variety of ways. Skilled managers have been able to take advantage of the continuing expansion and ongoing developments within the capital market to profit from pricing inefficiencies. Furthermore, with the decreased expense and increased access to information technology, skilled and talented managers are not constrained by infrastructure issues and are able to attract investment capital based purely on their ability. Because hedge fund management offers a better revenue flow for a manager, many of the most talented have left large, conservative firms with less interest in hedge funds to launch their own successful funds; investment capital has followed them.

The final major reason for the mass expansion of the hedge fund world during the last decade—and continuing even today—is that through the 1990s, in the biggest bull market in history, large amounts of personal wealth were created. Hedge funds have consistently turned in impressive performance results and, coupled with the high levels of investment wealth, have attracted allocation from astute investors.

As the hedge fund universe continues to grow, the range of investors who consider making allocations to them grows as well. Once dominated almost exclusively by high-net-worth investors, institutional investors now have channeled a great deal of capital into hedge funds as well. While the individual is still the predominant hedge fund investor, the amount of capital that this segment of the investment industry commands from elsewhere has grown as the industry continues to gain in popularity and acceptance. While currently peripheral, in the future this growth may affect both the constitution and regulations of the hedge fund industry.

ONE HUNDRED YEARS

As was previously mentioned, pairs trading and other market-neutral strategies have been around since the organization of listed markets. Jesse Livermore, perhaps the most famous trader of all time, is considered to have been the first pairs trader and, in fact, used certain principles of pairs trading in all of his analyses:

> *Tandem Trading, the use of sister stocks, was one of the great secrets of Livermore's trading techniques and remains just as valid today as it did in years gone by. This technique is an essential element in both Top Down Trading and in the maintenance of the trade after it has been completed. Livermore never looked at a single stock in a vacuum—rather, he looked at the two top stocks in an Industry Group and did his analysis on both stocks.*[*]

In this explanation of Livermore's trading style, monitoring "sister stocks," or two similar stocks in the same industry, was done to help confirm the analysis of either. Because Livermore made the assumption that trends

---

[*]Richard Smitten, *Trade Like Jesse Livermore* (Hoboken, NJ: John Wiley & Sons, 2005), 43–43.

within an industry would hold for the few largest issues within that industry, if the top stocks did in fact move in tandem, then he was comfortable declaring that a legitimate trend had been identified. Within this context, he was using tandem trading for directional trading that tended to be longer term. Livermore, also know as the "boy plunger," was famous for his ability to spot a long-term trend and ride it for significant profits.

Over the course of hundreds or thousands of tandem trades, it is not difficult to see how Livermore would have developed a feel for the regular fluctuations that occur between pairs of stocks. While primarily interested in the study of long-term trends, the inclusion of "sister stock" considerations in his analysis led to Livermore's reputation as the original pairs trader. If we accept this as the origin of pairs trading, the strategy on which the remainder of this book focuses has roughly one hundred years of history upon which to build. While the tools and technology that support the strategy have advanced immeasurably in that period, the principles at the core of the theory have, in fact, changed very little.

THE FUTURE

The future of the hedge fund industry, and market-neutral strategies with it, is a subject of increasingly heated debate. Hedge funds represent one of the few remaining unregulated investment vehicles available to the general public and, as a result, come under a level of scrutiny by the mass media that is missing from more traditional asset classes. Because most managers are not required to register with the Securities and Exchange Commission (SEC), a fact likely to change in the near future, the press seems to find particular pleasure in writing about those funds and managers who either behave dishonestly or meet with disaster. Because hedge funds have historically been limited to wealthy investors and have yet to make their way fully into the mainstream, another fact likely to change in the near future, stories of misconduct served as sensational material for news stories that were easily taken out of context.

The most famous story of hedge fund malfeasance is that of Long Term Capital Management (LTCM), which nearly brought the entire infrastructure of the financial world down in the late 1990s. LTCM, which employed both Wall Street and academia's elite, muscled its way into hugely overextended positions and forced its creditors to ignore the most basic of safeguards. When it became evident that many of their trades could not be salvaged and that billions of dollars would be needed to cover their losses, the chairman of the New York Federal Reserve Bank, in consultation with the heads of the largest investment banks on Wall Street, was forced to devise a plan to protect some of the oldest financial centers in the United States. While this is a gross oversimplification of a truly fascinating story, it serves as an example of a single story that has set the tone for the way much of the public views hedge funds.

The result of this type of media attention is that a plethora of myths exist about hedge funds: They are unsafe, they take unnecessary risk, and their managers are not trustworthy. In truth, much like other types of investments, hedge funds span the risk spectrum and employ the honest and dishonest alike. Some are quite conservative, following fundamental data on global macroeconomic trends, while others take significant risks, day-trading volatile futures contracts. The only real distinction between a hedge fund and a mutual fund is that a hedge fund has the ability to use leverage and sell short. The term *hedge funds* comes from the activity of selling short to "hedge" the risks of long-only portfolios; the ironic truth is that hedge funds were originally conceived to be more conservative than mutual funds.

In order to understand the likely future of the hedge fund industry, it will be useful to briefly consider the history of the mutual fund industry. Many individuals, the author included, believe that hedge funds will follow essentially the same path as mutual funds from the unregulated Wild West of the investment community to a staple found in any typical investment portfolio. The first mutual fund was created on March 21, 1924, when three Boston securities executives pooled their money; it was called the Massachusetts Investors Trust. (The first example of a pooled investment fund dates back to 1893 and was created for the faculty and staff of Harvard University.) The Massachusetts Investors Trust was launched with three shareholders and $50,000 in assets and grew to nearly $400,000 and 200 shareholders. Today, there are over 10,000 individual mutual funds with over $7 trillion in assets and approximately 83 million individual investors.

The stock market crash of 1929 slowed the growth of mutual funds and inspired Congress to pass the Securities Act of 1933 and the Securities Exchange Act of 1934. These laws require that a fund be registered with the SEC and provide prospective investors with a prospectus. The SEC helped create the Investment Company Act of 1940 that provides the guidelines that all funds must comply with today. This proliferation of regulation was a direct response to the decreased level of confidence evidenced in the stock market. The government felt that it needed to give investors a renewed sense of security to help encourage stock market participation at a time when confidence was at all-time lows.

With renewed confidence in the stock market, mutual funds began to grow steadily and by the end of the 1960s there were around 270 funds with $48 billion in assets. In 1976, John C. Bogle opened the first retail index fund, called the First Index Investment Trust. It is now called the Vanguard 500 Index fund and in November 2000 it became the largest mutual fund ever, with $100 billion in assets. The two largest contributors to mutual fund growth were the Employee Retirement Income Security Act (ERISA) of 1974, specifically clause 401(k), and the Individual Retirement Account (IRA) provisions made in 1981, allowing individuals (including those already in corporate pension plans) to contribute $2,000 a year. Each of these factors pushed individuals who previously considered their pensions to be their primary source of retirement income to turn to the stock market; many, if not most, of these individuals invested in mutual funds as a source of professional, yet accessible, money management. As this trend continued and mutual fund assets ballooned, technology was forced to keep pace. Today, these investors can change their investment allocation daily through online account management, can track their exact positions, and can even trade their own accounts through online brokerage services. Stock market participation is at an all-time high, and many investors are beginning to look for alternative approaches and vehicles by which to get ahead in sometimes confusing market conditions. Enter the hedge fund.

The stage has been set for the proliferation of hedge funds to follow a similar path to that just described for mutual funds. Accounting scandals, the Enron debacle, and the crusades of Eliot Spitzer coupled with the recent burst of the market bubble have all shaken investor confidence in the stock market. If history repeats, the government will step in, increase regulations, and seek to restore some of the lost confidence by establishing more rule of law. This process has already begun and will likely play out over the next few years until hedge funds become a part of the regulated mainstream.

The process is likely to be gradual, and one of the issues currently being debated is whether all hedge funds will be regulated under the same set of guidelines. The SEC voted in 2004 to require hedge funds to register by February 2006, concerned it needed to keep tabs on the freewheeling capital pools that once marketed exclusively to the rich but increasingly target less affluent investors. The Commodity Futures Trading Commission (CFTC) is currently attempting to come to an agreement with the SEC regarding registering hedge funds that invest in commodities. The CFTC does not want some of its hedge fund registrants to have to register with the SEC. Commodity pools collect investor contributions to trade in futures contracts and commodity options as well as other financial instruments. According to the CFTC, there are about 3,500 commodity pools with assets of more than $600 billion.

The debate is on, but both sides remain optimistic that a resolution will be reached. The SEC could potentially mandate that hedge funds dealing in commodities have to register with them, but spokespeople for the CFTC argue that the stringent guidelines set by the SEC are geared toward mutual funds and don't necessarily make sense for hedge funds. As of this writing, the SEC and the CFTC have not come to an agreement, but an announcement was due to be made in 2005.

This is but one of the issues currently being addressed by various regulatory bodies with regard to the hedge fund industry. Despite the lack of resolution, this debate represents a clear sign that the industry is changing and moving to a more conventional structure. The likely result of this paradigm shift is that within the next several years, hedge fund investing will not be limited to sophisticated, high-net-worth individuals who are thought to be more able to absorb the inherent risks of such an investment. Pension and 401(k) plans will likely begin to carry certain hedge fund election options and the Wild West will again be tamed.

One final piece of evidence that a change has already begun to occur is the introduction of fund-of-fund mutual funds that invest exclusively in hedge funds. These funds circumvent the typical long-only provisions of a mutual fund by owning long positions in hedge fund shares. They diversify risk by investing in a number of different funds and give less affluent investors the ability to participate in the returns of multiple hedge funds with a far lower threshold for participation. There are slightly more stringent requirements for the hedge fund managers that participate in such funds—they must be Registered Investment Advisors (RIA) and are required to report a net asset value (NAV) of their shares on a daily basis—but generally they provide a conduit to the hedge fund universe that was previously unavailable to an average investor.

The rapid acceptance and growth of such funds provides quantifiable proof that there is an increasing level of interest among the general public to participate in hedge funds. While there is significant and reasonable resistance by hedge fund managers, many of whom left more traditional investment firms to avoid the irritation and expense created by comprehensive regulation, industry-wide changes are inevitable. The transition will be slow and painful for many but should ultimately leave the industry in a better position to face the challenges of the future.

CHAPTER 2

Market Neutrality

M arket neutrality is the first of the three major features of pairs trading investigated here. The term *market-neutral* has come to be a quite appealing moniker in the last several years and can refer to a wide variety of strategies. Many investors mistake the term to mean risk-free; this misconception has been heavily capitalized on by those marketing these types of products, often applying it to anything than can be loosely considered to reduce market exposure or systematic risk. With the proliferation of so-called market-neutral products flooding the market, it is important to understand the key features, the different ways in which they can be applied, and how they relate to pairs trading.

A market-neutral strategy has three key features: the combination of long and short investing, the ability to use leverage, and the inclusion of an arbitrage situation. It is impossible to totally separate a discussion of market neutrality from a discussion of arbitrage, because relative value is the driving force behind all market-neutral strategies. In this section, however, the arbitrage discussion will be kept very informal and the more formal examination will be saved for Part Two. Instead, the exploration here will focus on the combination of long and short positions (leverage is not a necessary feature of either market-neutral investing or pairs trading, so it will not be discussed in great detail). The long/short relationship is the key aspect of pairs trading.

A broad definition that applies to all market-neutral strategies is as follows:

Market-neutral strategy: A trading strategy that derives its returns from the relationship between the performance of its long positions

and the performance of its short positions, regardless of whether this
relationship functions on the security or portfolio level.

This definition makes apparent the derivation of the idea of market
neutrality; portfolio performance is driven by relative performance
rather than by the absolute performance manifest in a traditional long-
only portfolio. In a market-neutral strategy, the return on the portfolio
is a function of the return differential between the securities that are
held long and those that are held short. As the market appreciates, both
the long and short positions appreciate in value, so the overall portfolio
value remains constant. Similarly, if the market declines, both the long
and short positions will decline in value. If the change in value of the
long positions equals that of the short positions, the value added from
equity selection will be zero, and the investor will earn close to the prevailing risk-free rate. If a manager has skill—which translates into the
long securities having a higher return than the short securities—investors will enjoy a consistently positive return regardless of the overall market return.

In more traditional long-only strategies, a manager is constrained by
the client-specified benchmark and is not permitted to maintain short positions. This long-only constraint reduces the ability of the manager to efficiently utilize his forecasts of the relative attractiveness of all the
securities in his investment universe. Suppose, for example, that a manager expects a large performance differential between two stocks in the
same industry—the first is expected to have a higher-than-average return
and the second to have a lower-than-average return. In a traditional strategy, the manager would exploit this information by buying the stock with
the higher expected alpha.* However, he could not effectively exploit the
information about the stock with the lower expected alpha. In a market-
neutral strategy, the manager could take a long position in a high alpha security and a short position in a low alpha security, thereby using all the
available information. This ability to "transfer" information to the portfolio enhances the return for a given level of risk. The ability to use more information translates into a higher information ratio for market-neutral
strategies.

---

*Alpha is defined as the portion of a stock's performance that is attributable to that
stock only having discounted the effect of movements in the general market.

TYPES OF MARKET NEUTRALITY

There are several types of neutrality, each of which has a different impact on the portfolio and relates differently to pairs trading. Understanding each and how to apply it appropriately will directly impact the portfolio construction process.

Share Neutrality

Share neutrality refers to balancing a trade with an equal number of long shares and short shares. This is a very uncommon approach because in terms of relationship investing, the share price of either security is somewhat irrelevant. While it is usually a good idea to trade in similarly priced securities, because it is unlikely that the two securities in question will be priced identically, share neutrality results in a disproportionate amount of exposure between the two legs of the trade. This explanation is not intended as a guideline for market-neutral investing but is included to answer a question about which many people express curiosity.

Share neutrality is much more frequently found in the portfolio of spread traders. While this subject is addressed in more detail later, it is useful to proceed with a basic understanding of the differences between pairs trading and spread trading. A spread is defined as the price difference between two stocks: price of stock A minus price of stock B. A spread trader will either buy ("go long") the spread, assuming it will get larger, or will sell ("go short") the spread, assuming it will become smaller. The result in either case is a share-neutral position, as one share of each stock is needed to own one spread of stock A and stock B. On the surface, this appears to be very similar to pairs trading because performance is driven, in a sense, by the relative performance of the two stocks. The difference, however, comes from the fact that there is a disproportionate dollar exposure to either the long or short side of the trade. If prevailing market conditions drive the trade away from the side with larger exposure, in spite of the fact that the trader's analysis was correct, the trade may still lose money.

Dollar Neutrality

Dollar neutrality is the most common type of market neutrality and is usually considered a requirement for market-neutral investing in equity securities. Dollar neutrality refers to buying equal amounts of long and short investments so that the dollar risk is equal on each side of the portfolio. By employing dollar neutrality in a market-neutral strategy, an investor ensures that his net dollar exposure to market swings is zero.

As an illustration, assume that all price relationships in the market are fixed; in other words, if the market goes up by 3 percent, the price of every security will also go up by the same 3 percent. Under such conditions, if one were to make a dollar-neutral investment, the net return on any trade would be zero because the dollar exposure to the long side of the market is equal to the dollar exposure to the short side of the market. Both sides of the trade move in tandem, never varying from the fixed price relationship at the time of the trade.

This example helps to explicate the relationship nature of market-neutral investing. Price relationships within the market are not fixed and are, in fact, very dynamic. In essence, therefore, when one makes a dollar-neutral investment, one is betting that the long side of the investment will perform better than the short side, regardless of the overall market direction. The rationale of dollar-neutral investing is elimination of the risk that, in the case of the price relationship remaining constant, a profit or loss could be generated anyway. Obviously, if a profit were generated, an investor would not be disappointed, but market-neutral investing seeks to eliminate or reduce the effects of general market fluctuations on the performance of a portfolio. The underlying premise of this type of strategy is that it is more difficult to accurately predict the direction of the general market than it is to predict the relative performance of related groups of securities.

Spreads versus Pairs   In order to demonstrate the importance of the differences between a spread trade (share neutral) and a pairs trade (dollar neutral), consider the following comparison of a spread trade relative to a corresponding pairs trade using two stocks:

Stock A, trading at $20/share, and Stock B, trading at $10/share.

Spread Trade

Long 100 shares of stock A: $2,000

Short 100 shares of stock B: $1,000

Net debit: $10/share ($1,000)

This is a hedged, bullish position.

Pairs Trade

Long 100 shares of stock A: $2,000

Short 200 shares of stock B: $2,000

Net credit/Debit: $0

This is a true market-neutral position.

Scenario 1: Market rises an equal percentage for all stocks (50 percent).

Stock A: $30
Stock B: $15

Scenario 2: Market falls an equal percentage for all stocks (50 percent).

Stock A: $10
Stock B: $5

The two things that should become immediately apparent in this example are that in a bull market (scenario 1) the spread trade will be profitable, and that in either case, the pairs trade will be flat. What should be noted is that in scenario 2, the spread trade will lose money in spite of the fact that the two stocks change by an equal percentage. In both scenarios, the specifics of the stock had no effect on the price; the entire move is explained by market fluctuations. The belief, correct or not, that stock A is a superior stock to stock B has not played out, but in scenario 2, the trade still lost money. In short, a spread trade is a market bet with a hedge feature built in, while a pairs trade is a market-neutral position. The central assumption behind pairs trading is that it is a far more straightforward process to predict the relative performance of two stocks than it is to predict the direction of the general market. In order to allow this assumption the chance to be successful, the trade must be executed as market-neutral to avoid the potential that an instance like scenario 2 will cause the trade to lose money without any difference in relative performance.

An alternate way to consider this concept is to assume that these two scenarios were instances of both stocks moving by equal dollar amounts. In either case, the spread will appear to be flat when in reality such cases represent a difference in relative performance. For example, if both stocks were to drop by $5, the spread trade would remain flat despite the fact that stock A had outperformed stock B (stock A loses 25 percent, while stock B loses 50 percent). This is the relative performance that a pairs trade is designed to capture, but it is only realized when the trade is executed as dollar-neutral.

Sector Neutrality

Sector neutrality has a special meaning in terms of a market-neutral strategy; in a traditional long-only portfolio, sector neutrality means balancing a portfolio along the lines of a benchmark. In other words, one sets up the portfolio in such a way that exposure to a given sector does not explain the performance differential between the portfolio and the benchmark. In a market-neutral strategy, sector neutrality means that portfolios are long/short balanced within each sector of the market to insulate the overall portfolio against the possibility that one sector will perform very well while another performs poorly. Being sector neutral avoids the risk of market swings affecting some industries or sectors differently from others—thus losing money when long a stock in a sector that suddenly plunges and short another in a sector that stays flat or rises.

This type of neutrality is of greater concern when one is following a long/short equity strategy in which a basket of long stocks is matched against a basket of short stocks. In a pairs trading strategy, because every pair is matched on a case-by-case basis, there may be instances in which sector neutrality is not followed. A pair that is not sector neutral, also known as a cross-sector trade, may find its way into a pairs portfolio depending on the methodology used for portfolio construction. For example, a portfolio that is constructed using fundamentals as the primary selection criteria is far less likely to include a cross-sector pair than a portfolio that is technically driven in its selection criteria.

Beta Neutrality

Beta neutrality refers to balancing the beta of the long side of the portfolio against the beta of the short side of the portfolio. Beta is the measurement of a stock's volatility relative to the market. A stock with a beta of 1 moves historically in sync with the market, while a stock with a higher beta tends to be more volatile than the market and a stock with a lower beta can be expected to rise and fall more slowly than the market. Beta neutrality, therefore, refers to the practice of matching the beta of the long portfolio with the beta of the short portfolio to ensure that market swings affect each portfolio in a similar way.

In a long/short equity strategy, this practice does require some attention, but if each portfolio is sufficiently large, the beta of any individual stock is somewhat muted by the group. In a pairs trading situation, matching betas can become a crucial part of the portfolio construction process because the success of each trade may depend on this step. If a pair has a net positive beta, the pair will, in essence, have greater long exposure and be dependent on positive market direction to be successful. Reciprocally, a pair with a negative beta will have its success tied to negative market direction. It is important to note that when matching two stocks it is virtually impossible to achieve total beta neutrality. The goal, however, is not to screen stocks until perfect beta neutrality can be achieved, but to be cognizant of the beta of each stock and to avoid matching stocks with widely variant beta scores.

Market Capitalization Neutrality

Market capitalization neutrality refers to balancing the portfolio in such a way as to keep the market capitalization exposure of the long side of the portfolio similar to the market capitalization exposure of the short side of the portfolio. Stocks of different market capitalization can be affected by market forces in various ways; while large cap stocks tend to be more stable and liquid, they may fall out of favor in times of explosive growth. While there are exceptions, stocks of similar market capitalization are more likely to react similarly to general economic conditions. For this reason, managers prefer to keep their portfolios relatively neutral to this type of exposure. It is important to remember that the ultimate goal of market-neutral investing is to reduce systematic risk whenever possible. Market capitalization represents such a systematic risk and should be neutralized.

As with beta neutralization, in a pairs trading situation the success of the trade may be dependent on this step of the portfolio construction process. Because a pairs trade involves only two stocks, the possibility that one will be affected differently from the other by a market swing must be carefully considered. When matching baskets of stocks, the effects of market capitalization are muted for any given stock in ways not present when only two stocks are being considered. A pairs trader, therefore, keeping in mind the ultimate goal of minimizing systematic risk, should try to keep the market capitalization of the two stocks he is pairing relatively similar.

CHOICE OF SECURITY TYPE

Market-neutral investing may be applied to almost any type of security. A market-neutral manager may invest in fixed income, convertible bonds, futures, options and, of course, equities. Many of the principles that affect one security type also affect the others, but some principles are very specific to an individual type of instrument. Keep in mind that for the purpose of this book the interest is only in equities. Other security types and the specific strategy characteristics unique to them are discussed later.

THE ADVANTAGES OF MARKET-NEUTRAL INVESTING

One of the most distinct ways to see the advantages of market-neutral investing is through the application of various statistical filters. Through their use and understanding, a trader can see where this approach differs and excels when compared with more traditional approaches.

Linear Regression Analysis

One of the ways to analyze the return characteristics of an investment strategy is through the process of linear regression analysis. This method compares the returns generated by a specific strategy with the returns of an appropriately selected benchmark. The purpose of the analysis is to determine what part of the return is generated as a result of market swings and what part can be attributed to the strategy. The two data streams are plotted and then, through regression analysis, a "best-fit" line is generated which describes the relationship between the two data sources. Figure 2.1 is the graphical representation of a simple regression analysis. When performing an actual regression analysis on a particular strategy, a significantly larger data pool is preferred as it gives a more accurate illustration of the relationship being studied.

Linear regression analysis leads directly to correlation, one of the most central mathematical relationships in pairs trading, so it is worthwhile to spend some time understanding the mathematics underlying it. If we assume that an x and a y represent each of our data points, then each point of the best-fit line is represented by an x and a y_{Δ}. Our data points don't always fall exactly on the best-fit line and, therefore, y does not al-

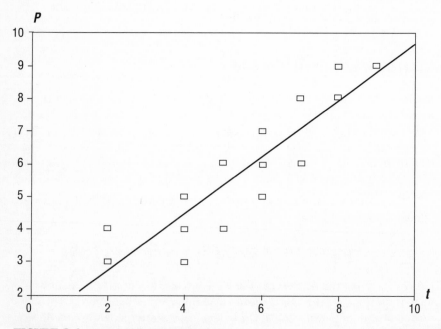

FIGURE 2.1 Simple Regression Analysis

ways equal y_Δ. The least squares method, the most common method for finding a regression line, uses the vertical deviation of each data point from the best-fit line (i.e., the deviation denoted as $y - y_\Delta$). The best-fit line results when there is the smallest value for the sum of the squares of the deviations between y and y_Δ. The sum of the squares of these deviations is called the *residual sum of squares* or sometimes the *error sum of squares*. This method produces the best line possible given that we have only a subset of all possible data.

Once the best-fit line is found, we need to find the equation for this line. To do this, one needs to know the slope and the y-intercept. These parameters have to be estimated from the subset of the data (thus, the more complete the data set, the better the estimates). To estimate these parameters, follow these seven steps:

1. Arrange the data into x, y pairs.
2. Compute the mean of all of the x values.
3. Compute the sum of the x^2 by squaring each value of x and adding the squares.
4. Compute the sum of the y^2 using the same method.
5. Compute the sum of each x value multiplied by its corresponding y value.
6. Calculate the slope (b) of the line as:

$$b = \frac{\sum x_i y_i - \left[\left(\sum x_i\right) \times \left(\sum y_i\right)/n\right]}{\sum x_i^2 \left[\left(\sum x_i\right)^2/n\right]}$$

7. Calculate the y-intercept (a) where $x = 0$ by the following formula:

$$a = y - bx$$

One is now ready to place the slope and y-intercept into a standard linear equations format:

$$y = a + bx$$

In this equation, y represents the strategy return, less the risk-free rate, and x represents the market return, also less the risk-free rate. The value b calculated above represents the beta of the strategy; in this case, beta refers to how sensitive the strategy return is to the market return. The value a represents the strategy's alpha, also known as the value-added return, attributable to the strategy. Market-neutral strategies tend to have very low beta scores and be very alpha driven.

This analysis also produces a correlation statistic, referred to as r, that describes the strength of the relationship between the two data sources (strategy return and market return). The main result of a correlation is called the *correlation coefficient* (or r). It ranges from -1.0 to $+1.0$. The closer r is to $+1$ or -1, the more closely the two variables are related. If r is close to 0, it means there is no relationship between the variables. If r is positive, it means that as one variable gets larger the other gets larger. If r is negative it means that as one gets larger, the other gets smaller (often called an inverse correlation).

While correlation coefficients are normally reported as r being a value between -1 and $+1$, squaring them makes them easier to understand. The square of the coefficient (or r squared) is equal to the percent of the variation in one variable that is related to the variation in the other. After squaring r, ignore the decimal point. An r of .5 means 25 percent of the variation is related ($.5^2 = .25$). An r-value of .7 means 49 percent of the variance is related ($.7^2 = .49$).

For two variables x and y, the correlation is defined by:

$$\text{cor}(x,y) \equiv \frac{\text{cov}(x,y)}{\sigma_x \sigma_y}$$

where σ_x denotes standard deviation and cov (x,y) is the covariance of these two variables.

Given n sets of variables denoted $x_i, \ldots, x_n$, the covariance $\sigma_{ij} \equiv \text{cov}$ (x_i, x_j) of x_i and x_j is defined by:

$$\text{cov}(x_i, x_j) \equiv [(x_i - \mu_i) \times (x_j - \mu_j)]$$
$$= (x_i x_j - x^{\wedge}i)(x^{\wedge}j)$$

where $x^{\wedge}_i = \mu_i$ and $x^{\wedge}_j = \mu_j$ are the means of x_i and x_j, respectively.

The correlation coefficient of a set of observations $\{(x_i, y_i): i = 1, \ldots, n\}$ is given by the formula:

$$r = \frac{\sum (x_i - x_{\text{avg}})(y_i - y_{\text{avg}})}{\sqrt{\sum (x_i - x_{\text{avg}})^2 \sum (y_i - y_{\text{avg}})^2}}$$

With correlation analysis there is always one dependent variable. There may be one or more independent variables. The dependent variable is always the security's price. The independent variable can be an indicator or one or more securities.

If we put this analysis in a slightly more basic format, when we choose a fund, we need to know if the direction of its price returns tends to be the same as a reference benchmark. If the value for correlation is positive, then the fund moves the same way as the benchmark. A negative correlation value shows that the fund tends to go up when the market goes down. A correlation near zero means that there isn't any significant relationship between the two price series.

Here is the formula:

$$\rho = \frac{\displaystyle\sum_{i=0}^{i=N}(rs_i - RS) \times (rr_i - RR)}{\sqrt{(rs_i - RS)^2} \times \sqrt{(rr_i - RR)^2}}$$

where N = number of weeks considered = 52
RS = security/fund mean return
RR = *reference index/benchmark mean return*
rs_i = security/fund return in week i
rr_i = reference index/benchmark return in week i

Much of the mathematics just described is unnecessary for the average trader wishing to implement a market-neutral strategy. There are countless programs, including any reliable spreadsheet program, that will perform these operations without a detailed understanding of the formulas supporting them. The formulas are included here for those traders who will need them when building an automated model. It is important, however, to understand what correlation is and what it measures. Specific applications are discussed in more detail in a later section.

Mean Variance Optimization

Mean variance optimization applies a quantitative model to historical return data to maximize expected return given a certain level of portfolio return; alternately, it can be used to minimize portfolio risk given a certain level of portfolio risk. In this type of model, risk is measured as variance and is plotted in graphical format. The output is known as the *efficient frontier* because it indicates the most efficient portfolio, given certain parameters, at each level of risk. Figure 2.2 is an example of what an efficient

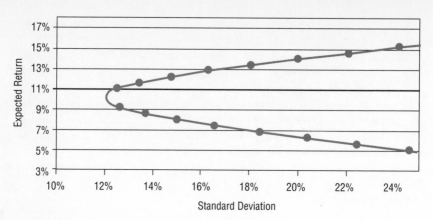

FIGURE 2.2   Efficient Frontier

frontier might look like for a given set of data. Each point on the line represents a possible portfolio's expected return and associated risk level.

At first examination, it seems counterintuitive to suggest that the efficient frontier could be shaped as it is, implying that there are two portfolios with the same level of risk and very different expected returns. For the purpose of illustration, consider two hypothetical portfolios: Portfolio A contains a basket of 20 equities and portfolio B contains a single bond. It is perfectly legitimate to predict that portfolio A will have an expected return of 15 percent, while portfolio B has an expected return of 5 percent. While it is well known that equities have a higher level of risk than do fixed income securities, by nature of having only one holding, portfolio B may have an equal amount of associated risk with a much lower expected return. It is unlikely that any manager would construct a portfolio with only a single holding, but the efficient frontier considers all possible portfolio combinations based on the data provided for the model.

The degree of risk of a portfolio as measured by variance of returns, the risk metric delineated by the efficient frontier, depends on the correlation between the portfolio's components, not on the average variance of each portfolio holding. By considering the relationship between the components, a mean variance optimization model maps the outputs of various portfolio combinations. Figure 2.3 shows the point on the efficient frontier that is considered to be the most efficient portfolio; this point, usually measured in terms of Sharpe ratio, represents the portfolio combination that has the highest level of expected return with the lowest level of risk, or, more simply, the portfolio with highest risk-adjusted returns.

The inputs to a mean variance optimization model can range from a group of securities to a group of portfolios. This is a very effective tool

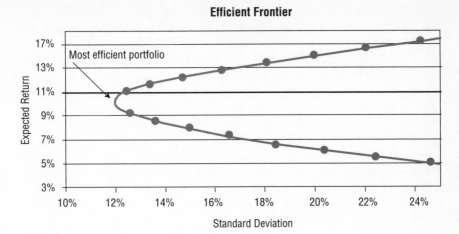

FIGURE 2.3 Most Efficient Portfolio

when making asset allocation decisions. By inputting a variety of portfolios, each with a different strategy—equities, fixed income, and alternatives, for example—it is possible to create a portfolio combination that should maximize returns while still carefully managing overall risk.

The reason that mean variance optimization is important to our discussion of market-neutral investing is that it has been shown that adding a market-neutral allocation to a portfolio of stocks and bonds can reduce risk without a proportional decrease in returns. This is largely driven by the fact that market-neutral strategies are not highly correlated with either stocks or bonds. These strategies offer returns that are higher than those offered by fixed income securities while still providing a lower level of volatility than equities.

Traditionally, investors have used an allocation to the bond market as a way of diversifying the risks associated with equity market exposure and achieving more stable results. An investor should now be able to replace that bond allocation with a market-neutral allocation and produce higher returns at the same level of risk.

RISKS OF MARKET-NEUTRAL INVESTING

Like any investment strategy, market-neutral investing comes with certain risks that are specific to this style of investing. While a good market-neutral manager may be able to reduce the level of systematic risk in his portfolio and produce superior risk-adjusted returns, he is more susceptible to other types of risk than a more traditional manager. Model risk, execution risk, and security selection risk are three of the most significant and should be considered before an investor decides to pursue this type of strategy.

Model risk refers to the ability of a manager's proprietary model to accurately predict the price movement for which it was designed. Different managers place various levels of importance on their models, but most use one to a greater or lesser extent as a part of their investment process. Statistical arbitrage managers, for example, rely almost exclusively on the buy and sell signals produced by their models; in many cases, complex computer systems execute trades automatically as they are generated by the model. Other market-neutral managers use their models as an initial screen before applying more detailed levels of analysis to the models' output. The specifics of model building and portfolio construction are discussed in more detail in the Chapter 3.

Some of the critics of market-neutral investing have coined the term *black box* to refer to the complex computer-driven models just described. They argue that trading based on this type of model makes it nearly impossible for investors to understand the criteria being used to trade their funds. With this lack of transparency, investors are making blind decisions. If the model is faulty, they will have no way to know this until they have already begun to lose money. The opposing side to this argument is that without their black box models, market-neutral managers are greatly constrained in the amount of data they can analyze in a timely fashion. Ultimately, an investor must make his decision based on the level of comfort that he feels with the manager and based on the manager's ability to explain the model without revealing the proprietary secrets it contains.

Another major risk factor facing the market-neutral manager is execution risk. Execution risk can be driven by liquidity concerns, commission restraints, margin ability issues, and short sale rules, but in each case the concern is that poor execution will adversely affect portfolio returns. Because a market-neutral strategy invests in the relationship between stocks and then profits as this relationship converges back toward its historical average, a market-neutral manager needs to be careful that he does not lose too much of his spread by paying high commissions. Another concern is that even after a trade has been placed successfully, liquidity problems may make it impossible to exit the trade and realize the gain. Margin rules can affect execution but are usually taken into account before a trade is placed; they are a part of execution risk but can be managed outside of usual market effects.

Each of these execution risks can be managed by an astute and experienced manager, but they should be understood by any investor considering this investment style since they affect portfolio returns differently from the way they might a more traditionally managed portfolio. This does not mean that these are the only risks facing a market-neutral fund manager, but they are some of the biggest and most easily recognizable. Delving deeper into various subjects surrounding market-neutral investing, and specifically pairs trading, will permit more thorough exploration of other risks.

The final major risk factor that should be taken into account by an investor considering adding a market-neutral allocation to his or her portfolio is security selection risk. This is the risk that the securities selected will experience adverse price action as the result of an outside and difficult to predict force, usually in the form of a news report or company announcement that changes the general perception of the stock being considered. This risk is present in all types of investing but play a slightly different role in a market-neutral portfolio. Critics of market-neutral investing, and of pairs trading in particular, argue that such strategies have twice the risk and half of the return. This argument is based on the fact that because a market-neutral position derives success from the relative performance of two securities, an investor is exposed to security selection risk on two stocks rather than one. The argument continues that because of the dual nature of the investment, the trade requires twice the capital exposure as a simple directional trade. While this is a vast oversimplification of how a market-neutral strategy works, it does point out a specific risk that should be considered.

There are two critical flaws with the argument above that will be highlighted here and fully investigated in later sections. The first flaw is that the argument assumes a skilled manager neither can nor does take into account the possibility of security-specific risk. Such consideration is a critical part of the market-neutral investment process and always figures into an experienced manager's approach. The second flaw with the preceding argument is that it does not give sufficient weight or understanding to the effects of correlation. Securities that are highly correlated tend to be so as a result of the fact that they react similarly to general market news. If one accepts this, it becomes apparent that the market-neutral approach to investing diminishes security-specific risk. Consider a simple market-neutral trade involving Coke and Pepsi. Should news come out that Coke had been found to contribute to obesity in children, Pepsi would likely be affected by such news as well. In a direction trade, owners of Coke will lose money. In a market-neutral trade, owners of Coke will lose money, but because the trade is hedged with a short position in Pepsi, the loss will be smaller. This results from the fact that these two stocks are highly correlated and tend to move in tandem; bad news for one company has negative effects for the other. While this is not always the case, in the majority of cases, market-neutral trades offer less risk than directional trades in the same securities.

CONCLUSION

This chapter has covered several types of market neutrality, the growth of this style of investing, and some of the advantages and risks of market-neutral investing. Understanding how each type of market neutrality can manage a particular aspect of systematic risk paves the way to begin making clear the advantages of market-neutral investing. It then becomes very clear why this industry has grown so much and so quickly and why so many marketing professionals are eager to include the term when extolling their particular investment product. By understanding some of the risks, one can see how to proceed before making a market-neutral investment. With this foundation it should now be possible to explore the various methods for building a model and ultimately constructing a market-neutral portfolio.

CHAPTER 3

The Market-Neutral Investment Process

The market-neutral investment process described here shows how a manager moves from the desire to follow a market-neutral investment discipline to the realization of a well-constructed market-neutral portfolio. The author focuses only on the equity universe, although several of the techniques described in this charter are applicable to other types of market-neutral portfolios. Some details of how these techniques apply to pairs trading specifically are included but comprehensive review of market neutrality and pairs trading is reserved for Chapter 4.

The process is broken down into three basic steps: the initial screen, the stock selection process, and the final portfolio construction. The initial screen is the part of the process that limits the universe of stocks that are to be considered for the portfolio. This is rather straightforward but differs from manager to manager. The stock selection process is the most involved step and the one that will require the most investigation. The discussion covers the steps involved in building a model and devotes a significant amount of time to both fundamental and contrarian analysis. Technical analysis might have been added to this section, but as it plays so central a role in pairs trading, it has been allotted its own section and only casual reference is made to it here.

The final portfolio construction step differs in its importance depending on how much manager discretion is left in the overall process. A statistical arbitrage manager is far less involved in portfolio construction than is the pairs trader. Whatever level of complexity this step involves, portfolio construction usually calls for applying risk-return optimization techniques to the stock selection process in order to make final portfolio decisions.

THE INITIAL SCREEN

Before a manager begins to select which stocks he would like to include in his portfolio, he performs an initial screen to limit the universe of stocks that may be considered. By taking this step, the manager can quickly eliminate a large percentage of stocks that he knows would not be candidates for the portfolio under any circumstances. There are usually four main criteria used during an initial screen:

Liquidity

Managers usually use market capitalization as the most salient way to judge the liquidity of a stock, and they may choose to limit their universe to stocks that meet minimum market capitalization requirements. Other managers may choose to look at average daily volume when deciding how to screen the investment universe. In either case, the manager is attempting to avoid the possibility that when the time comes to exit a particular trade he will not be able to do so at the prevailing market price. The greater the liquidity of a given security, the more assurance the manager can have that he will be able to quickly, easily, and efficiently exit a position when the time comes.

Short-Sale Ability

Market-neutral investing involves shorting securities as well as buying them long. A manager must, therefore, be able to short the equities he is considering in order to build a portfolio. Many of the largest brokerage houses keep lists, called "hard-to-borrow" lists, of securities that are not always easy to short sell. Many managers will obtain these lists in advance of their initial screen and exclude any stock that is listed on the "hard-to-borrow" list.

Involvement in Corporate Action

At any given time, there are many companies involved in some type of corporate action, ranging from mergers and acquisitions to secondary public offerings and stock repurchases. Such activities have a tendency to cause the price of the company's stock to fluctuate in ways that it might not otherwise. The stock of a company being considered for acquisition is more likely to feel upward price pressure than that of a company considering making acquisitions. Because the price action of these stocks is often less predictable than under normal conditions, many managers exclude from consideration stocks with pending corporate actions.

Restricted Sectors or Industries

Some managers, either for lack of expertise or a mandate constraint, will exclude certain sectors or industries from consideration. A company that falls into these categories will obviously be eliminated during the initial screen.

The initial screen is intended to allow a manager with a few very broad strokes to limit the number of stocks in his selection universe. This step saves valuable time and resources that otherwise would be used performing analysis on stocks that would be deemed unacceptable regardless of the opinion formed on the individual company. The initial screen is an important step because, depending on the specific parameters that the manager sets, he will conclude with a larger or smaller selection universe from which to build his portfolio.

STOCK SELECTION

Once a manager has limited his selection universe, he may now begin to select which stocks are to be included in the portfolio. This is a vital step for the market-neutral manager because of its significant value-added characteristics. Detailed return attribution analysis of a sample of equity market-neutral portfolios reveals that the majority of excess return, alpha, for each portfolio is attributable to stock selection. During the stock selection process, managers are looking for quantifiable metrics that have strong predictive ability across a wide range of stocks. For most managers, this involves the creation of a multifactor model that can be used to rank all of the stocks in the investment universe. Some managers create models based on fundamental data, while others use technical data or a combination of the two.

Before delving into the process of building such a model, a thorough investigation of both fundamental and contrarian analysis will be useful. Not only will this provide a foundation for later discussion of these topics in terms of pairs trading, but it will give some examples to work with in considering multifactor modeling. While neither subject is as central to pairs trading as technical analysis, each is an important tool for use in understanding a unified approach to pairs trading that is recommended at the end of Part Three.

Any reader who feels already in possession of a sound understanding of fundamental or contrarian analysis may wish to skip ahead to the "Model Construction" section of this chapter.

FUNDAMENTAL ANALYSIS

Fundamental analysis is the study of economic, industry, and company conditions in an effort to determine the value of a company's stock. Fundamental analysis typically focuses on key statistics in a company's financial statements to determine whether the stock price is correctly valued.

Fundamental analysis is the examination of the underlying forces that affect the well-being of the economy, industry groups, and companies. The goal here, similar to the purpose of most analysis, is to derive a forecast and to profit from future price movements. At the company level fundamental analysis may involve examination of financial data, management, business concept, and competition. At the industry level, there might be an examination of supply and demand forces for the products offered. For the national economy, fundamental analysis might focus on economic data to assess the present and future growth of the economy. To forecast future stock prices, fundamental analysis combines economic, industry, and company analysis to derive a stock's current fair value and to forecast future value. If fair value is not equal to the current stock price, fundamental analysts believe that the stock is either over- or undervalued and the market price will ultimately gravitate toward fair value.

If all the information regarding a corporation's future anticipated growth, sales figures, cost of operations, and industry structure, among other things, are available and examined, then the resulting analysis is said to provide the intrinsic value of the stock. To a fundamentalist, the market price of a stock tends to move toward its intrinsic value. If the intrinsic value of a stock is above the current market price, the investor will purchase the stock. However, if the investor finds through analysis that the intrinsic value of a stock is below the market price for the stock, the investor will sell the stock from his portfolio or take a short position in the stock.

The intrinsic value approach to the markets is based on a couple of big assumptions. The first is that the intrinsic value of an asset can differ from its market price. Purists of the efficient market hypothesis find this concept lacks any credibility. They feel that market price is the *only* reflection of true value for an asset and reflects all information available about its future prospects at any point in time.

Assuming you accept the notion of intrinsic value, the second big assumption of fundamental analysis is that, even though various elements fall off track from time to time, the market price of an asset will eventually gravitate toward its true value. This probably is a safe conclusion considering the long upward march of quality stocks in general despite regular setbacks and periods of so-called irrational exuberance. The key strategy for the fundamentalist is to buy when prices are at or below this intrinsic value and sell when they become overpriced.

The main source of information available to most investors wishing to perform some analysis is a company's financial statements. The masses of numbers can be bewildering and often intimidating to some, but these statements often provide a blueprint of the company's financial health. A corporation's annual report, usually a glossy and colorful document, is a statement of its financial operations. Annual reports are required by law and include a balance sheet, income statement, statement of cash flows, and auditor's report, along with a somewhat detailed description of the company's operations and prospects for the upcoming year. However, a company's 10-K form contains much more detailed financial information than many annual reports that are designed primarily for their appearance.

The information in an annual report is typically presented in this order:

- Summary of the previous year.
- Information about the company in general, its history, products, and line of business.
- Letter to shareholders from the president or CEO.
- An in-depth discussion of the financial results and other factors within the business.
- A complete set of financial statements for the current year (balance sheet, income statement, statement of retained earnings, and cash flow statement), including the notes.
- Auditor's report certifying the results as accurate according to accepted accounting standards (one should note that this does not vouch for the truth and accuracy of all the statements or numbers).

The Analysis

Most fundamental information focuses on economic, industry, and company statistics. The typical approach to analyzing a company involves four basic steps:

1. Determine the condition of the general economy.
2. Determine the condition of the industry.
3. Determine the condition of the company.
4. Determine the value of the company's stock.

This method employs a top-down approach that starts with the overall economy and then works down from industry groups to specific companies. As part of the analysis process, it is important to remember that all information is relative. Industry groups are compared against other industry groups and companies against other companies. Usually, companies are compared with others within the same industry group.

Economic Analysis

Preeminent in a top-down approach would be an overall evaluation of the general economy. The economy is studied to determine whether overall conditions are good for the stock market. Among the key factors to consider are inflation, interest rates, consumer spending, trade balances, and the overall money supply. Once these factors are evaluated, an analyst may form an opinion as to whether the economy is expanding or contracting. When the economy expands, most companies, regardless of industry, benefit and grow. When the economy declines, most sectors and companies usually suffer. Many economists link economic expansion and contraction to the level of interest rates. Interest rates are seen as a leading indicator for the stock market as well. Once a perspective on the overall economy has been developed, an investor can break down the economy into its various industry groups.

Industry Analysis

A company's industry obviously influences the outlook for the company. To assess an industry's potential, an investor would want to consider the overall growth rate, market size, and importance to the economy. Even the most attractive stocks can post weak returns if they are in an industry that is suffering. Often, it is more attractive to own a weak stock in a strong industry than a strong stock in an industry that is struggling. While the individual company is still important, its industry group is likely to exert just as much, or more, influence on the stock price.

Once an analyst has determined that the general economy appears strong, he may wish to decide which sectors will benefit most from economic expansion. For example, a growth strategy might be selected and involve the purchase of technology, biotech, semiconductor, and cyclical stocks. If the economy is forecast to contract, an investor might opt for a more conservative strategy and seek out stable income-oriented companies. A defensive strategy might involve the purchase of consumer staples, utilities, and energy-related stocks.

Once the industry group is chosen, an investor would need to narrow the list of companies before proceeding to a more detailed analysis. Investors are usually interested in finding the leaders and the innovators within an industry. The first task is to identify the current business and competitive environment within a group as well as the future trends. Comparative analysis of the competition within a sector helps to identify those companies with an edge and those most likely to keep it.

Company Analysis

After determining the economic and industry conditions, the company itself is analyzed to determine its financial health. This is usually done by studying the company's financial statements. From these statements a number of useful ratios can be calculated. Table 3.1 is a list of potential inputs into a financial analysis.

While this list may seem overwhelming, in time an analyst or investor will identify the statistics that work best and develop his own valuation model. There are many different valuation metrics, and much depends on the industry and stage of the economic cycle. A complete financial model can be built to forecast future revenues, expenses, and profits. An investor may also rely on the forecasts of other analysts and apply various multiples to arrive at a valuation. Some of the more popular ratios are found by dividing the stock price by a key value driver. Table 3.2 lists some of these ratios.

This methodology assumes that a company will sell at a specific multiple of its earnings, revenues, or growth. An investor may rank companies based on these valuation ratios. Those at the high end may be considered overvalued, while those at the low end may constitute relatively good value.

The ratios fall into five main categories: profitability, price, liquidity, leverage, and efficiency. When performing ratio analysis on a company, the ratios should be compared to those of other companies within the same or similar industry to get a sense of what is considered normal. At least one popular ratio from each category is described here.

Net Profit Margin   A company's net profit margin is a profitability ratio calculated by dividing net income by total sales. This ratio indicates how much profit the company generates per dollar of sales.

Return on Equity   The return on equity (ROE) is calculated by dividing the company's net income available to common shareholders by the average amount of common equity. This measure indicates the rate of return that is available to the equity providers of capital to the company. The calculation considers the amount of earnings available to common shareholders after all other capital providers have been paid their entitlement. The ROE incorporates the business and financial risk assumed by a common shareholder.

TABLE 3.1 Possible Inputs for a Company Analysis	
Accounts payable	Gross profit margin
Accounts receivable	Growth
Acid ratio	Industry
Amortization	Interest cover
Assets—current	International
Assets—fixed	Investment
Book value	Liabilities—current
Brand	Liabilities—long-term
Business cycle	Management
Business idea	Market growth
Business model	Market share
Business plan	Net profit margin
Capital expenses	Page view growth
Cash flow	Page views
Cash on hand	Patents
Current ratio	Price/book value ratio
Customer relationships	Price/earnings ratio
Days payable	PEG
Days receivable	Price/sales ratio
Debt	Product
Debt structure	Product placement
Debt/equity ratio	Regulations
Depreciation	R&D
Derivatives—hedging	Revenues
Discounted cash flow	Sector
Dividend	Stock options
Dividend cover	Strategy
Earnings	Subscriber growth
EBITDA	Subscribers
Economic growth	Supplier relationships
Equity	Taxes
Equity risk premium	Trademarks
Expenses	Weighted average cost of capital
Goodwill	

Price/Earnings (P/E) Ratio   The price/earnings (P/E) ratio is a price ratio calculated by dividing the security's current stock price by the previous year's earnings per share (EPS).

The P/E ratio shows how much an investor must pay to "buy" $1 of the company's earnings. In theory, this ratio is heavily influenced by an investor's view of the company's future earning potential; younger, growth-oriented companies tend to have higher P/E ratios than more mature companies.

TABLE 3.2 Ratios Commonly Used in a Company Analysis

Ratio	Company Type
Price/book value	Oil
Price/earnings	Retail
Price/earnings/growth	Networking
Price/sales	B2B
Price/subscribers	ISP or cable company
Price/lines	Telecom
Price/page views	Web site
Price/promises	Biotech

A common approach is to compare the P/E ratio of companies within the same industry. All else being equal, the company with the lower P/E ratio is the better value.

Book Value per Share A company's book value per share is a price ratio calculated by dividing total net assets (assets minus liabilities) by total shares outstanding. Depending on the accounting methods used and the age of the assets, book value can be helpful in determining whether a security is overpriced or underpriced. If a security is selling at a price far below book value, it may be an indication that the security is underpriced.

P/E to Growth (PEG) Ratio The P/E to growth (PEG) ratio is designed to address some of the shortcomings in the P/E ratio by adding another element to it. Principally, the P/E ratio is based on historical data and does not address expectations for continued operations of the company. But investors are typically more concerned with the future growth rate potential of a company than with its past performance when determining the suitability of an investment. The PEG ratio is calculated by dividing the P/E ratio by the company's historical or projected growth rate, but similar standards should be used in either case.

When using the PEG ratio as a valuation tool, an analyst typically assumes that the price/earnings ratio should equal the growth rate, resulting in a PEG ratio of 1.0. A ratio higher than 1.0 may indicate an overvalued stock, while a value less than 1.0 may indicate an undervalued stock. As a general rule, an investor should consider the average PEG for the industry in which the stock he is analyzing operates.

Current Ratio A company's current ratio is a liquidity ratio calculated by dividing current assets by current liabilities. This measures the company's ability to meet current debt obligations. A higher current ratio indicates the company is more liquid than does a lower ratio.

Quick Ratio   A company's quick, or acid-test, ratio is calculated by dividing the company's cash, cash equivalents, and accounts receivable by the current liabilities. The quick ratio is a refined measure of the current ratio that assumes that inventories should be deducted from current assets since they are less liquid than other assets.

Debt Ratio   A company's debt ratio is a leverage ratio calculated by dividing total liabilities by total assets. This ratio measures the extent to which total assets have been financed with debt. During times of economic stress or rising interest rates, companies with a high debt ratio can experience financial problems. However, during good times, debt can enhance profitability by financing growth at a lower cost.

Inventory Turnover   A company's inventory turnover is an efficiency ratio calculated by dividing cost of goods sold by inventories. It reflects how effectively the company manages its inventories by showing the number of times per year inventories are turned over (replaced). Of course, this type of ratio is highly dependent on the industry. A grocery store chain will have a much higher turnover than a commercial airplane manufacturer. As stated previously, it is important to compare ratios with those of other companies within the same industry.

After determining the condition and outlook of the economy, the industry, and the company, the fundamental analyst is prepared to determine whether the company's stock is overvalued, undervalued, or correctly valued.

Several valuation models have been developed to help determine the value of a stock. These include dividend models that focus on the present value of expected dividends, earnings models that focus on the present value of expected earnings, and asset models that focus on the value of the company's assets.

With a short list of companies, an investor might analyze the resources and capabilities within each company to identify those companies that are capable of creating and maintaining a competitive advantage. The analysis could focus on selecting companies with a sensible business plan, solid management, and sound financials.

Business Plan and Management

The business plan, model, or concept forms the bedrock upon which all else is built. If the plan, model, or concept is poor, there is little hope for the business. In order to execute a business plan, a company requires top-quality management. Investors might look at management to assess its capabilities, strengths, and weaknesses. Even the best-laid plans in the most dynamic industries can go awry with poor management. Alternatively, strong management sometimes creates extraordinary success in a mature industry.

Model Examples

The preceding steps provide qualitative perspective on a firm's position within its sector and the economy as a whole. Such a view indicates whether a quantitative analysis should be undertaken. If numbers are called for, there are two relatively simple models that can help investors wanting to better understand the firm being considered for investment. The two most commonly used methods for determining the intrinsic value of a firm are the dividend discount model and the price/earnings model. Both methods, if employed properly, should produce similar intrinsic values.

When using a dividend discount model, the type of industry involved and the dividend policy of the industry are important in choosing which of the dividend discount models to employ. As mentioned earlier, the intrinsic value of a share is the future value of all dividend cash flows discounted at the appropriate discount factor. For those familiar with the calculation of yield in fixed income analysis, the concepts are similar.

For constant dividends:

$$P = D_t / k_e$$

where P = intrinsic value
D_t = expected dividend
k_e = appropriate discount factor for the investment

This method is useful for analyzing preferred shares where the dividend is fixed. However, the constant dividend model is limited in that it does not allow for future growth in the dividend payments for growth industries. As a result the constant dividend growth model may be more useful in examining a firm.

For constant dividend growth:

$$P = D_t / (k_e - g)$$

where P = intrinsic value
D_t = expected dividend
k_e = appropriate discount factor for the investment
g = constant dividend growth rate

The constant dividend growth model is useful for mature industries, where the dividend growth is likely to be steady. Most mature blue chip stocks may be analyzed quickly with the constant dividend growth model. This model has its limitations when considering a firm that is in its growth phase and will move into a mature phase sometime in the future. A two-stage dividend growth model may be utilized in such situations. This model allows for adjustment to the assumptions of the timing and magnitude of the growth of the firm.

For the two-stage growth model:

$$P = {}^n\sum_{t=1} \frac{D_0(1+g_1)^t}{(1+k_e)^t} + \sum_{t=n+1}^{\infty} \frac{D_n(1+g_2)^{t-n}}{(1+k_e)^t}$$

where P = intrinsic value
D_0 = expected initial period dividend
D_n = expected dividend during mature period
k_e = appropriate discount factor for the investment
g_1 = expected dividend growth rate for initial growth period
g_2 = expected dividend growth rate for mature period

The two-stage model allows for greater flexibility in the testing of scenarios for the investor looking at a firm in its infancy or in a new industry.

CONTRARIAN ANALYSIS

The stock market is a combination of millions of traders and investors using their money to try to predict the future. It is important to keep in mind that they are all human beings who are affected by hope, greed, and fear. What differentiates them from one another is their level of experience and the amount of capital they have to invest. In spite of experience, however, large fund managers make the same mistakes as small individuals; if this were not the case, one would see more mutual funds consistently ahead of the S&P 500. Nevertheless, each of these investors leaves a mark every time they place a trade, and the contrarian analyst benefits from learning to read these marks and doing the opposite. If the majority of market participants are wrong (a fact supported by historical data), than if you do the opposite, you will be right. It is important to remember that opinions do not move the markets—money does. A true contrarian is not one who trades against the trend; a true contrarian is one who places bets against the opinion of the majority.

The contrarian believes fundamental analysis, economic reports, and news make for a good conversation but are less useful when it comes to predicting market movements. They provide an excuse for traders and investors to buy or sell stocks, options, and futures, and they create volatility and skew options prices. What these factors do not do is give an investor the jump on the market for which he or she is looking.

During primary bull and bear markets, the psychology of all investors moves from pessimism and fear to hope, overconfidence, and greed. For the majority, the feeling of confidence is built up over a period of rising prices, so that optimism reaches its peak around the same point that the market is also reaching its high. Conversely, the majority are most pessimistic at market bottoms, at precisely the point when the acquisition of stocks should be taking place. The better-informed market participants, such as insiders and stock exchange members, act in a contrary manner to the majority by selling at market tops and buying at market bottoms. Both groups go through a complete cycle of emotions, but in completely opposite phases. This is not to suggest that members of the public are always wrong at major market turns and that professionals are always correct, but that in aggregate the opinions of these groups are usually in direct conflict. Data is available on many of these market participants, so that over a period of years it has been possible to derive parameters that indicate when a particular group has moved to an extreme, historically associated with a major turning point.

The derivatives market is particularly useful as an indicator of sentiment, and many of the tools offered here make ample use of data from the derivatives market. While the primary focus here is on the equity markets, some examination of contrarian indicators is warranted. Any reader not well versed in derivatives should skip this section, as it is not critical to understanding either market-neutral investing or pairs trading.

The Put-Call Ratio

When an options trader buys a call, he does so with the belief that the price of the underlying stock will rise. Similarly, when he buys a put, he does so with the belief that the price of the underlying stock will decrease. From this behavior, it can be extrapolated that calls represent bullish sentiment and puts represent bearish sentiment. Taken one step further, a high ratio of calls to puts would represent bullish sentiment and a low ratio would represent bearish sentiment.

In practice, however, there are almost always fewer puts traded in the market than there are calls. We look at the put-call ratio to decide whether sentiment is bearish or bullish. A contrarian will mark out what he considers to be a safe put-call ratio level to move against the prevailing trend.

In practice, analysts use daily charts to mark these put-call levels with more accuracy. Overwhelmingly bearish sentiment (shown by a high put-call ratio) is associated with a low, and a technical analyst can mark the levels above which he considers it safe to go long. In reverse mode, the analyst can also mark the low put-call ratio levels of excessive optimism above which it may be safe to go short.

There are also certain contrarian indicators that are based on the level of open interest in a given derivative contract. The number of open contracts at the end of the day will vary according to demand for the underlying stock. In case of futures trades, the analyst must decide whether this is attributable to greater bullishness or bearishness, since futures contracts are not differentiated according to price—they are simply bought and sold at a certain spread. But options are differentiated according to price as well as position. Analysts can easily break down open interest into puts and calls. Then, the open interest put-call ratio can be analyzed in a fashion similar to the traded put-call ratio.

The peak put and call levels also will usually act as support and resistance levels. A heavy out-of-the-money call position (defined in Chapter 14) indicates excessive optimism, while a heavy out-of-the-money put position indicates excessive pessimism. In individual stocks, call sellers will usually own the stock and automatically create resistance by selling close to the peak open interest call levels. If it seems that the out-of-the-money puts will be triggered, then put sellers will buy and create support to prevent their positions being triggered.

Each time a trader analyzes a pair of stocks, it is useful to analyze put-call ratios of those stocks. Lets say a trader noticed a divergence between ABC stock and XYZ stock, which represents an attractive arbitrage opportunity (going long ABC and shorting XYZ). Let's also say that ABC's put-call ratio has historically fluctuated between 0.7 and 1.5 with a current reading of 1.4. From a contrarian standpoint a reading of 1.4 is bullish because it is closer to the high end of an historical range and therefore supports the trader's original analysis of going long ABC. Let's say that XYZ's historical put-call ratio range is between 0.3 and 1.2 with a current reading of 0.7. Although a reading of 0.7 looks neutral, it is less bullish than a reading of 1.2 of ABC stock on a relative percentile basis. All a trader needs is a confirmation from a comparative contrarian analysis to justify or rethink his original arbitrage opportunity.

It is very useful to chart put-call ratios of pairs candidates to identify better entry and exit points for individual stocks. It is especially helpful to chart the difference between put-call ratios of both stocks of a pair. Keep in mind that the absolute numbers are not as important as its relative stand in terms of their historical ranges.

Short Interest

Short interest is the total number of shares of a stock that have been sold short and not yet covered, usually expressed as a percentage. Most stock exchanges track the short interest in each stock and issue reports at the month end. This is very useful because it allows investors to see what action short-sellers are taking. A large increase or decrease in a stock's short interest can be a very telling indicator.

Short interest is considered a good indicator of investor sentiment. A high (or rising) short interest means that a large amount of people believe a stock will go down. When this is happening one should check the current research and news reports to understand the dynamics underlying the occurrence. In such cases, a high short interest stock should be approached with extreme caution but not necessarily avoided. From a contrarian standpoint, the conclusion is the opposite. Short-sellers (like all investors) are not perfect and some have been known to be wrong most of the time. Many contrarian investors use the short interest as a tool to determine direction and feel that a high short interest ratio (discussed next) is considered bullish because it indicates there eventually will be significant upward pressure as short-sellers cover their short positions.

Short Interest Ratio

The short interest ratio is defined as the number of shares sold short (short interest) divided by average daily volume. This is often called the days-to-cover ratio because it tells how many days, given the stock's average trading volume, that it would take short-sellers to cover their positions—if good news sent the price higher. The higher the ratio, the longer it would take to buy back the borrowed shares. This ratio is used by short-sellers because if too many shares of a given stock have been sold short and days-to-cover has stretched to a high number, covering a short position could prove difficult.

Short Squeeze

Some bullish investors see a high short interest as an opportunity; this is called the short interest theory. If an individual is short-selling a stock and the stock keeps rising, he will likely want to get out before his losses become too great. A short squeeze occurs when there is a lack of supply, and short-sellers, scrambling to replace their borrowed stock, force prices upward by exerting a great deal of buying pressure. A stock with a high short interest is an indicator that short position holders may be forced to liquidate and cover their position by purchasing the stock. If a short squeeze occurs and enough short-sellers buy back the stock, the price can be pushed even higher.

A pairs trader should always check short interest ratios of prospective pair candidates to make sure that their ratios are in line with each other and favorable to the pairing approach. In other words, a trader wants to see a high short interest ratio in a stock he intends to buy and a low ratio in a stock he intends to sell. Although this is not the indicator that will make or break a trade, it is essential to know the sentiment of stocks you trade.

Similar to the case of put-call ratios, absolute numbers play a less important role when compared to the relative value of an historical range. It is also very helpful to chart the difference of the short interest ratios of prospective stocks of a pair. Like most indicators, an investment decision should not be based entirely on the short interest in a stock, but it is a useful input when one considers the overall investment process.

MODEL CONSTRUCTION

Now that some of the concepts behind fundamental and contrarian analysis have been covered, exploration of the stock selection step of the investment process from the perspective of model construction is appropriate. It is important to remember that building a useful model involves choosing factors with a good predictive value applicable across a broad range of stocks. One must also be able to form a composite value from the individual factors that retains meaningfulness in terms of forward-looking predictive value. These factors may include technical, fundamental, and growth data, but all must be quantitative and statistically significant. Once a model has been created and the stocks within the selection universe have been ranked, the manager may begin picking stocks he wishes to include.

The standard form used in the creation of most market-neutral models is a linear equation with n terms:

$$r = bf_1 + bf_2 + bf_3 + \ldots bf_n$$

where r = the expected return of the security
b = is the sensitivity of r to the respective factor, f

The weighting of each factor within the model is based on that factor's estimated predictive value in terms of expected return. This can be determined using linear regression, as discussed in Chapter 2. Each factor serves as an independent variable and the regression coefficient for each becomes the respective weighting within the model. For example, within a fundamental model, a manager might choose to include P/E ratio, intrinsic value based on one of the previously described dividend models, current ratio, and debt ratio. Performing a linear regression analysis would make possible assignment of an appropriate model weight to each of these factors.

This process may seem simple and straightforward given the preceding explanation, but in execution it is quite complex. Various factor combinations must be tested under a variety of circumstances and a linear regression analysis must be performed for each combination. The back-testing, forward-testing, and linear regression analysis can involve millions of calculations to determine the relative predictive value of each factor and each combination of factors. The greater the number of factors that are involved in the model, the more complex and difficult the model is to construct.

Selection Criteria

After the model is created, it is applied to all of the stocks in the selection universe and they are ranked based on their expected return. The final step in the stock selection process is to create buy and sell rules based on the output of the model. In a typical long/short equity portfolio, the stocks with the highest ranking are bought for the long side of the portfolio and those with the lowest ranking are sold short for the short side of the portfolio. Some managers will take this process a step further and create a completely independent model for selecting the stocks for the short portfolio. These managers believe that including stocks with high scores in a negatively biased model creates superior choices to those with low scores in a positively biased model because the second model highlights different factors that have superior downside predictive value.

Once a stock has been placed in the portfolio, a manager will also set rules for when the stock should be removed. These criteria may be based on when the relative ranking of long stocks fall out of a certain range and when the relative ranking of short stocks rise above a certain range. These rules may also combine some time element with relative ranking to determine when a stock may be removed from the portfolio. Adherence to these rules is at the discretion of the manager, but they must be formulated very carefully and closely monitored.

Mean Reversion Managers

Certain specialized types of market-neutral fund management—of which pairs trading is one—require a different type of buy and sell rule. Where the long/short manager is simply trying to ensure that his long portfolio outperforms his short portfolio, there are managers, mainly statistically arbitragers, who try to capitalize on apparent price anomalies within a small group of related stocks. They operate on the assumption that while these anomalies may persist in the short term, over the long term they will disappear through natural market forces.

If one considers a group of stocks all within the same industry, historically, the group will trade at an average price relationship one to another. Perhaps an easier way to see this is to consider the same industry group of stocks relative to the index of that specific industry. In the long term the relationship of each stock to the index is fairly smooth. However, when one considers the same price relationship in the short term, the relative price of the stock will tend to fluctuate both above and below its average relationship.

A mean reversion manager will try to buy the stocks that are underpriced relative to the historical average and sell the ones that are overpriced relative to that average. In effect this type of manager will break his investment universe down into several small subsets, ranking each subset separately. The combination of longs from each subset comprises his long portfolio and the combination of shorts from each subset comprises his short portfolio. This type of management may use a different model for each group of stocks or may apply the same model to each subset individually.

Because the mean reversion manager is basing his price predictions on criteria different from the long/short manager, the buy and sell rules of the former likely will be different. The long/short manager, for example, might choose to remove a stock from the portfolio based on a change in model score or relative ranking, but the mean reversion manager is more likely to act on the basis of a historical average toward which he believes the price should revert. Some managers will remove a stock when its price reverts back to the mean as expected. Others will hold the stock until it has moved back through the mean and begun to diverge in the opposite direction to some extent. Again, there are no correct ways to formulate these rules, but their creation and execution likely will have a significant effect on portfolio performance.

PORTFOLIO CONSTRUCTION AND OPTIMIZATION

It is at this point that the types of market neutrality discussed in Chapter 2 can come into play. While the simplest approach to stock selection is to blindly select the highest and lowest ranked stocks of the group, the astute and careful manager will now begin neutralizing other factors as well, sometimes leaving out higher ranked stocks in order to achieve sector, market capitalization, and beta neutrality. Of course, all of these factors are in a state of constant flux and the manager must decide how frequently to rebalance the portfolio. A manager's style often can be directly linked to how often he makes rebalancing moves within the portfolio.

The process of trying to maximize the level of expected return while still neutralizing the various types of systematic risk described previously is known as *optimization*. Several programs have been created for just this purpose, but some managers prefer to use their own proprietary versions. Such programs are designed to allow the manager to track each risk factor as he adds stocks to each side of the portfolio. While it is usually impossible to build a portfolio with a net zero exposure to these risks, by being cognizant of them the manager can use his experience to minimize such risk whenever possible.

As discussed earlier, the manager must also decide how often to rebalance the portfolio based on these factors. By using an optimization program he can more accurately track his exposure to these risk factors, thus making more informed decisions on when a rebalancing is required.

CONCLUSION

The reader should now have a fairly comprehensive understanding of many of the factors that go into market-neutral investing. Some of the advantages and risks associated with this type of investment strategy as well as the steps one takes to build a market-neutral portfolio have been explored. In the following chapter, the concepts put forth in this section will be applied to pairs trading. Some of the concepts will not change, while others will be abandoned altogether. However, with a good foundation in the topic, it should be far less difficult for the reader to understand how to begin constructing the uniform pairs trading theory, which is the ultimate goal of this consideration.

CHAPTER 4

Market Neutrality and Pairs Trading

Building on the foundation put forth in the previous chapters, it should now be possible to place the central concepts of market neutrality into the context of pairs trading. Although pairs trading is a market-neutral strategy, not all of the elements of market neutrality apply in all situations. Practitioners of this strategy are often forced to decide which elements are most important and should be given the most consideration. Pairs trading does follow the general guidelines of a market-neutral strategy's investment process, but it is also subject to its own peculiarities. The similarities and differences are the subject of this chapter and will prove critical to constructing a unified pairs trading theory later in this book.

APPLYING PAIRS TO TYPES OF MARKET NEUTRALITY

A market-neutral investment strategy that focuses on matched pairs rather than the relationship between a basket of long stocks and a basket of short stocks must, by nature, consider the various types of market neutrality differently. Each pair is considered as a single trade; it is evaluated, analyzed, and closed as an individual unit, with its profit or loss based solely on the performance of the two stocks that make up the pair. This is a critical distinction because it means that the manager must consider all issues of market neutrality based only on the characteristics of the two equities. A traditional long/short equity manager who is considering a basket of stocks on each side of his portfolio is able to finely tune their characteristics because he is only concerned with the combined values of multiple inputs. A pairs trader has only a single input on each side of the trade with which to contend. As a result, it is nearly impossible for the pairs trader to totally mute the various systematic risks with which he is faced. Rather, the pairs trader must deal in ranges and often make choices between significant risk factors.

Dollar-Neutral Pairs

Dollar neutrality is the easiest type of market neutrality for the pairs trader to achieve because it is not specific to either of the equities involved in the trade. It may, in fact, be less complicated for the pairs trader to achieve dollar neutrality than for the long/short manager because he must only balance his dollar exposure to two equities at a time. While it is true that this process is repeated several times until the entire portfolio is constructed, this is in contrast to the long/short manager, who is dealing with much larger numbers.

Achieving this type of neutrality is relatively simple in a pairs trading strategy. One simply decides on the number of long shares that one wants to buy and then multiplies that number by the ratio of the long share price versus the short share price:

$$\text{Number of short shares} = \text{Number of long shares} \times \frac{\text{Price of long stock}}{\text{Price of short stock}}$$

While a degree of rounding may be required, depending on lot size restrictions, this ratio will determine the relationship that should exist between the position sizes to achieve dollar neutrality.

By employing dollar neutrality in a market-neutral strategy, an investor ensures that his net dollar exposure to market swings is zero. This is an easy systematic risk to remove from a pairs portfolio and it should be done in all cases. Some traders may consider either taking a disproportionately large position on one side of the trade or closing one side of the trade before the other in order to take advantage of a stronger opinion on one of the two stocks involved in the trade. This type of action might also be taken as a result of an opinion on which direction the market is likely to move in the short term. In either case, this is known as taking a directional bias. While there is nothing explicitly wrong with such an approach, it is not market-neutral pairs trading. There is always the temptation to attempt to squeeze a slightly larger profit out of a trade by taking a directional bias, but this, in essence, defeats the overall power of a market-neutral approach. While directional bias may improve performance for a number of trades, over an extended time horizon it will likely prove to be a detriment. Furthermore, if one has skill in this type of market timing, there are other, more powerful approaches that can be taken.

Sector-Neutral Pairs

In previous chapters, it was noted that sector has a special meaning in terms of market-neutral strategies; in these cases *sector-neutral* means that portfolios are long/short balanced within each sector of the market to insulate the overall portfolio against the possibility that one sector will perform very well while another performs poorly. In a matched pairs strategy, again, because equities are considered only two at a time, this term has an even more specialized meaning. Sector neutrality in pairs trading implies that the two equities selected for the pair must be in the same sector. Often this standard is taken one step further, requiring that both of the selected equities be in the same industry. Such a procedure is followed for the same reason in pairs trading as it is in more traditional portfolios; in a matched pair trade where sector neutrality is not observed, if one sector or industry experiences a sharp market swing, it will have a major effect on performance.

The degree to which this criterion is observed is usually a function of the approach taken to stock selection. If stock selection is driven primarily by fundamental factors, then sector and industry, and in some cases business model, neutrality is strictly observed. In order for the comparison between the two equities to have any meaning, one must be comparing the metrics of comparable companies. If, however, a technical approach is being applied, sector and industry neutrality may be of less concern. Cross-sector trading, while not common, may be used in specialized cases.

Under a technical model, the importance of sector neutrality is a measure of one's blind faith that technical factors correctly explain and predict market action. Cross-sector trades tend to be somewhat counterintuitive, but if one is basing stock selection on purely statistical inputs, then there is no compelling reason for these trades to have a lower probability of success than those in which sector and industry neutrality are observed. The limiting nature of this type of market neutrality means that the degree to which it is regimented is highly dependent on the manager.

Beta-Neutral Pairs

When trading matched pairs of equities, one should particularly consider the volatility as measured by the beta of each stock. While it is almost impossible to find two stocks that have both the same beta reading and all of the other criteria needed to qualify as a pairs trade, one must be careful to avoid matching two stocks with extremely different betas. This is a critical point. If a manager places a pairs trade in which each side of the trade has a very different beta, he runs an increased risk that the trade will be stopped out based on absolute dollar considerations, despite the fact that the pair is simply running through its normal fluctuations.

To understand this point, consider a trade in which the beta of the long side of the trade is twice the beta of the short side. If the general market declines, the short-term effect on the trade is that the long will depreciate at twice the rate of the short stock. Despite the fact that over time the long may outperform the short, as the trade is predicting, because of the beta disparity, if the market decline persists, the trade may lose enough in dollar terms to be stopped out before the performance differential has a chance to present itself. Under the same conditions a market advance would benefit the manager, driving his trade toward its profit objective with greater speed. The overall effect is that the manager has not hedged the market exposure out of his trade—this being both the goal and the power behind a market-neutral strategy.

The goal of the pairs trader is to eliminate or at least reduce systematic risk, so beta considerations must be made when considering a pair. It is not necessary to find two stocks with identical beta scores, but the beta score of each stock should be within a fairly tight range relative to the stock on the other side of the trade. If this standard is not met, the manager is, in effect, taking a market direction bet.

Market Capitalization–Neutral Pairs

In a pairs trading situation, market capitalization neutrality is of particular concern because, as in beta neutralization, the success of the trade may depend on this step of the portfolio construction process. Because a pairs trade deals with only two stocks, the possibility that one will be affected differently by a market swing must be carefully considered. When one is matching baskets of stocks, the effects of market capitalization are muted for any given stock in ways not present when only two stocks are being considered. A pairs trader, therefore, still with the ultimate goal of minimizing systematic risk, should try to keep the market capitalization of the two stocks being paired relatively similar.

PAIRS TRADING AND MARKET-NEUTRAL PORTFOLIO CONSTRUCTION

The procedures involved in the investment process when constructing a pairs trading portfolio are the same as those followed in any market-neutral strategy. First an initial screen is conducted, followed by stock selection, and finally a portfolio is constructed, paying special attention to various return-optimizing considerations. Where pairs trading is unique, and thus does not follow the same specifications as a typical long/short portfolio, is in the specifics of each of these steps. The driving force behind its differences is that, regardless of the size of the portfolio, one must design each trade two stocks at a time. The process is the same for a portfolio of 10 pairs as it is for a portfolio of 40 pairs.

The Initial Screen

The initial screen is intended to allow a manager to limit the number of stocks in his selection universe. Four main criteria are considered: liquidity, short-sale ability, involvement in a corporate action, and inclusion in a restricted sector or industry. The specifics of each of these criteria are covered in Chapter 3. By taking this step, a manager does not have to waste valuable time and resources performing analysis on stocks that would be deemed unacceptable regardless of the opinion formed on the individual company. The initial screen is an important step because, depending on the specific parameters that the manager sets, he will end up with a larger or smaller selection universe from which to build his portfolio.

Pairs trading does not require that the initial screen have any special features that differentiate it from any type of market-neutral strategy. The specifics of the initial screen are at the discretion of the individual manager and may differ depending on the equity universe with which the manager is comfortable. While the initial screen is an important step in any investment process, the general concept discussed in the preceding chapter applies to pairs trading.

Pairs Trading Stock Selection

Stock selection in a pairs trading strategy is the most important step of the investment process as well as the step that differentiates this strategy from other market-neutral strategies. During the stock selection process, managers are looking for quantifiable metrics that have strong predictive ability across a wide range of stocks. For most managers, this involves the creation of a multifactor model that can be used to rank all of the stocks in the investment universe. Pairs trading models can be fundamentally or technically driven, but they fall under the special case of mean reversion models. A mean reversion manager will try to buy the stocks that are underpriced relative to the historical average and sell the ones that are overpriced relative to that average. In effect, this type of manager will break his investment universe into several small subsets, ranking each subset separately. A pairs trader looks for stocks that, among other qualities, have a historical relationship, usually measured in terms of correlation; when that relationship moves away from its historical average, he trades on the assumption that the relationship will revert to its historical average.

This warrants additional examination, since it is both unique to pairs trading and critical to the success of the portfolio. Recall that the standard form used in the creation of most market-neutral models is a linear equation with n terms:

$$r = bf_1 + bf_2 + bf_3 + \ldots bf_n$$

where r = the expected return of the security
 b = is the sensitivity of r to the respective factor, f

The weighting of each factor within the model is based on that factor's estimated predictive value in terms of expected return. This can be determined using linear regression, as discussed in Chapter 3. Each factor serves as an independent variable and the regression coefficient for each becomes the respective weighting within the model. In pairs trading, the application of the model is dependent on whether the model is technically or fundamentally driven. When using a fundamentally driven model, one sorts stocks into their respective industries or sector groups, each stock ranked appropriately. The manager then decides, keeping optimization factors in mind, which stocks to pair. Fundamental models tend to be rare within the realm of pairs trading so they are not given a great deal of consideration here.

When using a technical approach, one applies the model to pairs of stocks rather than to individual equities. The implication here is that stocks must be paired before the model is applied. There are two possible approaches that a manager may take in order to apply his model to pairs rather than to individual stocks. First, he may include a secondary screen that examines the correlation between stocks in various groups within his equity universe and matches them based on preset criteria. These criteria may include factors other than correlation that the manager believes strengthen the relationship between the stocks he is matching. Many of the likely factor choices are technical indicators, discussed in a later section. Regardless of the specific factors selected, the goal of this secondary screen is to match stocks within the equity universe in such a way that the resulting pairs are highly related to one another and are likely candidates to revert to this historical relationship in cases where they have temporarily diverged.

The second approach the pairs trader may take is to build the correlation matching process into his model. This approach requires a higher degree of technical expertise and programming ability, but will simplify the process considerably. Either approach is equally legitimate; deciding which one to employ should be based on both technical expertise and the complexity of both the matching process and the trading model.

Once the stocks are paired and the model has been applied, buy and sell rules are established to dictate when a pair should be traded, what its profit objective will be, and at what level the stop-loss on the downside will be set. The manager can now begin selecting which pairs from his ranked universe will be included in the portfolio. This may be done based simply on model ranking or may include some parameters on sector, industry, and market capitalization.

Constructing a Pairs Portfolio

The portfolio construction step of the investment process for a matched pairs portfolio can be predicated on any number of criteria based on the rankings generated by the investment model. Pairs trading differs from other market-neutral strategies, however, when it comes to portfolio optimization. A traditional long/short portfolio often requires a highly technical optimization program because the manager is faced with a high number of inputs on each side of his portfolio. When trying to examine a number of types of neutrality, a manager using these programs is able to run the highly complex calculations necessary to process this data. While comparing the beta, sector, or market capitalization factor between a long and a short portfolio in which each side contains 20 or 30 stocks is very complicated, for matched pairs this comparison is relatively straightforward because one is only comparing two stocks. It may seem, therefore, that portfolio optimization is a relatively simple process in a pairs trading strategy, but other concerns do arise because the portfolio is comprised of pairs.

In pairs trading, portfolio optimization requires that each pair be analyzed and determined justifiable before it is included in the portfolio. During the stock selection process, the investment model is applied to pairs that have been matched based on statistical criteria that judge the pair to be both correlated and experiencing enough divergence away from the historical mean relationship to warrant the trade. Before the trade is included, a fundamental and technical overlay should be performed to assure that the pair could be justified as sound.

The fundamental overlay involves examining each stock in the pair from a fundamental analysis perspective. The manager is not trying to become an expert on the fundamentals of each company, but rather checking to be sure that the fundamentals do not contradict his statistical and model pairing. For example, a manager may be considering a trade that pairs a long position in stock A with a short position in stock B. When conducting a fundamental overlay, the manager accepts the trade when the fundamentals of stock A are superior to stock B or if the fundamental picture is unclear. The manager rejects the trade only when the fundamentals of stock B are far superior to those of stock A. In this instance, the manager would choose to avoid the trade so as not expose himself to the possibility that fundamentals will drive price action against him.

The other check that the manager performs during the fundamental overlay is on the recent and anticipated news on each stock. This check first ensures that a news-driven price shock is not responsible for a justified divergence that may persist. It also ensures that there is not a company announcement pending that could cause a price shock potentially detrimental to the trade. For example, if ABC Corporation has just announced they have lost a major income source and the price of the stock has fallen sharply, the observed divergence between ABC and its pair may be permanent as the price of ABC is unlikely to recover quickly. In this case, the manager would reject the pair because despite the historical price relationship between ABC and the company it is paired with, the manager believes that this relationship has changed in a fundamental and permanent way; in essence, he does not believe that mean reversion will occur.

Of equal significance when performing a fundamental overlay is anticipated news. The manager may know from historical data that during the past several quarters, when XYZ Corporation has announced earnings, the price of the stock has had a tendency to jump several points in either direction depending on the quality of the announcement. When performing the fundamental overlay, if the manager discovers that XYZ is scheduled to announce earnings within the projected time horizon of the trade, he may reject the pair to avoid the possibility that this news will interfere with the regular statistical mean reversion his model has predicted. By considering all of these factors, the manager is not looking for a reason to make the trade; rather, he is looking for reasons that would cause him to reject the trade and select another pair.

Similar to the fundamental overlay, the manager will also conduct technical and sentiment analysis on each of the stocks in his intended pair. He is again looking for arguments against the trade that would cause it to be rejected. A simple example of this would be a case in which the intended long stock appears to be under significant downward pressure and the intended short is under significant upward pressure. The technical review suggests that rather than mean reversion, the manager can expect the trade to continue its divergence. In this case, the manager would reject the trade, but continue to monitor it for a reversal in technical factors that would make the trade justifiable in the future.

In each of these cases, the manager is attempting to optimize his portfolio by excluding pairs that have strong external arguments against their success. This process is applied to those pairs that the manager is considering after they have been ranked by the model and optimized in terms of the various sorts of systematic risk. Failure to include this step in the investment process will severely decrease the percentage of profitable trades the manager makes and be a major drag on performance.

RISK MANAGEMENT

While formal risk management techniques are discussed in greater detail in later chapters, there is a significant consideration to pairs portfolio construction and management that should be addressed. It has been demonstrated that when a manager is constructing a pairs portfolio, because only two stocks are being matched, achieving beta, sector, or market capitalization neutrality is more challenging and often impossible. While it is useful to keep these relative factors similar between the stocks being paired, a more significant step in the process is to remain aware of the differences. This awareness allows a manager to actively manage open positions effectively in various types of market conditions.

To demonstrate the type of active management that can differentiate a successful manager from an unsuccessful one, consider a dollar-neutral matched equity pair in which the beta of the long position is greater than the beta of the short position. The implication of this disparity is that the pair itself is biased toward the long side, as one would expect the higher beta stock to be more volatile and have greater price changes for identical underlying changes in the general market. In other words, in addition to the pressures of mean reversion that are expected in the trade, a rise in the general market should be favorable for this trade while a decline would work against the original analysis. In such a situation, the skilled and experienced manager will pay attention to trends in the general market, as they will affect the success of this trade. Should he predict significant downward pressure, he might choose to close this trade early in order to avoid the negative beta impact. This is not to suggest that a manager should make a habit of second-guessing his own analysis, but simply that by being aware of the neutrality discrepancies he faces in each trade, a manager is more suited to actively and effectively manage his portfolio of open positions.

The general rule, therefore, can be stated that while perfect market neutrality is particularly difficult to achieve when one only has two individual securities to consider, awareness of the unavoidable discrepancies in market neutrality factors provides the manager with the tools needed to actively manage his positions. Pairs trading provides a unique set of challenges and opportunities that distinguish it from other types of market-neutral strategies. Understanding the characteristics of these differences is a key factor in becoming a proficient practitioner of the methodology.

CONCLUSION

While it may seem that the specifics of pairs trading and how they relate to market-neutral strategies require further exploration, it will be beneficial to first consider both arbitrage and technical analysis elements. The remaining connections will then become clear as a unified pairs trading theory is constructed.

PART TWO

The Arbitrage Element

Rule No. 1:
Never lose money.
Rule No. 2:
Never forget Rule No. 1.
—Warren Buffett

CHAPTER 5

Arbitrage Factors

The most basic definition of an arbitrage trade is one that seeks to exploit an inefficiency in the market by buying a security and simultaneously selling it for a profit. While such a situation would seem somewhat fantastic in today's era of information technology, it was once possible for a limited number of individuals with superior information and communication capabilities to exploit these types of situations. With the advent of real-time data on every desktop of even the most limited market participant, the days of simple arbitrage are basically gone. In the few cases that do still exist, the profit per transaction usually amounts to a mere fraction of a cent; therefore, these examples only become practical when millions, if not billions, of dollars can be applied to them to create a worthwhile profit.

While certain market inefficiencies do still exist, the majority of arbitrage activity today is based on perceived or implied pricing flaws, rather than on fixed price differences with incomplete information between or among certain individuals. In other words, these pricing flaws are not the result of incomplete or untimely information, but rather represent statistically significant anomalies of divergence from historically established average price relationships. In other terms, *relative-value arbitrage* is taking offsetting positions in securities that are historically or mathematically related, but taking those positions at times when a relationship is temporarily distorted. Thus, the most important feature of arbitrage, particularly in terms of how it relates to pairs trading, is the convergence of these flaws back to their expected values.

Trading based on this dynamic is essentially the same type of trading one sees in a *risk arbitrage* strategy but without the isolated fact of the underlying corporate event driving the thinking behind the trade. (Also referred to as M&A arbitrage, a risk arbitrage strategy involves identifying known corporate restructuring deals, buying the stock of the company being acquired, and shorting the stock of the acquiring company based on the assumption that each stock price will move toward the contractually agreed upon conversion prices as the deal moves toward fruition.) What drives relative-value arbitrage decisions is careful analysis rather than corporate news, per se devoid of analysis.

Comprehending *statistical arbitrage* is important to understanding pairs trading because they are in essential ways the same—or such that statistical arbitrage should be considered a *form* of pairs trading, as there are also some differences. While pairs trading may be driven by either fundamental or technical information and may have almost any time horizon, statistical arbitrage is based purely on historical, statistical data that is utilized in the very short term for numerous small positions. The most significant point of differentiation is that statistical arbitrage is almost purely model and computer driven, with very little human analysis affecting any single trade. Once a statistical arbitrage model is constructed and accepted, it is fed into a computer that makes all trading decisions based on the prescreened criteria. This often involves hundreds of trades a day, each trying to capture a very small positive price movement. This kind of trading obviously requires both very sophisticated modeling capabilities and a fairly extensive technology infrastructure.

Pairs trading has elements of both relative-value and statistical arbitrage. As previously discussed, a pairs trader selects his stocks via a method that is based on mean reversion. Traders utilizing mean reversion strategies work under an assumption that anomalies among stock valuations may occur in the short term, but in the long term these anomalies will correct themselves as the market processes the information. Thus, in a group of stocks that historically trade similarly, short-term events and the tendency of investors to overreact to unexpected news can create pricing disparities (stocks are over- and undervalued relative to the group) that are highly unlikely to hold in the long term. When one stock's statistical price anomaly reverts back to the mean price of its group of stocks, the move is known as mean reversion. The pairs trading strategy tries to take advantage of related securities whose prices have diverged from their historical norms. Traders search for groups of stocks for which the values, over the long term, are positively correlated. Usually, a common theme within each group links the individual equities together. A sector, an industry, a commodity, or a particular risk factor may define a group. The long-term trend line for the group is relatively smooth, but the short-term individual stock lines are full of peaks and valleys. Mean reversion traders try to sell short the stocks in the group that are at their peaks and buy those that have reached their likely bottom.

Pairs trading contains elements of both relative-value and statistical arbitrage in that it often uses a statistical model as the initial screen for creating a relative-value trade. A careful pairs trader will perform several layers of analysis on top of the model output before any pairs are actually executed, but it is the arbitrage element that is principally responsible for profit generation. Clearly arbitrage theory plays a central role in understanding pairs trading.

SECURITY TYPE

When considering arbitrage generally, one should keep in mind that classically traders specializing in this format have focused their efforts on fixed income and currency-related securities. The reason is that these types of securities are more easily tied to major economic metrics; the reactions of these securities to changes in macroeconomic factors are fairly straightforward and predictable. The result of this relationship is that with a basic understanding of macroeconomic principles, a trader has a good understanding of the price pressures affecting his portfolio. Equities tend to be more susceptible to subtle changes in mass sentiment, causing them to be more unpredictable. This sensitivity is partly attributable to participation in the equity markets by large numbers of laymen, while fixed income and currency trading usually are limited to professionals. The market behavior of professional traders tends to be more predictable and movement within their marketplace specialties more stable.

For the duration of Part Two, the investigation will continue to focus exclusively on the equity markets. Despite their differences from the fixed income and currency markets, the equity markets should provide a useful backdrop against which to understand the underlying concepts being presented. In later sections, Part Five specifically, some of the subtleties of currency arbitrage will be addressed to the extent that it furthers the reader's understanding of pairs trading. While fixed income arbitrage is not explored, it follows many of the same tenets explored here, and a separate consideration of it would do little to advance the current investigation.

THE EFFICIENT MARKET HYPOTHESIS

No exploration of arbitrage theory could be considered complete without including some discussion of the efficient market hypothesis. There are three forms of this theory, all premised on the idea that the market is able to efficiently process information and that, therefore, market prices will reflect all available information. This phenomenon is often referred to as the market's ability to "price-in" various pieces of information. It is most commonly discussed after the release of major economic news; one might hear an analyst say that the market did not move on the news because it had already "priced-in" the announcement.

The weak form of the hypothesis asserts that current market prices reflect all of the information contained in the historic prices of any given stock. The semi strong form asserts that current market prices represent all publicly available information, while the strong form takes the final step and claims that *all* information is incorporated, including inside information. Regardless of the form selected, the implication of the hypothesis is that stocks are fairly priced in the market and that arbitrage situations cannot exist. Despite the strength of this argument and the general empirical support ones finds for it, clearly arbitrage situations do exist. If they did not, professional arbitrageurs, such as the pairs trader, would soon face bankruptcy and find another line of work.

Thus the fact that the market appears to be efficient on the one hand and yet contains opportunities for arbitrage is something of a paradox. There are two possible explanations for how these seemingly contradictory situations exist simultaneously. One is that professionals who pursue arbitrage opportunities are themselves responsible for the creation of efficient markets. By seeking out and exploiting market inefficiencies, they essentially eliminate them in the process by driving prices toward their appropriate level. This argument is particularly appealing when one considers that all market participants are implicitly involved in arbitrage from time to time. It is not uncommon for a trader to look for undervalued options, futures, and even equities. These individual are not searching for arbitrage opportunities, but they take advantage of them when they present themselves. In this sense, if all traders are to a greater or lesser degree exploiting arbitrage opportunities, then the market efficiently distributes this information and eliminates these discrepancies whenever they occur. Meanwhile, the very small group of traders who actively seek such opportunities is irrelevant to market efficiency.

A second explanation for this paradox, while somewhat more elegant, is less compelling. If an opportunity for arbitrage is defined as one in which an individual may receive a risk-free profit, then a professional involved in arbitrage would fall outside this defined group. As was discussed in Part One, even when such a professional identifies an arbitrage opportunity, he is still faced with certain risks. Execution is the most severe of these, and by exposing himself to it, the professional is not receiving a risk-free profit. This argument is less compelling than the first because it hinges more on definition than practice. The skilled and experienced arbitrageur does face execution risk, but the risk is greatly diminished if the trade is well planned and backed by significant influences. Professionals tend to have both the means for careful planning and the influence required to ensure reasonably sound execution.

The conclusion that can be drawn from the efficient market hypothesis is that while the market is generally efficient, there is often a time lag in this efficiency which can be exploited by solid analysis and careful planning. Resolution of the paradox is, therefore, not necessary.

TYPES OF ARBITRAGE CONVERGENCE

An arbitrage position is built on convergence expectations and relies on the comparison between traded market prices and the relationship that the trader believes should exist based on historical analysis. This convergence comes in three varieties and is dependent on the type of arbitrage position one takes. While only one of these types of convergence is relevant to pairs trading, understanding each will make the pairs case more solid.

Absolute Convergence

This type of convergence is representative of the purest form of arbitrage position and is most commonly observed in cases of *index arbitrage,* which involves capturing pricing discrepancies between a derivative and its underlying reference. In taking an index arbitrage position, a trader may buy a futures contract in one market and simultaneously sell the same contract in a different market. This is done with futures contracts on indexes, hence the name index arbitrage. While one is dealing with the same contract, this is still a derivative and reference situation because one market usually commands the most volume and liquidity, and thus sets the price on which the foreign contract is established. For example, some Japanese Index futures trade on both the Japanese and Singapore exchanges, as well as in U.S. markets. If a trader identifies a pricing discrepancy between two of these markets, an arbitrage situation exists and can be exploited.

This type of convergence is referred to as absolute because after execution it is set, in the sense that it has been captured. The trader may have to wait until the individual contracts expire to realize his profit, but he knows the amount he will receive at that time. These positions are subject to execution risk, but once the trade has been placed, the remaining risks that the arbitrageur faces can be managed. For example, the trader may face foreign exchange risk, but this can be managed easily through forward contracts that expire simultaneously with the contracts that make up the arbitrage. Other risk management techniques may need to be applied to the position over its life, but if a skillful trader does this, his profit is guaranteed.

Index arbitrage is the best example of absolute convergence because not only does it exploit an identifiable pricing discrepancy, but it also is subject to a wide variety of risk factors that must be understood if the trade is to be managed properly. Each of these features helps to explain why this type of trading is fairly rare and limited to a small number of individuals. To both identify these opportunities and then successfully manage them requires a great deal of technology as well as experience in a wide range of risk management techniques. Absolute convergence situations are not present in pairs trading, but understanding them helps one to define or recognize what a pairs trading strategy is not. Such recognition will remove any confusion that the would-be practitioner may have and will help him to avoid any surprises once the enterprise has been accepted.

Overt Convergence

This type of convergence is most commonly associated with *risk arbitrage* and occurs when the convergence is planned but not certain. When two companies are planning a corporate action, such as a merger or acquisition, and this news is announced, there is frequently a difference between the current market prices of the two stocks and the contractually agreed-upon conversion price. As the time remaining until the announced conversion decreases and the certainty that the action will occur increases, the prices of the two stocks involved tend to move toward parity with the agreed-on conversion price.

In risk arbitrage, the trader takes a long position in the company being acquired and an offsetting short position in the company doing the acquisition. These positions are based on the fact that the acquirer usually pays a premium for the market price, putting upward pressure on share price; the stock of the acquiring company feels downward pressure as share price is adjusted to compensate for the expenditure and share dilution. If the deal is consummated, the expected convergence occurs and, on the day of conversion, the prices of the two equities should be at the agreed-on conversion price as the result of normal market pressure.

The greatest risk in this type of arbitrage is that the corporate action will not take place as planned. If this occurs, the relationship between the two involved stock prices ceases to be meaningful and convergence becomes unlikely. Risk arbitrageurs perform detailed analysis of the announced action prior to taking a position and usually possess broad networks through which information can be collected. They attempt to get a clear picture of both the respective shareholder perspectives and the regulatory environment in which the deal must be approved. Judgment and experience, however, are ultimately the best risk management tools available in this type of situation.

This type of convergence is called overt because it involves publicly announced information that should lead to the convergence. Both of the companies involved will have spent time performing their own analyses and are not likely to announce a deal that they do not believe is possible. Furthermore, both sides will have negotiated terms that they believe are favorable and will have made a strong commitment to seeing the action take place. When the announcement is made, the risk arbitrageur can feel comfortable that each company will be working toward realizing the end action of the deal that will, in turn, result in the desired convergence.

This is not a speculative situation because there is ample evidence at the time such an announcement is made that the convergence is the goal of the two companies involved. The trader does not need to seek out the opportunity and speculate on whether it will result in convergence; if the deal happens, the convergence is contractually guaranteed. The historical relationship between the two stock prices does not play a role in his analysis; he must simply judge whether he believes the action will take place. This, again, is not the situation faced by a pairs trader, but an understanding of it will help to define the limitations of the speculative convergence that a pairs trader faces.

Implied Convergence

Implied convergence is the basis of pairs trading and is based on the assumption that statistically related securities that have experienced a divergence from their historical relationship will, at some point in the future, converge back toward their historical average. The phenomenon is the mean reversion theory discussed in Part One. This type of arbitrage is often termed *speculative* because it relies on convergence occurring without a strong fundamental reason behind it; where absolute convergence occurs by definition and overt convergence is the result of contractual stipulations, implied convergence is the result of the speculative belief that history will repeat. This is the weakest of the three types and is often overlooked. The result is that strategies that rely on implied convergence have not received the same attention as the others; therefore, there are more opportunities available to capitalize on this type of pricing discrepancy.

By definition, an arbitrage position that is based on implied convergence is proprietary because it relies on the analysis of only a small group
of traders who believe the convergence is justified. Because there is no
underlying force driving the convergence it is subject to price shocks, and
the actuality of convergence is the greatest risk facing the arbitrageur.
Through careful and rigorous analysis, tight stop-loss measures, and solid
model construction, this type of arbitrage system can produce stable and
sustainable profits with very limited risk.

RISK ANALYSIS

When hedging risk in an arbitrage situation, there are two types of hedges
that can be used: static and dynamic. A static hedge refers to a position
that is considered hedged at the time of initiation and will not be adjusted
through the duration of the trade. Dynamic hedges, conversely, are hedge
positions that will be regularly adjusted; as they do not apply to the pairs
trading strategy, they will not be discussed.

Static hedges are most commonly defined in terms of quantity. A fixed
quantity of each stock is used on each side of the trade and is not changed
until the trade is ultimately closed. In the type of arbitrage situation specific to pairs trading, these quantities are fixed based on a historical relationship. The various types of relationship that may be considered are the
types of neutrality discussed in Chapter 4. Exploring some of these relationships more deeply will help to flesh out the nature of arbitrage valuation and why it is so critical to pairs trading.

In the case of a beta-neutral trade, beta can be defined as follows:

$$\beta_{a/b} = \frac{\text{Cov}(r_a, r_b)}{\sigma_b^2}$$

$$= p_{a/b} \times \frac{\sigma_a^2}{\sigma_b^2}$$

where $\beta_{a/b}$ = beta of a versus b
        Cov (r_a, r_b) = covariance of the returns of a and b for the
                relevant period
        $p_{a/b}$ = the correlation coefficient between a and b
    σ_b^2 and σ_a^2 = the respective variances

In such a case, each dollar of exposure to a is hedged with $\beta_{a/b}$ dollars
of exposure to b; this creates the desired beta-neutral trade. If nominal ex-

posure is now assigned the terms N_a and N_b, respectively, then the relationship becomes:

$$N_b = \beta_{a/b} \times N_a$$

and the valuation of the trade is

$$V = N_a - N_b$$

From this relationship, it follows that the change in V, the value of the position, is dependent on the change in the value of the nominal exposure to both a and b. If this logic is followed through, then the only way for V to be a nonzero figure is if the relationship between a and b diverges from its historical norm. Beta-neutral trades can therefore be thought of as historically based, while convergence-based dollar-neutral trades come from on a forward-looking perspective. This is relevant to an understanding of arbitrage risk because it illustrates that the very idea of a hedged trade is heavily based on the type of metric with which one chooses to evaluate risk.

The advantage of a static hedge is that it tends to be fairly stable over time because the probability of convergence does not vary greatly from day to day. The specific positions that are initiated may vary somewhat in terms of the nominal exposure that the trader accepts based on the type of hedge and neutrality criteria he is seeking in the short term. However, because he is predicting the future value of the relationship between the long position and the short position, his hedge relationship will not fluctuate much. In a dynamic hedge situation, because the nature of the hedge is in a state of constant fluctuation, the timing and nominal exposure of each leg of the trade can be very uncertain.

NONCONVERGENCE

Nonconvergence is the biggest risk facing the speculative arbitrageur. In the case of an implied convergence, the trader is basing his position on the statistical probability that mean reversion will occur. The manager believes that he has identified a short-term divergence from a historically significant relative average and that this relationship will normalize over time. Nonconvergence is considered to have occurred when either the divergence increases in magnitude to the point that a stop-loss limit is reached and the trade is closed, or the duration of the trade extends beyond a predetermined time frame in which the manager believed the convergence would occur. In the latter case, because an implied convergence has no specific expiration, as do absolute and overt convergences, the chosen period is determined based on the historical volatility of the relationship and the opportunity cost of staying with the trade. This metric will differ from case to case and is somewhat at the discretion of the manager.

Given the importance of managing nonconvergence to the speculative arbitrageur, and given the somewhat arbitrary nature of duration limitation, the most important risk management tool that can be employed is the stop-loss. By analyzing the level at which stop-losses are set, the manager of this type of strategy can not only gain insight into the efficacy of his trades, but also evaluate the legitimacy of the strategy as a whole.

Consider the following equation:

$$(W \times W_m) - (L \times L_m) = 0$$

where W = the percentage of winning (profitable) trades
          W_m = magnitude of winning trades
          L = the percentage of losing trades
          L_m = magnitude of losing trades

If the manager of a speculative arbitrage portfolio examines the statistics of his trades to determine the values for the first three terms of the equation, then, by solving the equation for L_m, he can determine the maximum allowable loss on each losing trade to keep the strategy at the breakeven level. If his analysis reveals that this stop-loss level is lower than he believes is achievable, the entire strategy must be abandoned. If, however, the manager can set his stop-loss level below the calculated value, he can be comfortable that the strategy is profitable in design.

The level at which one sets a stop-loss is extremely important to the success of an implied convergence strategy. As previously discussed, it must be sufficiently tight to guarantee the ability of the manager to stay in business; if his strategy losses money consistently, he will not be able to keep trading. The other concern that bears some consideration is the case in which the stop-loss level is too tight. While the manager wants to limit the amount of money he may lose on a given trade, by closing a trade, he runs the risk that convergence will begin after the trade is closed and an opportunity will have been lost. Since it is unlikely that a manager will open every trade at the very instant that convergence begins, his stop-loss must be sufficiently loose to absorb some losses while he waits for convergence to begin and the trade to ultimately become profitable.

The specific level differs for each manager and may be gradually adjusted over time as he becomes more comfortable with the behavior of the trades he is placing. The level may also differ from trade to trade based on the specific characteristics of the securities being traded. Adjusting stop-loss levels can be a risky proposition but may be necessary when dealing with more or less volatile securities. It is important to remember that regardless of these subtleties, the manager must keep the level above the break-even figure calculated with the preceding equation. If he departs from this too frequently, he is liable to lose his overall profitability chasing minor incremental increases.

The specific stop-loss percentage that a manager may wish to use can be calculated if the preceding equation is rewritten:

$$(W \times W_m) - (L \times L_m) = P$$

where P = the expected profit from the strategy

In this case, still assuming that the percentage of winning and losing trades as well as the magnitude of the winning trades are known, if the equation is again solved for L_m, the appropriate stop-loss level is determined. The equation has many powerful applications because it may be used in a variety of ways. If, for example, statistical analysis reveals that after a trade has lost 6 percent it is unlikely to become profitable and should be stopped out, assuming the profit objective and win/loss percentages are known, the required profit objective can be calculated. In this example, if 70 percent of trades are profitable and the required return of the strategy is 10 percent, then the required profit objective can be calculated:

$$(70\% \times W_m) - (30\% \times 6\%) = 10\%$$

$$W_m = 2.7\%$$

In this case, in order for the strategy to return 10 percent, the required profit on each winning trade must be 2.7 percent. The equation may also be used to calculate the expected strategy return if both profit objective and stop-loss can be statistically revealed and win/loss percentage is known.

NORMALIZING DIVERGENCE

This technique is used in any mean reversion strategy and allows the trader to compare divergence to a normalized distribution. This provides cleaner data with which to analyze any given trade. The technique is commonly used to compare a stock's price with its moving average, the assumption being that the stock price will tend to oscillate around its moving average.

The chart in Figure 5.1 shows the normalized deviation between Microsoft and its 10-day moving average over the period of one year. This process is referred to as a *Z transformation* and is obtained by taking the difference between the price of Microsoft and its 10-day moving average, subtracting the average of the difference, and dividing by the standard deviation of this difference. As can be seen from the chart, this normalized deviation oscillates around zero fairly symmetrically. This relationship could be exploited by trading on the assumption that at a given level of divergence, there is a high probability that the deviation will revert to zero.

The problem with this relationship is that it is not possible to trade the moving average. If a market-neutral speculative arbitrageur takes a position in Microsoft only, he is exposed to the very systematic risk he is trying to eliminate. While there is a likelihood that Microsoft will revert to its moving average in the short term, there is no guarantee as to the direction in which the stock's price will move, relative to entry, in order to reach that moving average. There is a solution to this problem that can be used by the pairs trader, but that discussion is reserved for Chapter 6. What is important to understand here is that by normalizing a divergence, the arbitrageur will find mean reversion can become a very powerful tool.

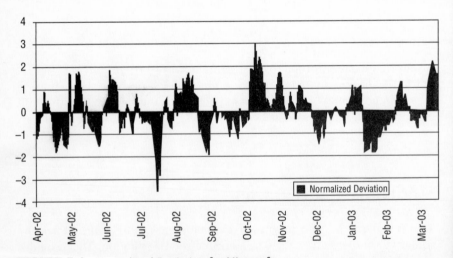

FIGURE 5.1 Normalized Deviation for Microsoft

CONCLUSION

While this discussion of arbitrage may seem somewhat cursory, it should be more than sufficient to provide a framework for understanding the arbitrage element of pairs trading which will be discussed in Chapter 6. Because pairs trading relies on implied convergence, it should be considered a speculative arbitrage situation. This understanding will help to define some of the risk factors that affect the strategy, as well as how they can best be dealt with. Using some of the tools offered here, coupled with those offered in Part One, the reader will gain an even better understanding of how to approach the strategy and trade it successfully.

CHAPTER 6

Arbitrage and Pairs Trading

A rbitrage is the second key element that defines pairs trading and gives it shape as an investment strategy. In this chapter, the factors considered in Chapter 5 are directly related to the strategy, toward the end of giving the reader a way to relate the two theories. Many of the features of this relationship are similar to those of pairs trading and market-neutral investing. Some redundancy is therefore inevitable.

RELATIVE-VALUE AND STATISTICAL ARBITRAGE

Before beginning the discussion relating pairs trading and arbitrage, it may be useful to provide explicit definitions of the two types of arbitrage that are most relevant to a matched pairs strategy: relative-value and statistical arbitrage. Pairs trading possesses many of the characteristics of each of these strategies and yet has some key features that make it unique.

Relative-Value Arbitrage

Relative-value arbitrage encompasses a broad range of investment approaches including convertible, merger, fixed income arbitrage, and the strategies being explored here. The common element of each of these approaches is that the manager is making a spread trade, rather than seeking exposure to the general market. Returns are derived from the behavior of the relationship between two related securities rather than stemming from market direction. Generally, the manager takes offsetting long and short positions in these securities when their relationship, which historically has been statistically related, is experiencing a short-term distortion. As this distortion is eliminated, the manager profits. Relative-value arbitrage is another name for what is called a mean reversion strategy in pairs trading terminology.

What differentiates a relative value arbitrageur from a pairs trader is that a relative value manager considers all types of relative value strategies and picks one or more to include in his portfolio at a given time. While such a portfolio may contain a pairs trading allocation, it may simultaneously contain convertible and fixed income arbitrage positions. The manager's decision about which strategies to include in his portfolio is usually a function of his experience, expertise, and resources. The greater the number of strategies he chooses to include, the more resources he must dedicate to assuring that each strategy is accurately covered.

As a result of combining multiple strategies, the relative value manager is exposed to certain unique risk factors. While he is obviously exposed to the individual risk factors associated with each strategy, he must also monitor the risks associated with his strategy mix and allocation. *Strategy mix risk* refers to the additional risk the manager accepts by adding different strategies to his portfolio. By diluting his area of expertise, his returns may suffer from lack of adequate attention to any one approach. *Strategy allocation risk* is derived from the manager's ability to identify which strategy offers the best risk/return profile at a given time. He may make good trades in each strategy but decrease his overall return potential by allocating too much to relatively underperforming areas of the portfolio.

In connection with pairs trading, it is the philosophical approach taken by the relative value arbitrageur that is of interest. This style of arbitrage is concerned with relationship investing as opposed to directional trading. This is the central philosophical approach that motivates the pairs trader. In seeking to eliminate or reduce exposure to the various types of systematic risk, the pairs trader chooses to invest in the relationship between two securities or groups of securities that he believes are related. As a result of this principle, pairs trading is one of the strategies available to the relative value arbitrageur.

Statistical Arbitrage

Statistical arbitrage is the relative-value arbitrage strategy that is most similar to pairs trading. The strategy involves analyzing various groups of stocks that are statistically related and then buying the ones that are undervalued for the long portfolio and selling short those that are overvalued for the short portfolio. This is another example of a mean reversion strategy, because the manager believes that over time the two groups will converge back to their historically established mean relationship. The selection of each group of stocks is based on a complex model that can quickly evaluate the data and provide the manager with a simplified ranking output.

What differentiates statistical arbitrage from pairs trading is the amount of human intervention that is allowed. Statistical arbitrage models are usually followed automatically, with little interaction from the manager. This type of portfolio tends to employ heavy turnover and extremely active trading. The model generates trades and executes them with the goal of finding hundreds or thousands of very small gains over a given time frame. The advantage of this type of trading is that it eliminates human emotion from the trading equation; emotion, it is believed, often causes the failure of a successful system. The pairs trader may use a statistical model as a screening tool but will apply his own analysis and discretion to the process. His trades tend to be longer in duration and generate both larger profits and losses on a per trade basis.

THE IMPLIED CONVERGENCE OF MATCHED EQUITY PAIRS

A pairs trading strategy is based on implied convergence because there is no fundamental or identified reason that the stocks involved should revert back to their historical average—rather, the expectation is based on statistical probability. The pairs trader takes a position in the belief that a relationship that has behaved in a certain way for an extended period of time will continue to do so in the future. This expectation is, of course, based on a stipulation or assumption that the relationship is not acted on by some outside force that will change the basic characteristics of its structure.

It may be helpful to consider a scientific corollary from the world of physics. The popular maxim, "An object in motion tends to stay in motion," is a good parallel to the principle on which the pairs trader relies. It is important, however, to remember the second part of this rule that is often omitted from discussion: "An object in motion tends to stay in motion unless acted on by an outside force." It is the search for the presence of this outside force that leads the pairs trader to perform additional layers of analysis after receiving the output of his statistical model. Forces like news-driven price shocks and fundamental economic changes can alter the historical relationship between two stocks; in such cases, the pair is rejected and replaced with pairs in which no such forces portend.

That a matched equity pairs strategy is driven by implied convergence results in it being labeled a *speculative arbitrage* situation. This label can be misleading because it connotes a great deal of risk inherent in the strategy. Factually, when this strategy is executed with the appropriate level of skill, experience, and caution, it is one of the more stable investment approaches available. Still, as a speculative arbitrage strategy, many investors have overlooked it and have omitted it when fashioning their allocation options. In this time of increased volatility, relative-value arbitrage strategies should be a part of every investor's allocation considerations.

NORMALIZING PAIRS DIVERGENCE

As discussed in Chapter 5, normalized deviation is a technique used in any mean reversion strategy and allows the trader to compare divergence to a normalized distribution. Such a technique provides cleaner data with which to analyze a given trade. It is commonly used to compare a stock's price with its moving average, an assumption being that the stock price will tend to oscillate around its moving average. One problem, of course, with this exercise is that it is not possible to trade a moving average, and it is therefore impossible to capitalize on the information that this relationship provides. It is possible, however, to introduce the same calculation when considering a pairs relationship.

Consider the following equation:

$$\Delta_{norm} = \frac{\left(\Delta - MA_{10-day}(\Delta) \right)}{\sigma_{10-day}(\Delta)}$$

where Δ_{norm} = the normalized divergence
             Δ = the absolute difference
      $MA_{10-day}(\Delta)$ = the 10-day moving average
       $\sigma_{10-day}(\Delta)$ = the 10-day standard deviation

The output of this equation represents the degree of divergence in terms of standard deviations. The implicit approximation in this process is that divergence is a random variable normally distributed. This operation provides far more useful information than does the divergence expressed in absolute terms, because it offers some predictive qualities about the relationship. For example, there is only a 15 percent chance that the deviation is either above 1 or below –1, and only a 2.3 percent chance that the divergence is either above 2 or below –2. This information should prove extremely useful because it gives the pairs trader a very high level of confidence that when the above conditions exist, he is dealing with a true anomaly that can be exploited.

As an illustration, consider the chart in Figure 6.1. It is clear from the chart that it is rare to find the relationship represented here, General Motors versus Daimler Chrysler, more than 1 standard deviation away from its mean value, and even more rare to find the relationship more than 2 standard deviations away from its mean. This is the type of information that a matched equity pairs manager hopes to find, since it confirms his belief that when the relationship does move beyond its normal range, it can be considered an abnormal divergence that can be exploited. What the chart also shows is that over the one-year period represented, the relationship does exhibit regular oscillation characteristics around its mean. In other words, the manager can observe that the chart is relatively symmetric and frequently crosses its mean value, in this case, the moving average. The more frequently the relationship oscillates about its mean, the more volatile the relationship is considered to be; more volatile relationships are easier to trade on a short-term basis as they provide more frequent opportunities to capitalize on the implied mispricing.

Once the manager has performed the necessary Z transformation (as described in Chapter 5) and become comfortable with the strength of the relationship, he may begin to set buy and sell rules based on the observed

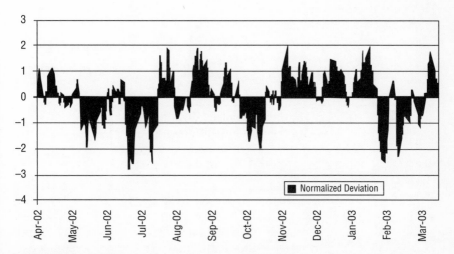

FIGURE 6.1 Normalized Deviation for General Motors and Daimler Chrysler

behavior of the relationship. This level may be set at 1.5, 2, or 2.5 standard deviations of divergence, but the level should be selected in such a way that the pair may be traded regularly. If the level is set too low, the manager will decrease the likelihood that the pair will quickly enough revert to its mean and he may defeat the power of his analysis. If the level is set too high, the manager will decrease the frequency with which the pair may be traded and he may miss many profitable trading opportunities. Finding the ideal level that best fits a particular manager's style is somewhat subjective and can be dependent on the underlying volatility of the securities that the individual manager selects to trade.

This type of analysis may also be used to examine the legitimacy of a pairs relationship. Figure 6.2 shows the chart of a pair that would be unsuitable for trading. Two features of this chart would lead the matched pairs trader to reject this pair during his stock selection process. First, notice how infrequently the relationship demonstrates a significant divergence from its mean. In such situations, it becomes very difficult for the manager to determine whether the pair is well positioned to begin the mean reversion process or if the observed diversion is likely to continue to increase in magnitude. While it may be possible to set buy and sell rules in such a situation, the probability of success is very limited. These rules would have to be set to such a low degree of divergence that the relationship would likely demonstrate a high probability of reaching this level of divergence. If the divergence does not represent a significant mispricing situation, the manager will not have a sufficient level of comfort to trade the pair.

The other feature of the chart in Figure 6.2 that would lead a pairs

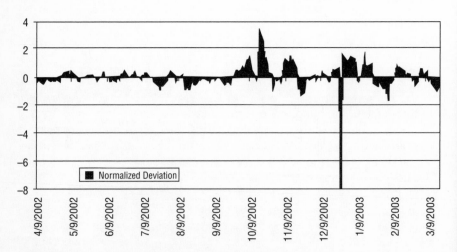

FIGURE 6.2   Normalized Deviation for U.S. Steel and Sears

manager to reject this trade is the huge level of divergence observed in December 2002. The chance of a 3 standard deviation degree of divergence is less than 1 percent; in December 2002, the relationship between U.S. Steel and Sears diverged to a level of greater than 8 standard deviations. The chance that this kind of divergence will be observed again in the future is nearly impossible, but it reveals something about the relationship to the manager. During the period of relevant historical observation, upon which the manager would evaluate the strength of the statistical relationship between these two stocks, this pair had clearly experienced a significant price shock. Despite the fact that it is statistically unlikely that a similar level of divergence will be observed in the future, the pair has revealed itself to be susceptible to price shocks and therefore not a good candidate for inclusion in the portfolio. The manager must understand the difference between statistical significance and practical significance in order to trade effectively. In such an instance, the manager's experience comes into play and proves most important.

If the two stocks depicted in Figure 6.2 are considered outside the parameters of the normalized deviation analysis, it is not surprising that the relationship does not play out as a good trade candidate. One need not be an experienced trader to realize that the relationship between U.S. Steel and Sears is a tenuous one at best. These two companies are in very different lines of business, and one would not expect to find a significant correlation between the two. This is an extreme example, used for demonstrative purposes only. In the regular course of portfolio construction, a pairs trading manager may encounter such a relationship between two stocks that his model and analysis have deemed otherwise acceptable. Normalizing the deviation helps the manager to identify questionable trades that other methods of analysis might not identify.

CONCLUSION

In this section, the importance of arbitrage as an element of pairs trading has been explored and confirmed. Arbitrage strategies are as complex as they are varied, covering most types of securities and the relationships between them. Pairs trading is but a microcosm of the arbitrage world, but a discussion of its importance is necessary to a complete exploration of the strategy. Readers who want a deeper understanding of the various types of arbitrage, how they can be used, and the specific advantages and constraints of each, should consult one of the many works dedicated to the subject. The information contained here is deemed sufficient to aid in the formulation of a unified pairs trading theory that will be developed in Part Four.

PART THREE

The Technical Analysis Element

One of the funny things about the stock market is that every time one man buys, another sells, and both think they are astute.

—William Feather

CHAPTER 7

Technical Tools and Indicators

I t should be fairly clear by this point that technical analysis plays a very central role in pairs trading. Although it is certainly possible to create fundamentally driven pairs trades, the methodology suggested throughout this text uses technicals to perform the majority of analyses required before trading; fundamentals are used simply as an overlay to ensure that there are no glaringly obvious reasons not captured in the technical indicators to wave managers off trades. Other books are available on the subject of technical analysis for those readers who wish to delve more deeply into the subject. While some necessary information about technical indicators is included here, this is not intended to be another book on the subject. The goal in this section is to explain technicals as they relate to pairs trading and to specific methodologies.

While a fundamental analyst considers a huge amount of very subjective data, the technical analyst deals with only three pieces of data: price, trading volume, and sentiment. He evaluates them to form an opinion on the likely direction of prices over a shorter period of time. The complete analyst looks at the fundamentals to decide whether a significant movement is likely or to compare two or more companies on a longer-term scale; he employs technical analysis to determine the most propitious time to enter the market. From a pairs trading standpoint, technical analysis plays a much more important role and, in the majority of cases, is the driving force behind most trades.

Technical analysts use computers to reconstruct past market activity and test trading theories. The underlying assumption is that a trading system that worked well in the past will work well in the future. System traders analyze their technical findings in the form of trading methods that have worked well in the past (over recent months and years) and try to determine a set of rules in order to project future trading results. This process, which is called *optimizing*, seeks the optimum balance between the values that produce the greatest profit and the values that produce the smallest loss.

The problem is, of course, that today's price behavior may not resemble yesterday's price behavior at all. Factors that affect prices are almost countless and in constant flux. This is one of the most significant risks facing a pairs trader and is called *model risk*. If there is a major flaw in the trading model, the entire system is likely to go awry and not produce a profit. The pairs trading approach, however, offers a great advantage over other methods because it allows a trader to incorporate different indicators and techniques (correlation, technical tools, fundamentals, and risk management, for example) to achieve a high probability of success without sacrificing statistical relevance. Opportunities are countless.

In this chapter, the major technical indicators most relevant to pairs trading are defined and discussed. While there are literally thousands of indicators in use worldwide, ranging from public indicators, available to everyone, to proprietary ones, this exploration will be limited to those that help form a solid foundation for a unified pairs trading theory. At the end of this section, the reader should have a solid, basic understanding of those elements of technical analysis needed to become a successful pairs trader.

The indicators discussed in this chapter are broken into three groups: market strength indicators, moving average indicators, and volume as an indicator. Market strength indicators compare the number of buyers apparent in the market with the number of sellers apparent in the market. When this relationship becomes distorted, the market for a given stock is said to be either overbought or oversold. Moving average indicators, as the name suggests, center on a stock's moving average for the period of the indicator. These numbers can be helpful because they give a smoothed picture of the stock's price action over a given period of time. Volume as an indicator is used primarily to confirm a trader's view of other information; it is used to gauge the intensity of the underlying market move.

MARKET STRENGTH INDICATORS

Before examining the specific indicators in this group, it will be helpful to give formal definitions of the terms that these indicators are trying to measure.

Overbought: When the market, or an individual stock, is said to be in an overbought condition, it means that the recent number of buyers has been disproportionately high compared to the number of sellers. Regular market forces tend to keep the number of buyers and sellers in equilibrium. Therefore, when an overbought condition exists, one expects downward pressure on the stock as the number of sellers catches up with the number of buyers until equilibrium is restored.

Oversold: This condition is the exact opposite of an overbought condition: The recent number of sellers has been disproportionately high compared to the number of buyers. In an oversold condition, upward pressure is exerted on the stock as the number of buyers catches up with the number of sellers—again, as equilibrium is restored.

Relative Strength Index

The relative strength index (RSI) is an interesting indicator because it does not measure relative strength in the classic sense. Usually, when a trader refers to the relative strength of a position, he is referring to the strength of that position relative to the strength of an index or benchmark. In the case of RSI, the indicator is measuring the relative internal strength of the position relative to itself. While this seems counterintuitive, consideration of the equation and the appropriate use of its output should clarify this problem.

The RSI formula is as follows:

$$\text{RSI} = 100 - \frac{100}{1+\text{RS}}$$

where   RS = Average for net up closing changes for N days divided by average of net down closing changes for N days.

The trader selects the number of days to be used; 5, 9, and 14 are standards used by most traders and are included in most commercial software programs.

The RSI will range from just above 0 to just under 100, but it is extremely rare to see a number close to either of these extremes. Most commonly, an RSI reading will fluctuate between 30 and 70. At extremes, it will move under 30 or above 70. Many traders prefer to use 20 and 80 to indicate oversold and overbought conditions, but the level selected is left to the individual trader.

An RSI number that becomes too small or too large theoretically indicates that the trader should begin monitoring a position carefully; when a stock becomes overbought or oversold, the trader expects a reversal to occur in the immediate future. Figure 7.1 shows the chart of a stock's price action and the corresponding RSI reading; it is apparent that extreme RSI readings often are associated with price reversals in the stock under scrutiny. These reversals tend to occur when or shortly after the extreme reading is taken, so the trader should not consider such a reading to be an immediate trading catalyst.

RSI measurements can be used to examine the relationship between two stocks as well. The specifics of RSI for a price relationship are similar to those for an individual stock, but they may be even more pronounced. One of the ways to use RSI is to look for a divergence between the chart of the stock and RSI readings. Figure 7.2 shows the chart of a ratio's price action and the correspondent RSI reading. When a divergence is detected, it may indicate a major trend reversal rather than a regular fluctuation.

Perhaps the most important observation that can be made from Figures 7.1 and 7.2 is that extreme RSI readings are almost always associated with reversals in price direction. It is important to observe, however, that the degree of the reversal is not reflected in the RSI reading. Some of the most extreme readings are associated with only small reversals. Remember that RSI is but one of the many indicators available to a trader, a

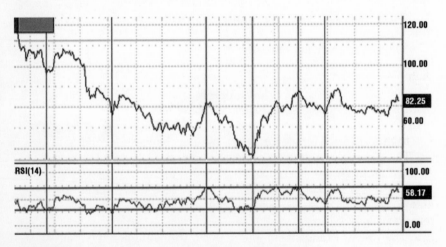

FIGURE 7.1 Price Action and RSI Reading for One Stock

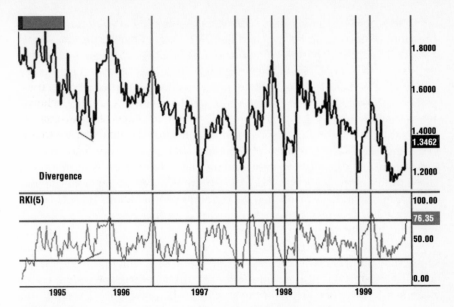

FIGURE 7.2 Two Stocks' Price Relationship and RSE Reading

combination of multiple indicators is needed to provide a picture of the market derived from technical analysis. No single indicator is either flawless or sufficient as a rule for all trading decisions.

Stochastics

Stochastics are another popular market strength indicator. The stochastic oscillator compares the point at which a stock's price has closed relative to its price range over a specific period of time. The theory behind this indicator is that in an upwardly trending market, prices tend to close near their high; conversely, during a downward trending market, prices tend to close near their low. In an upward trending market, as the trend begins to mature and near reversal, the closing price tends to be farther from the high than observed early in the trend. The same characteristic is true relative to the low price for a downward trending market.

The stochastic indicator attempts to determine when prices begin to close at an increasing distance from their trading range highs. In an upward trending market, as this begins to occur and closing prices are grouped near the day's low, such occurrence signals that a reversal is imminent. Similarly, in a downward trending market, when the closing prices are grouped near the day's high, a trader can also begin to look for a reversal.

The stochastic indicator is plotted as two lines. They are the %D line, the more important of the two, and the %K line. The stochastic, like RSI, is bounded by a range between 0 and 100. Readings above 80 are strong and indicate that price is closing near its high. Readings below 20 are strong and indicate that price is closing near its low. Under regular circumstances, the %K line will change direction before the %D line. In cases when the %D line changes direction prior to the %K line, a slow and steady reversal is usually indicated. When both %K and %D lines change direction, and the faster %K line subsequently changes direction to retest a crossing of the %D line, one may assume this to be a good confirmation of the stability of the prior reversal. An extremely powerful reversal is under way when the indicator reaches its extremes around 0 and 100. When the indicator retests these extremes following a pullback in price, a good entry point is indicated.

Many times, when the %K or %D lines begin to flatten, one may conclude that the trend will reverse during the next trading range. Quite often, just as with the RSI, a trader may identify a divergence on the chart. Specifically, the price action of the stock may be making higher highs, but the stochastic oscillator is making lower highs. In this case, the indicator usually is demonstrating a change in price before the price itself is changing. The same characteristics may be observed when price action is at new lows.

The formula for %K is as follows:

$$\%K = 100 \times \frac{C - L5_{close}}{H5 - L5}$$

where   C = the most recent close
          L5 = the lowest low for the last five trading periods
          H5 = highest high for the same five trading periods

The %D line is a smoothed version of the %K line that utilizes three periods. The %D formula is as follows:

$$\%D = 100 \times \frac{H3}{L3}$$

where   H3 = the three-period sum of (C − L5)
         L3 = the three-period sum of (H5 − L5)

Figure 7.3 shows the chart of the same stock used in Figure 7.1 over a slightly different time period. An examination of the chart reveals that the

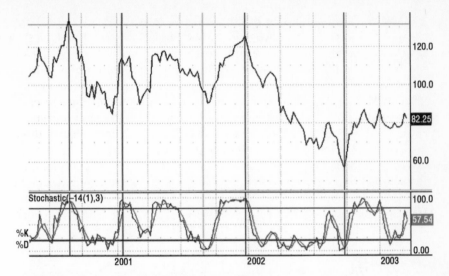

FIGURE 7.3 Stochastic Indicator for One Stock

stochastic indicator often reaches an extreme level before the reversal begins. This indicator is most helpful for alerting a trader that a price reversal is imminent. As in the RSI case, one should not use an extreme stochastic reading as an absolute catalyst for trading action.

Like RSI, stochastics can be applied to the relationship between two stocks. Figure 7.4 shows the chart of the same relationship represented in Figure 7.2. It illustrates how a 14 and 5 period stochastics oscillator attempts to identify overbought and oversold conditions for the ratio between stocks. As can be seen, in a majority of cases, entry points are nearly ideal when both %K and %D lines get below 20 or above 80 and cross each other.

It is very important to search for overbought and oversold conditions in a ratio between two stocks within a time frame suitable to a particular trader's style. While the example in Figure 7.4 deals with a relatively long period of time, shorter periods can be used. If the trader's time horizon is five days, it may not be appropriate to use a long-term weekly chart with indicators pointing to long-term reversals. The same indicators can be applied to daily, intraday and even one-minute charts.

Regardless of the specific time frame being considered, both RSI and stochastics are very useful for determining the relative degree to which a stock has reached those overbought or oversold conditions that exist within the market, with an individual stock, or within the relationship between two different stocks. These indicators prove very helpful to a trader in determining appropriate entry and exit points for whatever strategy he

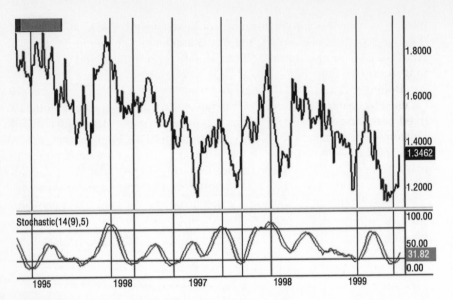

FIGURE 7.4   Stochastic Indicator for Relationship between Two Stocks

is trading. The application to pairs trading will be made even more explicit in Chapter 8 and in Part Four.

MOVING AVERAGE INDICATORS

The moving average is a technical indicator that is widely used by almost all technical traders. In its simplest form, the moving average is calculated by finding the average price for a given stock or index over a set period of time. Traders use this information to determine how a stock is behaving today relative to how it has behaved in the past. Moving averages, and the indicators based on them, are very powerful because they represent strict mathematical relationships. Where chart patterns are open to interpretation, moving average indicators, like market strength indicators, are objective measures of past activity. The advantage of this type of indicator is that they lend themselves to computerization and are easily included in trading models.

Bollinger Bands

Bollinger Bands are envelopes that surround the price bars on a chart. Bollinger Bands are plotted two standard deviations away from a simple moving average, which may or may not be displayed. The time period for this moving average can vary, but Mr. Bollinger recommends 10 days for short-term trading, 20 days for intermediate-term trading, and 50 days for longer-term trading.

Bollinger Bands are differentiated from simple envelopes by the criteria used to space them from the moving average; envelopes are plotted a fixed percentage above and below a moving average. Because standard deviation is a measure of volatility, the Bollinger Bands adjust themselves to the prevailing volatility within the market. They widen during volatile market periods and contract during less volatile periods. Many technicians increase the value of the standard deviation from 2 standard deviations to 2.5 standard deviations away from the moving average when using a 50-day moving average. Conversely, many technicians may lower the value of the standard deviation from 2 to 1.5 standard deviations when using a 10-day moving average.

It is important to keep in mind that Bollinger Bands alone do not generate buy and sell signals; they should be used with another indicator. The best combination is Bollinger Bands and RSI because when price touches one of the bands, it can indicate one of two things: It could indicate a continuation of the trend, or it could indicate a reaction the other way. Bollinger Bands, like many other indicators, need to be used in conjunction with another indicator to release their predictive ability. When combined with an indicator such as RSI, an excellent indicator with respect to overbought and oversold conditions, Bollinger Bands become quite powerful.

Generally, when a stock's price touches the upper Bollinger Band and RSI is below 70, a trader reads this as an indication that the trend will continue. Similarly, when price touches the lower Bollinger Band and RSI is above 30, a trader reads this as a signal that the trend will continue lower. In situations where the stock price touches the upper Bollinger Band and RSI is above 70, he understands that the trend may reverse itself and move downward.

Bollinger Bands can be used to evaluate the relationship between two stocks as well as to evaluate a single stock or index. Because it is the analysis of stock relationships that is most applicable to pairs trading, that will be the focus of this investigation. The vertical bars on the chart in Figure 7.5 indicate where the price of this ratio between two stocks is above the upper Bollinger Band or below the lower Bollinger Band. As can be seen, almost all of them are associated with turning points.

Bollinger Bands used in conjunction with other indicators can provide a trader with a good frame of reference for the price action of a stock or pair of stocks in which he is interested. The strength of this indicator is that it builds volatility into a process that is already easy to use as a result

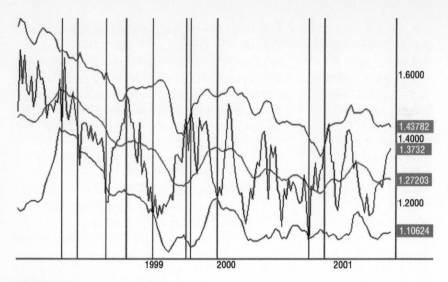

FIGURE 7.5   Bollinger Bands

of its mathematical basis. When it is paralleled with market strength indicators, like RSI or stochastics, an experienced technician can get a strong signal about the future direction in which the entity is likely to move. This is of particular importance in a traditional investment situation where market direction is the central factor driving performance. In a market-neutral situation, this ability to discern direction is still of great importance because the trader can apply the same indicators to the relationships between stocks that he is using as his trading vehicles.

Moving Average Convergence/Divergence (MACD)

The moving average convergence/divergence (MACD) indicator combines some of the principles of oscillators, like those already discussed, with a dual moving average crossover approach. It uses two metrics, both represented with lines. The faster of the two lines (called the MACD line) is the difference between exponentially smoothed moving averages of closing prices; the 12- and 26-day moving averages are most commonly used. The slower of the two lines is the exponentially smooth average of the trailing nine MACD periods. These metrics can be adjusted, but they are the most common examples and are used by a majority of traders.

There are two ways in which traders use MACD to generate buy and sell signals. The first involves a classic moving average crossover event. When the MACD line, the faster of the two, crosses the signal line, a signal is generated. If the MACD crosses and becomes higher than the signal line, this is a buy signal; if the MACD line crosses and becomes lower than the signal line, this is a sell signal. The second way that MACD gives buy and sell signals is as an oscillator. MACD fluctuates above and below a zero reading. Similar to RSI, when MACD is well above its median position—for this indicator that is zero—the position can be considered overbought. An oversold condition exists when the lines are too far below the zero median. Used in conjunction, the two indicators contained within MACD can be very powerful.

Figure 7.6 shows the chart of a stock's movement as compared to the MACD indicator.

Two important observations can be made from the graph. The first is that in most cases, when the MACD line crosses the signal line, a price reversal occurs. The second observation, perhaps a subtler one, is that the magnitude of the price move that follows a reversal tends to be proportionate to the distance MACD is from zero. In cases where MACD is well above or below zero, representing an oversold or overbought condition, the price move that follows the reversal tends to be larger in magnitude.

As was the case with both RSI and stochastics, a divergence may occur between the price action of the stock or index and the indicator itself. Such a case is represented in Figure 7.6. A divergence of this kind occurs when the MACD lines shift direction and the price action continues. These observations usually signal a more significant reversal pattern in the near future. In fact, this type of indicator divergence is often associated with either a major top or a major bottom, depending on whether the divergence is bullish or bearish in nature.

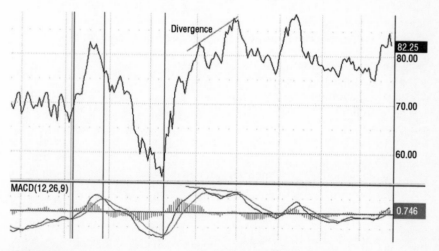

FIGURE 7.6 Moving Average Convergence/Divergence Indicator

VOLUME AS AN INDICATOR

The use of volume as an indicator can be applied to all types of markets and all types of securities. It is usually referred to as a secondary indicator because it must be placed in the context of some other market information to have any practical application. A trader may know that the daily trading volume of a particular stock is climbing, but without any market context behind it, this information is useless. When volume trends are used as a backdrop for other information, however, they can be used as confirmation of another indicator.

Generally, the level of volume is used to measure the intensity of the action observed in a price move within the market. What is relevant to a trader is not the absolute level of volume but the relative trend it displays within a specific time frame. If volume is increasing during an observed price event, the intensity of the move is confirmed by the market's growing conviction in its continuation. It is important to remember that regardless of what other traders may think or say, a technical trader is only concerned with what they do; increasing volume confirms that regardless of previously stated opinions, a growing number of market participants are getting behind the price move and driving it to a larger degree. Of course, if a trader observes declining volume behind a price move, this signals to him that there is not much conviction behind the move and interest is tapering.

Increasing or decreasing volume, and the strength of belief in the price movement that it represents, indicates market pressure to the trader. When a stock is in an upward trend and volume is increasing, there is upward pressure on the stock as more individuals compete to become part of the trend. Conversely, with the same upward-trending stock, if volume is decreasing, there is downward pressure on the stock, as sellers must accept lower prices in order to close their positions. Implicit in this argument is the fact that volume movement tends to precede price movement. This is a result of the fact that the changing number of traders interested in the stock creates the price pressure just described.

The same factors apply to a stock that is in a downtrend. If increasing volume is observed in a down-trending stock, the technician confirms the strength of that trend and believes it will continue. In simpler terms, volume should increase or expand in the direction of the prevailing price trend. When volume decreases in the direction of the prevailing price trend, this suggests that a reversal may occur in the near future.

Figure 7.7 shows the chart of a common stock and the daily volume measurement that corresponds with each trading day's price action. A careful examination of the chart shows that preceding most changes in the price trend of the stock, volume began to decrease or contract. After the reversal occurred, the volume began to increase or to expand in the di-

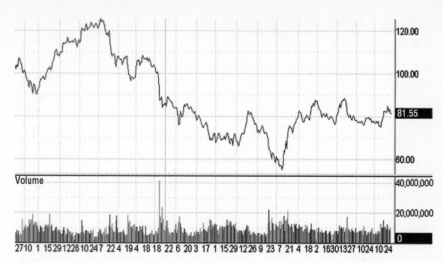

FIGURE 7.7 Daily Volume Measurement

rection of the new trend. It should not be assumed that simply because one observes falling volume, a reversal is imminent. What can be assumed is that when the technical trader has applied other indicators to the stock he is considering, volume may be used to help confirm whether his analysis is accurate. A trader may believe that a reversal is coming, but the increasing volume he observes in the direction of the trend will cause him to question his analysis and consider other factors. As with any indicator, volume is not a perfect predictor of future price action; when used as a secondary indicator, however, it can help a trader strengthen or weaken his comfort level with the signals provided by primary indicators.

CONCLUSION

This is not a book on technical analysis; readers who require more information are encouraged to find a more comprehensive source.

The indicators discussed in this chapter are but a few of the thousands being used every day by traders in all arenas. There are indicators that are specialized for trading certain types of securities and those designed to be superimposed on others. The indicators considered here are the ones most necessary to a discussion and understanding of pairs trading. In the next chapter, the techniques for applying these indicators to matched pairs trading are discussed and placed in context.

CHAPTER 8

The Technicals of Pairs Trading

The previous chapter discussed the use and application of many technical indicators, which were broken into three distinct groups: market strength indicators, moving average indicators, and volume as an indicator. The application of market strength indicators has already been discussed, and volume behaves the same way regardless of situation. This chapter discusses the application of some moving average indicators to pairs trading, and explains some specific techniques that are relevant to this strategy. At the conclusion of this chapter, sufficient foundation will have been laid to delve into the creation, formulation, and understanding of a unified pairs trading theory.

PAIRS APPLICATION OF MOVING AVERAGE INDICATORS

Moving average indicators can be a powerful tool when considered in the context of pairs trading. Over time and with experience a trader will develop a sense of which ones work best within his or her particular style.

Using Bollinger Bands to Trade Pairs

Chapter 7 introduced the general usage of Bollinger Bands. Another method for using Bollinger Bands to determine an entry point for a pair of stocks requires charting the two stocks separately. Often the best entry point is when the price of one stock closes above its 20-day upper band

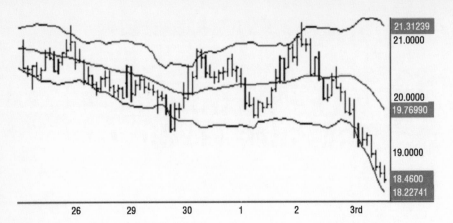

FIGURE 8.1 ABC Company, 30-Minute Chart with 20-Bar Bollinger Bands

and the other stock does not. The stock that closed above the upper band is considered overbought while the second stock is not overbought enough. If both correlated stocks are in a strong upward trend, the probability is that the second stock will catch up with the first one. Another possibility is that the first stock will reverse. In this case, the probability is that it will correct the overbought condition faster than the second stock.

The charts in Figures 8.1 through 8.3 help to illuminate this argument graphically. The vertical lines on the chart in Figure 8.3 point to the instances when one of the stocks is outside the statistical deviations while the other one is not. These instances represent good entry points for a pairs trader. Following the rules just expressed, he can feel comfortable

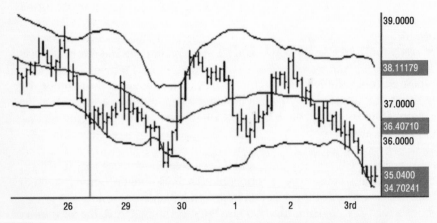

FIGURE 8.2 XYZ Company, 30-Minute Chart with 20-Bar Bollinger Bands

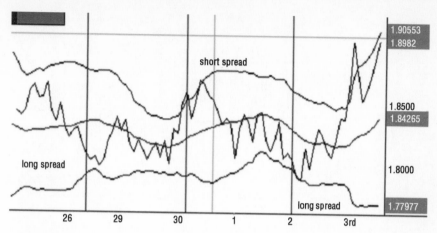

FIGURE 8.3   XYZ and ABC, 30-Minute Chart with 20-Bar Bollinger Bands

that these entry points offer profitable trading points, if all other assumptions hold true.

The Flatness Coefficient

The Flatness Coefficient is a proprietary moving average indicator that was developed specifically to be used in pairs trading. It is used to measure the amount of trend or flatness that is observable in the moving average of a pair of stocks. This information can be an excellent predictor of the probable success of a pairs trade as it begins mean reversion. The Flatness Coefficient is not specifically applicable to single stocks or indexes, and its application will not produce any reliable analysis. While the specific mathematics behind the indicator are proprietary and cannot be discussed, the concept is very useful in understanding a pairs relationship.

The flatter the moving average, or the smaller the degree of observable trend in that moving average, the higher the Flatness Coefficient. When a pairs trader examines the relationship between two stocks, he will find that a high score for this indicator represents a more stable price relationship. Figures 8.4 and 8.5 show the charts of two different pairs relationships with very different characteristics in terms of Flatness Coefficient. The relationship depicted in Figure 8.4 is stable and the moving average is quite flat; this pair would have a relatively high Flatness Coefficient because over time the relationship displays very little trend. Keep in mind that the trader is interested in pairs that display very little trend over the relevant period but which still have significant and tradable oscillation about the moving average. A pair that does not move is just as difficult to

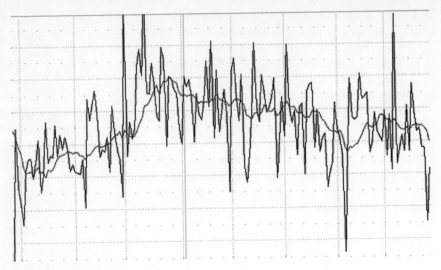

FIGURE 8.4 Stable Pair Relationship with Flat Moving Average

trade as one that displays too much trend. The moving average in Figure 8.5 begins fairly stably, but in the second half of the price action becomes very trending. Despite some small fluctuations in the relationship, the pair goes straight down and, more importantly, does not cross its moving average for a significant time period.

A general rule observed by some pairs traders is that crossing the

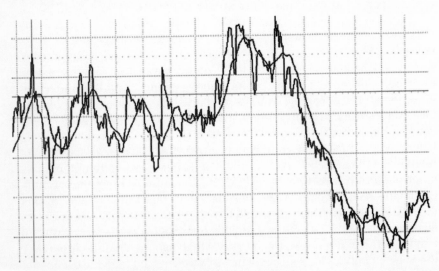

FIGURE 8.5 Moving Average That Becomes Trending

moving average is the desired exit point. In the case of Figure 8.5, this could be a very costly strategy because, despite the fact that the pair does eventually cross above the moving average, signaling that mean reversion has occurred, it does so at a much lower price than the likely entry price. Such a situation is unlikely in the case of Figure 8.4 because the moving average does not waiver a great deal, but rather is very flat.

Some general observations can be made from comparing the two charts and applying them to pairs trading. The first is that the higher the degree of observable flatness in the moving average of a pair, the more stable that pair is likely to be. Intuitively this relationship suggests that the probability of successful and profitable mean reversion increases in the case of stable pairs. The pair in Figure 8.5 demonstrates successful but not profitable mean reversion. Since traders are interested in profits, this is an important point.

The second and somewhat more subtle conclusion issuing from this discussion is that the magnitude of a profitable move is more predictable in cases where the moving average is very flat. The stability of this figure over time allows the trader increased confidence in future price action. Increasing the predictive value of any indicator or price move opinion allows a trader to move carefully and to aggressively manage his portfolio. The flatness coefficient is useful to the pairs trader because it not only gives him insight into the likely degree of price movement with which to associate mean reversion, it also gives him some indication of how stable the pairs have been over time.

The Technical Approach

Part of what distinguishes a technical trader from other types of traders is that charting and pattern recognition are central to his understanding of the market. When the technical trader is dealing with highly correlated pairs of stocks, before he begins to explore the technical indicators that are applicable to pairs trading he must chart and analyze each prospective pair. The first step is to select a reasonable time horizon defining the length of time between the initiation of a trade and the anticipated exit from it. By looking at the ratio between two equities, a trader can see the intervals between convergence and mean reversions and can thereby intelligently project the time it is likely to take a trade to achieve a desired profit objective. If a correlation analysis is done on a relatively long period of time, it is not prudent to engage in short-term trading based on this analysis. Obviously, short-term traders should apply more weight toward short-term correlation computations in order not to create a disconnect between their analysis and their expectations.

The simplest way to visualize a relationship between two equities is to chart the ratio between those two equities. A chart should be constructed by dividing one stock by the other. By doing this, a new trading vehicle is created; from a technical viewpoint, considering it as one trading unit rather than as a relationship between two stocks is preferable.

The chart in Figure 8.6 illustrates a long-term relationship between two securities that are strongly correlated. It quickly becomes apparent that there were plenty of profitable opportunities in trading these two stocks as a pair. A brief consideration of the chart reveals two basic tenets that are very useful when trading matched equity pairs:

1. Pairs trading is an example of range-bound trading (buying when this ratio is low and selling when this ratio is high).
2. Expectations in terms of time horizon are identifiable from chart analysis.

No matter what the stock market does, the correlation remains the constant on which the trade is premised. When considering any range-bound trading strategy, the trader attempts to buy near the bottom of the range and sell near the top. When a trader is considering a pair of stocks, "buying at the bottom" means buying one issue and shorting the other when the difference in price is historically significant. This same theme recurs through all of the topics that have been covered. A pairs trader is not concerned with whether these stocks go up or down after initiating a position; he is only concerned with the difference in price move between these two stocks, or whether his long position outperforms his short position.

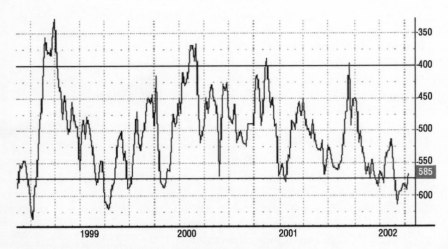

FIGURE 8.6   Ratio between Two Strongly Correlated Stocks

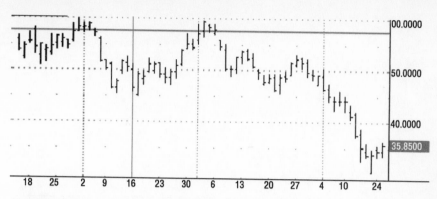

FIGURE 8.7 Stock A Price Action

The charts in Figures 8.7 and 8.8 show the price action of two stocks from the same sector. Note how closely correlated these stocks are. Instead of predicting the future direction of these equities, a pairs trading strategist tries to identify a deviation from the historical price ratio of this pair, and acts on the temporary contraction or expansion of this difference. The chart in Figure 8.9 represents the price relationship graphically. A technical trader will use all of the tools described to this point, but as a last check, he looks for charting behavior consistent with his predictions.

When a chart pattern similar to the one shown in Figure 8.9 is identified, the chart confirms the trader's analysis. This last graphical check is highly subjective and the ability to perform it evolves with experience. It is, however, central to the nature of technical trading because it relies heavily on graphical behavior recognition to confirm an underlying belief about market activity.

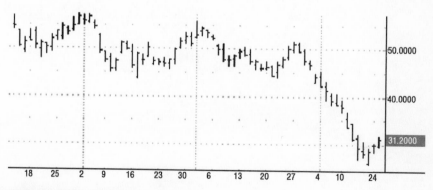

FIGURE 8.8 Stock B Price Action

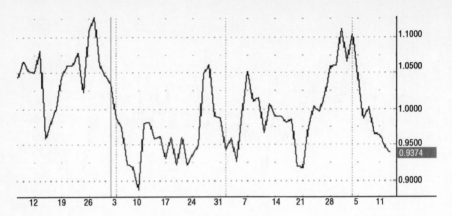

FIGURE 8.9 Stock A/Stock B Price Relationship

PRICE TREND IN PAIRS TRADING

A trend is the tendency for price or any other value to move more in one direction than another. Identifying and analyzing a price trend is the foundation of technical analysis. A familiar maxim often heard on Wall Street declares, "A trend is your friend." Although this is true for directional trading, the opposite is true for pairs trading. When a pairs trader analyzes two stocks as one trading unit, the last thing he wants to see is a trend. In the case of a chart showing a ratio between two stock prices, a trend means that two stocks are constantly diverging and do not return to the mean. What a pairs trader is looking for is a range.

Figure 8.10 shows the chart of a common stock over a five-year pe-

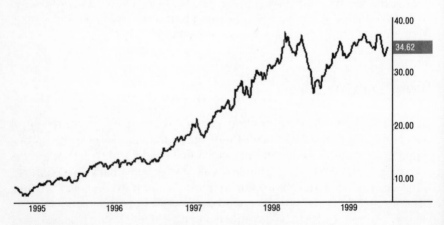

FIGURE 8.10 Price Action of a Stock over Five Years

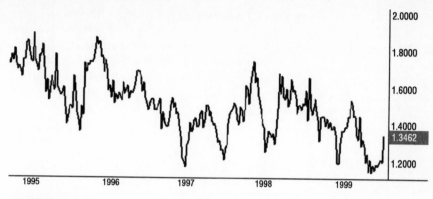

FIGURE 8.11   Price Relationship between Two Stocks Showing No Trend

riod. Clearly this stock has been trending for a long period and would be an ideal candidate for a buy-and-hold strategy if that trend continues. In the midst of a strong bull market, this is a reasonable assumption, but the trade is susceptible to a high degree of market risk. If the trend reverses, the buy-and-hold investor will have no protection and may end up losing money very rapidly.

A pairs trader seeks to eliminate this risk by matching stocks that have a high probability of behaving similarly. Figure 8.11 shows the chart of this same stock plotted as a price relationship with another stock with which it is highly correlated. The chart in Figure 8.11 shows a complete lack of trend, which is what the pairs trader is seeking. This relationship presents dozens of short- or intermediate-term opportunities to capitalize on the price action of the two stocks without being exposed to systematic risk. Regardless of the direction or trend in the general market, the pairs trader can profit from trading this relationship.

CONCLUSION

It should now be clear that trading matched equity pairs is very technical in nature. There are hundreds of indicators and approaches that can be applied to the price action of both individual stocks and the relationships between them. While the technician will always come back to a chart for final confirmation that his other analysis is accurate, in pairs trading, those indicators that represent solid mathematical relationships are preferred because they can be quantified and placed within the framework of an investment model.

In Part Four, all of the elements covered to this point will be combined and a unified pairs trading theory developed. Parts One through Three have been designed to give the reader a framework for understanding this final step and applying it to his own trading. While none of these sections are exhaustive on the subject matter they address, they should prove more than sufficient for preparing the reader to understand the unified pairs theory that follows.

PART FOUR

The Unified Theory

The man who makes everything that leads to happiness depends upon himself, and not upon other men, has adopted the very best plan for living happily. This is the man of moderation, the man of manly character and wisdom.

—Plato

CHAPTER 9

Reviewing the Elements

The pairs trading investment strategy is comprised of three central elements: the market-neutral element, the arbitrage element, and the technical analysis element. From the preceding exploration of these elements, a reader should now have a sufficiently comprehensive understanding of each to integrate the parts into a unified theory. This section is designed to give any prospective pairs trader the final tools that he will need to begin to apply the methodologies that drive the strategy.

For those ambitious readers who have chosen to skip ahead to this section of the book, a brief review of each element is provided. It is highly recommended that any questions about the individual elements be addressed before proceeding to the discussion of the unified theory.

THE MARKET-NEUTRAL ELEMENT

The first step to understanding this element of pairs trading is to provide a broad definition that applies to all market-neutral strategies.

Market-neutral strategy: A trading strategy that derives its returns from the relationship between the performance of its long positions and the performance of its short positions, regardless of whether this relationship is created on the security or portfolio level.

From this definition, the derivation of the idea of market neutrality becomes apparent; portfolio performance is driven by relative performance rather than by the absolute performance one would expect to find in a traditional long-only portfolio. In a market-neutral strategy, the return on the portfolio is a function of the return differential between the securities that are held long and those that are held short. In more traditional long-only strategies, a manager is constrained by the client-specified benchmark and is not permitted to maintain short positions. This long-only constraint reduces the ability of the manager to efficiently utilize his forecasts of the relative attractiveness of all the securities in his investment universe.

Types of Market Neutrality

Share Neutrality   Share neutrality refers to balancing a trade with an equal number of long shares and short shares. This is a very uncommon approach because in terms of relationship investing, the share price of either security is somewhat irrelevant.

Dollar Neutrality   Dollar neutrality is the most common type of market neutrality and is usually considered a requirement for market-neutral investing in equity securities. Dollar neutrality refers to buying equal amounts of long and short investments so that the dollar risk is equal on each side of the portfolio. By employing dollar neutrality in a market-neutral strategy, an investor ensures that his net dollar exposure to market swings is zero.

Sector Neutrality   In a traditional long-only portfolio, sector neutrality means balancing a portfolio along the lines of the benchmark. In other words, one sets up a portfolio in such a way that exposure to a given sector does not explain the performance differential between the portfolio and the benchmark. In a market-neutral strategy, sector-neutral means that portfolios are long/short balanced within each sector of the market to insulate the overall portfolio against the possibility that one sector will perform very well while another performs poorly. By making the portfolio sector-neutral, one avoids the risk of market swings affecting some industries or sectors differently from others and thereby losing money when long a stock in a sector that suddenly plunges and short another in a sector that stays flat or goes up.

Beta Neutrality   Beta neutrality refers to balancing the beta of the long side of the portfolio against the beta of the short side of the portfolio. Beta is the measurement of a stock's volatility relative to the market. A stock with a beta of 1 moves historically in sync with the market, a stock with a higher beta tends to be more volatile than the market, and a stock with a lower beta can be expected to rise and fall more slowly than the market. Beta neutrality, therefore, refers to the practice of matching the beta of the long portfolio with the beta of the short portfolio to ensure that market swings affect each portfolio similarly.

Market Capitalization Neutrality Market capitalization neutrality refers to balancing the portfolio in such a way as to keep the market capitalization exposure of the long side of the portfolio similar to the market capitalization exposure of the short side of the portfolio. Stocks of different market capitalization can be affected by market forces in various ways; while large cap stocks tend to be more stable and liquid, they may fall out of favor in times of explosive growth.

Linear Regression Analysis

Perhaps one of the best ways to analyze the return characteristics of an investment strategy is through the process of linear regression analysis. This method compares the returns generated by a specific strategy with the returns of an appropriately selected benchmark. The purpose of the analysis is to determine what part of the return is generated as a result of market swings and what part can be attributed to the strategy. The two data streams are plotted and then, through regression analysis, a best-fit line is generated which describes the relationship between the two data sources.

Linear regression analysis leads directly to correlation, one of the most central mathematical relationships in pairs trading. The analysis that generates the equation for the best-fit line also produces a correlation statistic, referred to as r, that describes the strength of the relationship between the two data sources (strategy return and market return). The main result of a correlation is called the *correlation coefficient* (or r). It ranges from -1.0 to $+1.0$. The closer r is to $+1$ or -1, the more closely the two variables are related. If r is close to 0, there is no relationship between the variables. If r is positive, as one variable gets larger the other gets larger. If r is negative, as one variable gets larger, the other gets smaller (often called an *inverse correlation*). Finding highly correlated pairs of stocks is a key step in finding suitable trades in a pairs strategy.

Mean Variance Optimization

Mean variance optimization applies a quantitative model to historical return data to maximize expected return, given a certain level of portfolio return; alternatively, it can be used to minimize portfolio risk, given a certain level of portfolio risk. In this type of model, risk is measured as variance and is plotted in graphical format. The output is known as the *efficient frontier* because it indicates the most efficient portfolio, given certain parameters at each level of risk.

It has been shown that adding a market-neutral allocation to a portfolio of stocks and bonds can reduce risk without a proportional decrease in returns. This is largely driven by the fact that market-neutral strategies are not highly correlated to either stocks or bonds. These strategies offer returns that are higher than those offered by fixed income securities, while still providing a lower level of volatility than equities.

The Market-Neutral Investment Process

The process is broken down into three basic steps: the initial screen, the stock selection process, and the final portfolio construction. The initial screen limits the universe of stocks that are to be considered for the portfolio. This is rather straightforward but differs from manager to manager. The stock selection process is the most involved step and often involves building a model. The final portfolio construction step differs in importance depending on how much manager discretion is left in the overall process.

Stock Selection   Once a manager has limited his selection universe, he can begin to decide which stocks are to be included in the portfolio. During the stock selection process, managers are looking for quantified metrics that have strong predictive value across a wide range of stocks. For most managers, the use of these metrics involves the creation of a multifactor model that can be used to rank all of the stocks in an investment universe. Some managers create models based on fundamental data; others use technical data or a combination of the two.

The standard form used in the creation of most market-neutral models is a linear equation with n terms:

$$r = bf_1 + bf_2 + bf_3 + \ldots bf_n$$

where r = the expected return of the security
b = is the sensitivity of r to the respective factor, f

The weighting of each factor within the model is based on that factor's estimated predictive value in terms of expected return. The predictive value can be determined using linear regression, as discussed in Chapter 2. Each factor serves as an independent variable and the regression coefficient for each becomes the respective weighting within the model.

THE ARBITRAGE ELEMENT

The most basic definition of an arbitrage trade is one that seeks to exploit an inefficiency in the market by buying a security and simultaneously selling it for a profit. While certain market inefficiencies do still exist, the majority of arbitrage activity today is based on perceived or implied pricing flaws rather than on real ones. In other words, these pricing flaws are not the result of incomplete or untimely information, but rather represent statistically significant anomalies of divergence from historically established average price relationships. In simple terms, relative-value arbitrage is the activity of taking offsetting positions in securities that are historically or mathematically related but are currently related in ways considered temporarily distorted. Thus, the most important feature of arbitrage, particularly in terms of how it relates to pairs trading, is the convergence of these flaws back to their expected values.

The Efficient Market Hypothesis

There are three forms of this theory, all premised on the idea that the market is able to efficiently process information in the sense that market prices will reflect all available information. The weak form of the hypothesis asserts that current market prices reflect all of the information contained in the historic prices of any given stock. The semi strong form asserts that current market prices represent all publicly available information, and the strong form asserts inclusion of all information, including inside information. Regardless of the form selected, the implication of the hypothesis is that stocks are fairly priced in the market and that arbitrage situations cannot exist. Despite the strength of this argument and the general empirical support one finds for it, arbitrage situations clearly do exist.

Types of Arbitrage Convergence

An arbitrage position is built on convergence expectations and relies on the comparison between traded market prices and the relationship that the trader believes should exist based on historical analysis. This convergence comes in three varieties and is dependent on the type of arbitrage position one takes.

Absolute Convergence This type of convergence represents the purest form of arbitrage position and is most commonly observed in cases of index arbitrage, which involves capturing pricing discrepancies between a derivative and its underlying reference. This type of convergence is referred to as absolute because after execution it is set, in the sense that it has been captured. The trader may need wait until the individual contracts expire to realize his profit, but he knows the amount he will receive at that time.

Overt Convergence This type of convergence is most commonly associated with risk arbitrage and occurs when the convergence is planned but not certain. When two companies are planning a corporate action like a merger or acquisition and the news has been announced, frequently a difference occurs between the current market prices of the two stocks and the contractually agreed-upon conversion price. As the time remaining until the announced conversion decreases and the certainty that the action will occur increases, the prices of the two stocks tend to move toward parity with the agreed-upon conversion price.

Implied Convergence Implied convergence is the foundation of pairs trading and is based on the assumption that statistically related securities that have diverged from their historical relationship will at some point in the future reconverge toward their historical average.

Nonconvergence Nonconvergence is the biggest risk facing the speculative arbitrageur. In the case of an implied convergence, the trader is basing his position on the statistical probability that mean reversion will occur. The manager believes he has identified a short-term divergence from a historically significant relative average and that this relationship will normalize over time. Nonconvergence is considered to have occurred when either the divergence increases in magnitude to the point that a stop-loss limit is reached and the trade is closed, or the duration of the trade extends beyond a predetermined time frame in which the manager believed the convergence would occur.

THE TECHNICAL ANALYSIS ELEMENT

Technical analysts use computers to reconstruct past market activity and to test trading theories. The underlying assumption is that a trading system that worked well in the past will work well in the future. System traders analyze their findings, which are based on technical analysis, in the form of trading methods that have worked well over recent months and years, and try to evolve a set of rules to extrapolate trading results, seeking the optimum balance between the values that produce the greatest profit and the values that produce the smallest loss.

A complete review of the technical indicators most relevant to pairs trading can be found in Chapter 7 and will not be repeated here. It is recommended that any reader not familiar and comfortable with major technical indicators take the time to consider Chapter 7 thoroughly.

The Technical Approach

Charting and pattern recognition are central to the technical trader's understanding of the market. Before he begins to explore the technical indicators that are applicable to pairs trading, it is essential to chart and analyze each prospective pair, assuming that the stocks are highly correlated. He first selects a reasonable time horizon to define the length of time from when a trade is initiated to when he anticipates exiting it. By looking at the ratio between two equities, a trader can see the intervals between convergence and mean reversions, and therefore can intelligently project the time it would take a trade to achieve the desired profit objective. The most straightforward way to visualize a relationship between two equities is to create a chart showing the performance ratio between those two equities. A chart should be constructed by dividing one stock by the other. This creates a new trading vehicle and from a technical standpoint permits viewing it as one trading unit rather than as a relationship between two stocks.

Price Trend in Pairs Trading

A trend is the tendency for prices or any other value to move more in one direction than another. Identifying and analyzing a price trend is a foundation of technical analysis. Although the Wall Street maxim "A trend is your friend" is apt for directional trading, the opposite is the case for pairs trading. When a pairs trader analyzes two stocks as one trading unit, the last thing he wants to see is a trend. In the case of a chart of the ratio between two stocks, a trend means that two stocks are constantly diverging and do not return to the mean. What a pairs trader seeks is a range.

As noted earlier, what is offered here is far from a comprehensive look at technical analysis. Readers wishing to learn more on this subject should either read the Part Three of this book or purchase a separate book that covers the topic more thoroughly. The information contained herein is only intended to give the reader enough information to implement one specific strategy—not to work professionally as a technical trader.

CHAPTER 10

Trading Pairs Fundamentally

Throughout the investment world pairs trading takes many forms, and the various forms rely more or less heavily on different factors. While none of these approaches is inherently better than the others, some parallel the approach laid out in this book more closely than others. One approach that differs greatly from the one explored in this book relies heavily on fundamental data rather than technical factors. This particular approach falls largely outside of the focus of this book (hence the inclusion of technical rather than fundamental analysis as the third element), but it should be addressed in order for the reader to gain a comprehensive understanding of the strategy. It should not be assumed that the fundamental approach is a less legitimate form of pairs trading than the technical approach, but rather that it is not the preferred methodology of this particular writer.

THE FUNDAMENTAL APPROACH

While fundamentals should play a role in any pairs trading approach, many practitioners of this strategy use fundamental analysis as the basis of their model and research. This method tends to be preferred by institutional investors for a number of reasons. Large institutional investment houses tend to build their long-only portfolios using fundamental analysis and employ small armies of analysts in order to thoroughly cover large investment universes. Those houses that choose to include pairs trading in their investment approach are already in possession of the infrastructure, data, and manpower required to use the fundamental approach to pairs trading. Furthermore, because these managers prefer fundamental analysis generally, they are hesitant to abandon such preferences when constructing a pairs portfolio. Institutional investors also prefer the fundamental approach because they believe that they possess the best research on the street and wish to leverage that expertise when expanding beyond traditional portfolio construction methods. By using their existing knowledge base to construct a pairs portfolio, these managers are able to stretch the usefulness of their information further and take advantage of opportunities presented by stocks that their analysts deem poor long candidates.

FUNDAMENTALS APPLIED

The manager using the fundamental approach looks to pair stocks in the same industry when he believes that one will outperform the other based on the fundamentals of the two companies. The specific metrics the manager considers will vary from manager to manager, but the characteristics of those metrics will follow some general themes. For the duration of this explanation, consider the example of Coke and Pepsi; both companies are in the same industry, follow a very similar business plan, and are similarly affected by major macroeconomic news events. While these conditions are preferential to the technical manager, they are virtually required by the fundamental manager. The first condition of a pairs trading strategy using the fundamental approach is that the companies be as close to identical in terms of their businesses as possible.

Once two such companies are identified and paired, the fundamental manager may begin to apply his analysis to each. The three main areas that the manager will consider are product line and profitability, management, and relative position within the industry. Again, the specific metrics may differ from manager to manager, but each of these areas will be considered. The manager is trying to identify which company will perform better in the immediate future—in other words, which company is a better value. There are three possible outcomes of this investigation: stock A is a better value, stock B is a better value, or there is insufficient evidence to make a strong argument for either company being a better value. In order to determine the general guidelines by which a manager reaches the appropriate conclusion, it will be useful to explore each of these as major themes.

Product Line and Profitability

In an attempt to determine which company will likely outperform in the short to intermediate term, the manager will consider both the product lines and profitability of each company. Each of these factors affects the success of the company in executing its business plan and in controlling market share. Perhaps more importantly, these factors have a significant impact on how each company is viewed by the market, both individually and relative to one another.

In the example of Coke and Pepsi, if a manager learned that Coke was about to release a new cola which might sweep through the beverage industry as a great success, he would adjust his opinion of the relative strength of the two companies accordingly. New product lines often affect a company's relative strength and should be carefully considered. Likewise, if the manager learned that Pepsi had just signed a contract with the National Football League to sell only Pepsi products at all stadiums, he obviously would reevaluate the strength of Pepsi relative to Coke. Negative news should be considered as well; if a newly released study reported a specific ingredient of Pepsi had been found suspect as a possible cause of cancer, a very negative impact on Pepsi sales and its stock would follow.

Product line analysis is rarely as straightforward as in the above examples. In most cases the manager must examine subtle differences in both the products offered and the market's reaction to them. Minor changes in consumer perception can have a significant impact on the bottom line and affect the performance of the stock. This type of analysis takes careful research as well as the experience to know how to classify the available information. While the public can be fickle and prone to overreaction, news events can sharply affect the price of a stock in the short term and leave the manager in a position of choosing between weathering the storm or taking large unwarranted losses.

Fundamental managers employ a variety of techniques for collecting and analyzing information about the companies in which they are interested. These techniques range from examining the sales figures released by a company to discussing general sales trends with both company officials and the vendors that sell the company's products. Clearly, this type of research is quite time consuming, and usually a single analyst is responsible for only a small number of companies within a specific industry or sector. A fundamental manager usually is forced to rely on the research of other analysts in order to build a comprehensive portfolio. While this approach has no inherent weaknesses, the manager's comfort level is often closely tied to his sense of the reliability of the analysts.

Profitability analysis tends to be less subtle and relies more heavily on statistics as the fixed standard. Such figures are directly tied to product line analysis and the two usually are considered together. By juxtaposing these figures with the results of the product line analysis, a fundamental manager tries to form an opinion about the likely future performance of a company's stock. Some of the most common profitability statistics are:

- Profit margin
- Earnings per share
- EBITDA
- Operating margin
- Sales
- Price/earnings (P/E) ratio

These metrics give the manager quantified measures for comparing the two companies he is considering. As is the case with product line analysis, a manager must have the necessary experience to interpret these figures appropriately. For example, an experienced manager would not expect a mature, stable company to have the same profitability figures as a start-up, growth company, even though both may be in the same business and suitable for pairing.

Profitability measures do not always have an immediate impact on the company's stock price, but because the average duration of a fundamental pairs trade tends to be several months, these figures may be quite important. Examining these figures in the context of product line analysis and general company information can give the manager a glimpse of the likely future earnings the company will report. This kind of information does have a significant impact on stock price, so the manager should always be keenly aware of scheduled earnings announcements to be made by any of the companies in which he is investing.

The fundamental approach requires that the manager consider both the product lines and the profitability of the companies being paired. Both of these factors can have a significant impact on the future performance of the stock's price and can help the manager to determine whether his pairing is appropriate. Appropriateness is judged in terms of the trade generally and the direction, which stock is long and which is short. If no clear distinction can be made between the two stocks, the pair may not be a good candidate for including in the portfolio.

Management

The second general area of consideration that the manager employing the fundamental approach will consider is the management of the two respective companies. While there are some financial metrics that can be utilized in performing such an analysis, this type of comparison is often very subjective, relying on the skill and insights of the investment manager. In many cases, a lack of any definitive information in this arena can be as useful as a mountain of data, indicating that there are no major concerns pending for either company and that the manager may rely on other metrics when making his decision.

The statistical measurements of management efficiency that are most commonly used by fundamental managers are:

- Return on equity
- Return on assets
- Various growth rates

These numbers let the manager judge whether management is effectively using the resources at its disposal to run the company. It is again important to note that this judgment requires a degree of experience. The analyst must take into account differences between the two companies when analyzing these figures; mature companies will have different results from start-ups, and companies in different industries may have completely unrelated values for these measurements. The manager's ability to interpret these statistics is central to his ability to make positive use of them.

The other management factors that prove most important to the fundamental manager are any recent, ongoing, or upcoming changes in the ranks of upper management. Such a change usually indicates that the company is experiencing some degree of internal turmoil. While this tends to be negative, in certain instances it is positive. If, for example, a new chief executive has been hired to revamp the operations of a struggling business, this may be seen as a positive sign that potentially could drive performance. The speed with which such information can impact stock price differs from situation to situation, and it is up to the analyst to decide how pertinent the information may be to the trade in question.

Another piece of information that should be considered is the trading activity of insiders in company stock. This information is a public record and can give an analyst some insight into the opinion various officers of the company may have about the future performance of the stock. While this is not an absolute measure—the officer may be selling stock to raise funds to purchase another house—if there is an observable trend in the trading activity of insiders the manager should consider such information. As is the case with all fundamental data, this piece of information has to be considered in the proper context.

The other concern that also falls into this category is ongoing instances of accounting scandal and illegal insider trading. Such events are almost always unforeseeable but should be considered as they can have devastating results on a stock's price. Companies related to those under investigation should be avoided as new developments can come at any point and affect the partners of the primary target. This concern is obviously somewhat limited, but given the ease of avoiding such companies, the mention of this concern is warranted.

Regardless of the determination made by a manager about the strength or weakness of any management teams in charge of the companies in which he is investing, the research must be done. A news release that a major change is taking place can have a great impact on the company's stock price and thus on the trade. The manager who fails to capture such information when it is available may find himself with a substantial loss on his books. In most cases, an analysis of company management has very little impact on the decisions made by a fundamental manager, but in those cases where there is pertinent information it often is of vital importance and should not be overlooked.

Relative Industry Position

The fundamental approach to pairs trading requires that a manager consider the position of each of the companies he is considering relative to others within the same industry, especially those being paired against each other. This should be fairly obvious, since the goal of the fundamental analyst is to identify stocks that are undervalued in the marketplace relative to their intrinsic value—but it is even more critical in pairs trading. The manager is seeking to pair undervalued stocks on the long side with overvalued stocks on the short side in most instances and thus must know the relative position of each. This analysis will help not only to determine whether a pairing is justified, but it may provide insight into a pairing that would have an even greater potential.

Consider the previous example of pairing Coke against Pepsi, and assume that Coke is the intended long side of the pair with Pepsi as the intended short. During analysis, a manager discovers that within the beverage industry, Pepsi has experienced the greatest price advance over the last several months and that Coke has remained basically unchanged. If all other fundamental data is excluded, or assumed to be equivalent across the two companies, the manager could conclude that his pairing is appropriate. There is no evidence that Pepsi is a substantially better company than Coke, so the disparity between their price activity is unwarranted; Pepsi has become overvalued relative both to the industry and to Coke specifically. Because the manager is building a market-neutral portfolio that is designed to capitalize on relative-value arbitrage, he is not concerned with the future performance of either stock explicitly. The manager concludes that this relative price disparity will correct itself and make his pair profitable. It is irrelevant whether Coke begins to perform and catches up with Pepsi (making the long side of the trade profitable) or if the price of Pepsi corrects and drops back to a level more in keeping with other companies in the industry (making the short side of the trade profitable). The key to the success of the trade is that Coke outperforms relative to Pepsi.

In this example, if the manager's analysis reveals that there is a reason that Pepsi has risen over the period being considered, making a judgment about the quality of the pair becomes significantly more complex. It must first be determined whether the rise in Pepsi's price is commensurate with the catalyst that caused the rise to occur. Simply stated, the manager must try to judge whether the stock went up too much, too little, or an appropriate amount given the forces behind the move. If he determines that the move was too great, the trade might still be considered sound. If, however, the stock's rise is judged to be too small, the manager will conclude that the stock will continue to rise and not wish to be short the stock. Finally, if the manager believes that the rise was appropriate in terms of degree, he will have no strong basis upon which to judge the future behavior of the stock's price, whether explicitly or versus Coke. In such a case, the manager will reject the pair, because he is trying to capitalize on implied market inefficiencies, not simply make baseless bets.

Clearly understanding the relative position of each stock being considered within its respective industry is vital to analyzing the quality and appropriateness of a potential pairs trade. The manager must consider where each stock stands relative to its peers, why it is there, and how the stock is likely to perform in the immediate future. This part of the analysis gives the manager a chance to judge each of the stocks in his universe not only individually but also relative to one another. In most cases, the manager will try to avoid buying stocks that are already positioned at or near the top of their industry and avoid shorting stocks that are already positioned at or near the bottom of their industry.

Decisions of this type are based on the underlying belief that each industry has a metaphorical center of gravity around which each of the stocks it contains fluctuates. It is very rare for the same companies to be consistently on one side of this continuum; rather, each company tends to bounce back and forth between being one of the strongest in the industry and being one of the weakest. While this is a belief rather than an undisputed fact, there is some empirical data to support such a belief, and this phenomenon is generally accepted among pairs traders.

PORTFOLIO CONSTRUCTION

Judging pairs, even when a strong fundamental case exists, is a very subtle process that relies on the experience of a manager. While Pepsi may
have outperformed Coke during recent months and become overvalued,
there is no market rule that forces this disparity to be corrected. The manager may know that Coke is a better run company, with stronger financials, a better product line, and favorable news in the pipeline, but that
does not ensure that it will begin to outperform Pepsi at any certain time.
Pepsi may inexplicably continue its run while Coke remains dormant for
many months to come, despite informed opinion that this behavior is unwarranted. The manager must continue his time horizon, consider how
long he can wait for the disparity to correct itself, and weigh how much of
a loss he is willing to sustain on paper while he waits for a correction to
occur. It is very uncommon for a manager to perfectly judge the correct
entry time into a pair based on fundamental data. His experience may give
him a rough feel for how long the market will require to incorporate the
data into the stock's price, but this process is more art than science.

In some cases, the manager will enter a trade, sustain his maximum
acceptable loss, close the trade, and then watch the pair behave exactly as
he believed it should have—but too late for him to participate in the profit.
While this is clearly a great frustration to the manager, he must maintain
his discipline in order to survive. Had he chosen to remain in the pair beyond his predetermined loss maximum and the trade had continued to decline, the manager could easily have destroyed his portfolio. A more
comprehensive investigation of profit objectives and stop-loss limits is described in Chapter 11, but the discipline they represent is important to
keep in mind when considering the fundamental approach.

The specifics of portfolio construction differ from manager to manager, based in part on the level of sophistication and human participation
desired. In the simplest form, a manager will consider the market industry by industry and pair the stocks he believes will appropriately comple-
ment each other in a given trade. After this process is complete, the
manager will perform his analysis on the stocks he has selected and decide which of the pairs survive to be included in the portfolio. This type
of portfolio construction relies heavily on the manager's ability to make
the initial pairing and to correctly interpret the data he encounters during
his research. While this approach is very time consuming, it allows a
skilled manager to bring his greatest expertise into play when designing
his portfolio.

A more sophisticated approach entails the use of a model to rank the
stocks within each respective industry. Such a model, based on fundamental data, will consider quantified metrics such as P/E ratio, earnings per

share, debt/equity ratio, or return of assets; the metrics chosen will be based on the manager's decision about which provide the best predictive value when considering future performance. The manager then will pair the stocks with the highest scores with those with the lowest scores. After this is done, the manager may wish to further investigate each pair to satisfy himself that the pairing, made purely on quantified data, has not failed to take into account some subtle yet important piece of information that will affect the trade. After this final piece of analysis is completed, the manager will be left with a group of pairs from which to build the portfolio. Depending on the number of pairs remaining, a decision may be made to include all of these pairs or a further screen may be developed by which to limit the number of pairs in the portfolio. This further screen can be based on which pairs have the most extreme scores, which pairs exhibit the most market-neutral characteristics (including beta, market capitalization, etc.), or with which pairs a manager is most familiar. Regardless of criteria, this final screen is focused on maximizing return and limiting risk.

The final, and most sophisticated, approach uses a model to evaluate the pairs being considered for inclusion in the portfolio. This approach may entail either model-ranking every possible combination of stocks from the investment universe or using a secondary model to rank the pairs that are formed from the output of the primary model. In either case, this level of sophistication requires both a thorough understanding of the process and an ability to statistically quantify huge amounts of data. The manager may still wish to evaluate any pairs that are being considered for inclusion to ensure that some nonquantifiable piece of information has not been overlooked.

Regardless of which of these three methods is used, it is during the portfolio construction process that the manager sets buy and sell rules. He must have a set criterion to determine when a pair is considered unsuccessful and should be closed, as well as criteria for determining when it should be considered to have succeeded. The specifics of these rules may be based on changes in model score, percentage or dollar value gains and losses, or a combination of other various factors, but by setting these rules, the manager forces himself to be disciplined when making critical portfolio decisions.

PROBLEMS WITH THE FUNDAMENTAL APPROACH

Despite the fundamental approach being the method preferred by institutional investors for trading pairs, there are a variety of flaws in it. This is not to suggest that other approaches are not without shortcomings, but it is important for the reader to understand why this writer prefers other approaches. The three most obvious weaknesses of the fundamental approach are the huge amount of data and research required to put it into practice, its high reliance on manager judgment, and its lack of clear timing indicators to the manager using it. Proponents of the approach would argue that these are not weaknesses but rather peculiarities similar to those of any investment theory. Regardless of how these features are classified, they should be understood when trying to evaluate the approach.

The fundamental approach to pairs trading requires extensive research and the analysis of huge amounts of data. While fundamental data is available through many information vendors, there are literally hundreds of different metrics that can be obtained, many of which are industry specific. Furthermore, some of this data is specific not only to a given industry, but to segments of that industry. The metrics for a mature technology company will be very different from those for a growth company engaged in the same type of business. As a result of this level of specialization a manager has a difficult time developing general rules for the overall portfolio. It also causes him to favor pairing companies that not only are in the same industry but follow similar business plans. This is not an inherent weakness but it does cause the manager to miss or overlook a great number of potentially profitable pair candidates.

In cases in which the manager has both the experience and the resources to evaluate this plethora of industry-specific data, the ongoing level of research remains quite high. Again, this is not inherently problematic but to some will seem unnecessary when other equally successful approaches are readily available. The fundamental manager justifies his approach by assuring himself and others that his success is tied to his superior level of research, but, because of the vast number of metrics at his disposal, it can be quite difficult to separate statistics that have good predictive value from those that do not.

The second shortcoming of the fundamental approach is its high reliance on the judgment of the manager. This feature makes it very difficult for nonspecialists to trade the theory, and, while simplicity of execution is not a prerequisite for a successful investment methodology, this approach is just not accessible to the majority of the investment community. While practitioners on the inside find this appealing, few readers would derive benefit beyond satisfying some level of curiosity from a book about this approach.

Another, more significant, problem with an approach that is this reliant on personal judgment is that it is likely to fail over time, as a manager's span of experience is exceeded by changing market conditions. A system based heavily on experience and instinct relies on the manager's ability to accurately pick stocks. This implies that in order for the system to be successful over time, the manager must be able to pick stocks in all types of market conditions without permitting his personal predispositions or his emotions to affect his decisions. This may seem relatively straightforward, but some managers are good at picking stocks during bear markets, for example, but less successful during bull markets. A manager who can be successful under all conditions is rare. A system that can take a greater degree of the human element out of the equation is more likely to be successful.

The final major weakness of the fundamental approach is that it does little to assist the manager in determining the proper timing for entering a given trade. The manager may be able to clearly ascertain that Coke is a better value than Pepsi, but this information alone does not predict when the stock prices will reflect this information. The market may incorporate the value information quickly in some cases and take several months in other cases. What this means practically for a fundamental pairs manager is that he must look for a specific catalyst to motivate him to enter a given trade. Some possible catalysts for entering a trade may include a major news release, the development of a new product, or a shake-up in management. While all of these are good indicators that a stock may behave in a certain way, they are far from guaranteed. Furthermore, pairs may perform as expected without the presence of any such catalyst. If the manager makes a trade without a catalyst, he is in essence betting blindly. If, however, he waits for a specific catalyst to prompt his trading decisions, many profitable opportunities may be lost.

While there are certainly weaknesses in other approaches to pairs trading, many of the others tend to be easier to manage or eliminate. The fundamental approach does bring a specific type of expertise to a manager's trading, but it requires both more time and experience than do other approaches. Each manager must decide for himself what approach will be the most successful and must capitalize on his specific experience, but other approaches are easier to learn and hone.

THE VERDICT

The fundamental approach to pairs trading, most commonly used by institutional investors, has its basis in a manager's ability to bring his experience to the stock selection process. If the manager has the resources and the experience required to thoroughly evaluate a reasonably sized investment universe, the approach can be quite effective and allow the manager to leverage the tools he already has at his disposal.

For most potential pairs traders, this approach requires more resources than they will have. However, there are other pairs approaches that are easier both to execute and to understand. Overall, the fundamental approach, while sound in most ways, should be reserved for the professional manager who employs a team of analysts and can dedicate large and varied resources to the pairs enterprise.

CHAPTER 11

The Technical Approach

U nderstanding each of the elements of pairs trading is a major step toward obtaining a firm grasp of the comprehensive theory. In practical application, a pairs trader often will need to make judgments about the issues he is facing on the basis of nuances that would be impossible to discern had he studied the theory only from one narrow perspective. Having understood and then synthesized these three elements—market neutrality, arbitrage, and technical analysis—the reader will be able to practically apply the theory.

THE ELEMENTS COMBINED

Now that each of the elements of the theory have been thoroughly explored, it will prove useful to consider a broad, generalized definition upon which the discussion can build:

Pairs trading: A market-neutral, relative-value arbitrage strategy that is based heavily on technical factors. The strategy uses technical and fundamental inputs to match correlated equities; it derives its return from the performance of a pair's long position relative to the performance of its matched short position.

While this definition is clearly an oversimplification of the strategy, it touches on all the major pieces of the theory. While it may seem odd that a single strategy can be classified as drawing on three distinct areas of investment management, this anomaly becomes understandable when the relationship between these areas is explored. While relative-value arbitrage is driven by the relationship between various sets of securities, such a portfolio is often constructed using market-neutral principles. Similarly, while market-neutral strategies are focused on removing market exposure to limit portfolio risk, this process usually involves betting on the relative value of one group of securities versus another group. In essence, a market-neutral portfolio may be a special case of relative-value arbitrage, and a relative-value arbitrage portfolio may be a special case of market neutrality.

Technical analysis may be used when constructing either type of portfolio; it is simply the means by which the manager judges the securities he intends to include. When constructing a market-neutral or a relative-value arbitrage portfolio, the manager may rely on technical factors to determine which stocks meet the criteria that he wishes to satisfy. Taking this logic an additional step, one sees that a technically driven market-neutral portfolio may be a special case of relative-value arbitrage. While these relationships may seem obvious, a student of arbitrage may never come across the term *market-neutral* and may never practice technical analysis. Making these seemingly obvious relationships more concrete helps to strengthen the foundation upon which the unified theory is being constructed.

GETTING STARTED

As with any investment strategy, the first step the pairs trader must take is to identify his investment universe. This group of potential trading vehicles may include anything from stocks and bonds to commodities or derivatives, but it is usually important to select a universe of similar instruments; in other words, one should not set out to pair stocks with bonds or grain futures against the euro. As previously mentioned, the investigation in this book is specific to equities, but the concepts may be applied to other markets as well.

Within the equity markets, the trader will likely wish to limit his universe further in order to keep his field of inquiry manageable. This may entail focusing on the United States equity market and excluding foreign markets, or it may entail narrowing the field to a specific index or group of indexes. The type of analysis favored by the individual trader (technical versus fundamental) coupled with the extent of that trader's resources will be the driving force behind universe selection. The less experienced trader who favors fundamental analysis and has limited resources will be better served by choosing a smaller universe than will a professional technical analyst, who can bring the resources of a large firm to bear on any decisions. Fundamental analysis tends to be more time consuming and require more manual research and calculation than technical analysis; most technical indicators can be easily obtained through subscription to a single service.

The importance of a trader's level of resources should be obvious; the greater the extent of his resources, the more able he will be to analyze a large number of stocks. This is particularly the case with technology resources as well as programming and mathematical experience. The greater the number of elements in the universe, the more complex the required model will be and the greater the amount of computing power required to analyze each possible combination. It is important to remember that looking at pairs of stocks—inherent to the strategy—makes the possible number of pairs increase exponentially as more stocks are added into the universe.

The other factors that a trader should consider when selecting his universe are diversity and uniformity. While these two concepts may seem diametrically opposed, both are key to the successful implementation of the theory. The selected universe must have sufficient diversity to give the trader a reasonable breadth of choice when constructing his portfolio as well as the opportunity to spread his financial resources across many trades. While appropriate diversification is discussed later, it is worth noting here that a portfolio of 30 pairs contains less risk and is better balanced than one constructed of only two pairs.

Uniformity is important in terms of subsets of the selected universe. The trader must be able to find within that universe a sufficient number of similar stocks that can be paired with one another to make reasonable choices. For example, selecting one stock per industry for the investment universe would make it difficult to pair any two stocks in such a way that the two companies paired would be affected similarly by prevailing macroeconomic factors. While not a requirement but a preference, the fundamental analyst in particular will tend to minimize his market risk by pairing stocks that are unlikely to react in substantially different ways to macroeconomic news.

The general guidelines for selecting an investment universe can be subsumed into one basic principle: The pairs trader should select a universe of manageable size that contains a diverse group of equities which display uniformity within various subsets of the larger group. This elementary rule of thumb is far easier to state than to practice. One of the most common pitfalls a new practitioner of the theory faces is beginning with an investment universe that is either too large to manage or too narrowly focused. A good starting point for the average trader with average resources is to choose the S&P 500 as the investment universe. These 500 stocks contain all of the necessary attributes to effectively apply the theory and should not overwhelm a novice. After this index has been mastered, in the sense of comfort and successful execution, other indexes may be added, but care should be taken not to overextend beyond the trader's resources.

UNDERSTANDING PAIRS TECHNICALLY

Once an investment universe is selected, a manager employing a pairs trading strategy will begin to construct potential pairs for consideration for the portfolio. This can be done using a variety of methods, including the construction and application of a model, manual comparison of stocks within the same industry, or the use of a third party matching service.[*] What is common to all of these approaches is that they are tied to understanding pairs from the standpoint of a technical analysis. For any of these methods to work, the manager must consider historical statistical data to determine the nature of the relationship between the two stocks being matched. As discussed previously, the model construction and application approach builds most of the technical review into an automated process, while the other two approaches rely more heavily on a manager's ability to analyze a chart. Regardless of which method a trader intends to rely on, a closer look at the technicals and chart patterns found in pairs trading will help to solidify understanding of the technical approach. While many of the specifics discussed in this chapter can also be used while following a fundamental approach, they are the foundation and basis of a technical approach and should be understood as such.

TECHNICAL CHARTING AND MARKET NEUTRALITY

Market neutrality is one of the cornerstones of the technical approach and, as such, must be built into any analysis of technical charting. The power of market neutrality can be illustrated by analyzing a potential

---

[*]While several services of this nature are available, the writer has a clear bias toward the services offered by PairTrader.com. It should be noted that the writer is associated with PairTrader.com but has reviewed many of the other services available and found them to be neither as comprehensive nor as easy to use.

pairs trade, examining the chart of each stock individually as well as a chart of the two stocks combined in a variety of ways. Figures 11.1 and 11.2 are the charts of Fortune Brands (FO) and ITT Industries (ITT), respectively, over the same time period. An initial examination of the two charts reveals a great deal of similarity in the price action of these two stocks, but it impossible to determine how closely these price movements mirror one another. Without further analysis, a manager might decide that these stocks are likely to have a high statistical correlation to each other, but he has no basis upon which to turn this assumption into a potentially profitable trading opportunity.

In Figure 11.3, the price action for the two stocks for the same time period is plotted on the same graph. This information is more useful, because it makes clear that the prices of these two stocks go through periods of relative over- or underperformance. It would be easy for a manager to oversimplify the results of this analysis and conclude that the points where the graphs of the two stocks crossed each other represented appropriate entry or exit spots for the trade. In such a scenario, the stock whose graph was on top would be the long and the stock whose graph was on the bottom would be the short. At points where the two graphs cross, the manager would enter the pair and wait for an acceptable profit before closing the pair. This is a form of pairs trading at the most elementary level and can succeed in certain situations.

A problem with this approach is that should the two stocks not follow their historical relationship, the manager has very little guidance information with which to make trading decisions. Furthermore, the manager has no basis to judge when the pair should be considered successful and when it should be considered unsuccessful and closed. At a more basic

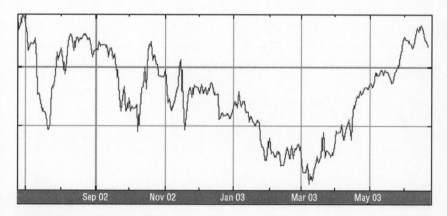

FIGURE 11.1 Fortune Brands

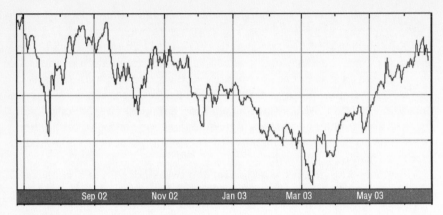

FIGURE 11.2 ITT Industries

level, were the manager to wait until the two graphs cross for the second time before closing the trade, his net profit would be zero. While Figure 11.3 demonstrates that there is a relationship between these two stocks, the exact nature of that relationship is erratic and almost impossible to consistently trade for a profit.

In order to gain useful information about the likely behavior of the price relationship, the manager must consider the pair from a market-neutral point of view. By graphing the price ratio between the two stocks (FO/ITT), the manager is considering the price action of the relationship from a dollar-neutral perspective. Figure 11.4 represents the chart of the dollar-neutral price action over a specified period of time. Once the rela-

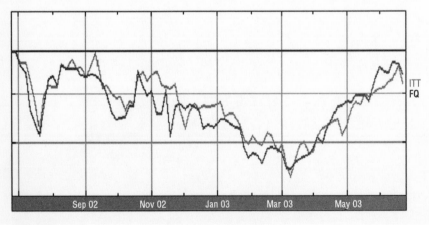

FIGURE 11.3 Fortune Brands and ITT Industries

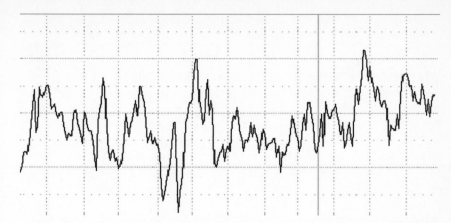

FIGURE 11.4   Dollar-Neutral Price Ratio between Fortune Brands and ITT Industries

tionship is considered from this perspective, one sees quickly that employing a type of market neutrality makes trading this pair a far easier proposition. The chart in Figure 11.4 displays a price relationship that moves in a definite range over the period of time being considered. This is useful for the manager because he can now predict not only the likely direction that the pair will move, but also the degree to which the relationship is likely to change. The manager is now able to set reasonable profit objectives and stop-loss levels. In essence, by bringing market neutrality to technical charting, the manager has gone from making low-probability guesses to carefully calculated predictions about the future action of the pair.

TECHNICAL CHARTING AND RELATIVE-VALUE ARBITRAGE

Applying technical charting to relative-value or statistical arbitrage provides a graphical representation of the central concept behind pairs trading. From this perspective, the goal of the pairs trader is to identify two highly correlated stocks that have oscillated around a statistically significant average. The chart in Figure 11.5 represents the same pair that was examined in Figure 11.4 with the addition of a graphical representation of the moving average. As is seen in the chart, the price relationship regularly diverges away from the moving average to an extreme, reverses, and then passes through the moving average to a new extreme on the opposite side. Some of these extremes are marked with the vertical lines on

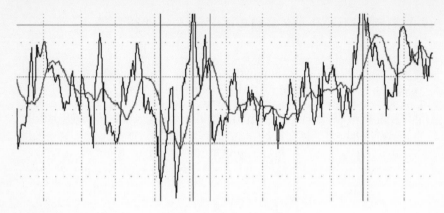

FIGURE 11.5   Price Ratio plus 14-Day Moving Average

the chart. The successful pairs trader learns to capitalize on this stable relationship by making high-probability, relative-value bets on the pair. When the price relationship is at a low extreme, the manager buys the numerator stock (FO in this case) long and sells short the denominator stock (ITT in this case). When the pair is at a high extreme, the process is reversed (long ITT and short FO).

While it is not always clear when the price relationship is at an extreme, there are several other technical tools on which the manager may rely when making this determination; these are discussed, applied, and illustrated later. When the pair is considered graphically, the nature of the relative-value arbitrage becomes much more explicit; the manager is betting that the price relationship between the two stocks will mean-revert back to the moving average. The arbitrage element of this process is in the assumption that the divergence between the two stock prices represents a short-term pricing discrepancy that will be corrected over time. Recall that this type of arbitrage is often termed speculative because it relies on convergence occurring without a strong fundamental reason behind it; whereas absolute convergence occurs by definition and overt convergence is the result of contractual stipulations, implied convergence is the result of a speculative belief that history will repeat. There is no guarantee that the matched equities will ever begin mean reversion and converge back to their historically average relationship. Statistical analysis may reveal that the desired convergence is a high-probability event, but there is no certainty that the process will occur. Lack of any identifying criteria that ensure this process will occur is one of the main risk factors that a manager faces and attempts to control.

APPLYING OTHER TECHNICAL INDICATORS

In previous sections, the integral connection between the various elements of pairs trading was demonstrated. In order to fully understand the technical approach, the use of various other indicators must now be explored and integrated into the theory. While the indicators explored in this section do not represent an exhaustive list, the connections demonstrated here can be applied to whatever indicators a manager finds most useful. In addition to the moving average indicator already mentioned, Bollinger Bands and the relative strength index are useful in helping a manager determine when to enter a pair. Like most other technical indicators that a pairs trader will consider, these two indicators are used primarily to determine timing.

One of the most difficult skills to develop for a manager using the technical approach is proficiency is selecting entry points. Because the convergence on which he is basing his trades is speculative, selecting a good entry point is critical. If the manager enters the trade too early and the trade moves against him, it may be difficult to determine whether mean reversion has yet to begin or whether the historical relationship on which the manager is speculating has broken down. At some point, the manager may need to accept a realized loss in order to protect the portfolio. If this loss turns out to be a function of entering the trade too early, the manager has not only lost money in the trade, but has missed a good opportunity. Over time, and through the use of other technical indicators, the manager will become more skilled at selecting entry points. While it is impossible to expect a manager to pick a major reversal point for his entry every time, by using the tools at his disposal, the manager can increase the probability that his selected entry point is near a major reversal point.

Bollinger Bands

In Part Three, the specific application of Bollinger Bands to pairs trading was discussed. The chart in Figure 11.6 will make that explanation even more explicit and help the reader integrate the use of this indicator into the general theory. This is the same chart as in Figures 11.4 and 11.5, with the addition of the Bollinger Band indicator; the vertical lines represent the same extreme reversal points as observed previously. An experienced pairs trader would note that at the indicated reversal points, the graph of the price action touches the Bollinger Bands. Although there are several instances in which the price action reverses without touching one of the bands, a manager can conclude that when one of the bands is touched, the probability of a reversal is very high.

Bollinger Bands alone are not sufficient for the manager to identify

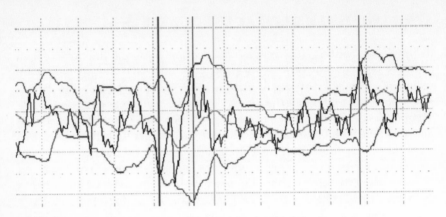

FIGURE 11.6   Price Ratio, Moving Average, and Bollinger Bands

and analyze potential matched equity pair candidates, but the application of this indicator after candidates are identified can be quite useful in confirming the manager's opinion and helping to determine appropriate entry points. It should be noted that the pair selected for this example is a particularly good one and not all pairs will demonstrate such straightforward compliance with these principles. This is not to suggest that only matches deemed perfect pairs are tradable; less well-suited pairs can be traded, but they may be repeated less frequently. Furthermore, an experienced manager may not require a pair to actually touch one of the bands, but will still use the pair's proximity to the band as a gauge for the likelihood of a reversal.

Relative Strength Index

The relative strength index is very similar in its application to Bollinger Bands; it is another tool that the manager uses to determine whether the observed divergence in a given pair is at or near an extreme. Figure 11.7 presents the same relationship depicted in the preceding charts, with the addition of the relative strength index indicator applied; again, some of the major reversal points are indicated by the vertical lines. Upon initial observation, it may appear that these two indicators are simply different expressions of the same information. It is, however, just this type of redundancy that adds confidence to a manager's belief that he has identified an appropriate entry point. In some cases, the various indicators that a manager considers will not provide the same support and may present opposing views of the trade. When this occurs, the manager is less confident that he has identified the appropriate entry point and may pass on

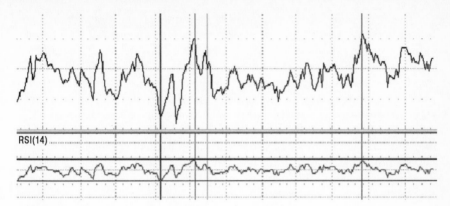

FIGURE 11.7 Price Ratio and Relative Strength Index

the trade. Different managers rely more or less heavily on different indicators and will build different levels of significance for each indicator into their models.

One indicator is not necessarily better than another, and the usefulness of an indicator may be highly dependent on other factors within the portfolio. Most important for the novice pairs trader is to select a group of indicators, become familiar and comfortable with them, and then begin to focus on discerning which of the group provides the most predictive ability. In some cases, a manager may rely on different indicators depending on the type of market he is facing or on the particular strategy he is trading. No indicator is perfect nor guaranteed to be successful, but the addition of a selected group can be useful to a manager in improving his skill at selecting good entry points.

SELECTING PROFIT OBJECTIVE AND STOP-LOSS LEVELS

One of the keys to success in pairs trading is knowing when an open trade should be closed for either a profit or a loss. Setting profit objective and stop-loss levels aids a manager, not only in the efficient management of his portfolio but also in remaining disciplined when approaching trades. If a manager leaves a trade open too long, he may see his profit disappear or his loss hemorrhage to a disastrous level. Such decisions should be made at the time the trade is opened and only changed in rare cases of discovering strong evidence to support such a change. While the stop-loss levels may differ slightly from trade to trade, there are some general guidelines that will aid the manager in setting these levels.

As the premise for this explanation, assume that the manager, in addition to his other analyses, uses Bollinger Bands as his primary timing indicator. If one remembers that Bollinger Bands are drawn two standard deviations on either side of the moving average, it is reasonable to assume that two standard deviations of divergence can be considered an extreme move. Following this logic, the trader's profit objective should be set two standard deviations above the entry point (this point is represented by the moving average when the pair is opened), and the stop-loss can be set at two standard deviations below the entry point (this can be calculated by determining the distance from the moving average to the Bollinger Band and then subtracting this figure from the entry ratio). The result of using this method is an unencumbered, easy to calculate level for each of these potential exit points. This methodology is particularly useful for those managers who wish to create models that are purely mathematical while still being unique to each pair.

Basing profit objective and stop-loss levels on standard deviations of divergence allows the manager to use a common methodology across all pairs while still accounting for the unique characteristics of each. Some pairs are clearly more volatile than others and display a greater magnitude of oscillation than others. Furthermore, the magnitude of oscillation will likely change over time for any given pair. Both of these factors are accounted for using this methodology. At the time the trade is initiated, the specific volatility characteristics and degree of divergence are built into the standard deviation calculation.

Some of the most common variations of this method include choosing a smaller or larger number of standard deviations, choosing a different number of standard deviations for the profit objective and the stop-loss, or simply choosing a specific percentage move to use for all cases in either direction. The percentage method is less sophisticated than the method just described, but it may be selected by managers who operate under specific mandated investment restraints. The number of standard deviations that a manager selects tends to be a function of how aggressive he wishes to be; because selecting a higher number involves more upside risk and more downside potential, such a choice would be considered more aggressive.

The general goal that the manager is trying to accomplish by setting these levels, other than creating important investment discipline, has two components. On the upside, the manager tries to set the profit objective high enough to capture the majority of the potential profit involved with each trade, without setting it so high that the trade will reverse before it is closed. In most cases, long-term performance will be better if the manager sets this level too low and takes smaller profits than it will be if the manager loses winning trades by setting the level too high.

On the downside, the manager attempts to set the stop-loss low enough that he does not close the trade for a loss before it reverses and becomes profitable but high enough to limit his loses on unsuccessful pairs. If the stop-loss level is set too low, the manager will cannibalize much of his trading profits waiting for bad trades to turn around; if this level is set too high, the manager will find himself getting stopped out of many trades just before they reverse and become profitable. In the long run, performance will be better if the manager sets stop-loss levels a bit too high and misses some potentially profitable trades than it would be if he sets them too low and takes larger realized losses than are necessary.

Some of the more advanced concepts that a manager may wish to employ when setting these levels include trailing stops and the consideration of resistance and support levels. The term *trailing stops* refers to stop-loss levels that are progressively raised as a trade moves in a profitable direction. For example, assume that a manager is using a plus or minus 5 percent exit strategy when a trade is opened. If the trade quickly moves up 3 percent, the manager may wish to raise the stop level to a maximum loss on the trade of 1 percent, or perhaps limit his downside to close the trade, if it slips back to showing less than a gain of 1 percent. This is an example of a trailing stop. Such a process is followed most often when a trade moves quickly in the first several days that it is open. It is usually inadvisable to move the profit objective under any circumstances; doing so usually results in a manager's eagerness taking over, with long-term negative results.

Some managers may wish to customize the levels they select for profit objectives and stop-losses based on recent support or resistance levels. The rationale behind this decision is that if one of these levels is broken, the manager feels that the pair will continue in the given direction of breakout regardless of the number of standard deviations of divergence this represents. Figure 11.8 depicts the price relationship of IBM and Microsoft over the past several months. As can be seen from the graph, there is a short-term support level that has held for a large part of the examined

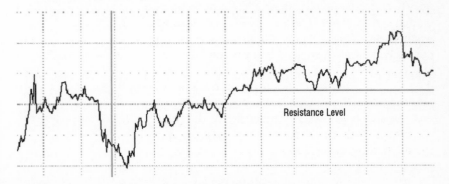

Resistance Level

FIGURE 11.8   Price Ratio between IBM and Microsoft

time period. The manager may decide to set his stop-loss at or just below this level, under the assumption that if the support level is broken, the price ratio is likely to fall a great deal. While this type of analysis is not required, more experienced pairs traders often consider this type of factor.

The other major consideration when setting profit objective and stop-loss levels is the expected duration of the intended trade. This will be affected by the trader's observation of how quickly the pair has oscillated in the past. In most cases, a trade will hit either its profit objective or its stop-loss within roughly the expected time frame, but a maximum duration should still be determined. A common mistake made by novice pairs traders is to assume that a trade should remain open until one of the two extremes is reached. What they fail to realize is that there is an opportunity cost associated with sitting in a pair that does not move significantly. With the vast number of potentially profitable trades that exist in the market, a dormant pair should not be held too long.

Determining a sound exit strategy is one of the more complex aspects of pairs trading, but it is vital to the eventual success of the strategy. Over time, a manager will gain, both through research and experience, a sense for what strategy is most in keeping with successful execution of his particular style. The two standard deviation rule is a solid starting point for any manager applying the technical approach. It will give him both the discipline and the variability necessary to manage his portfolio successfully while he develops his own unique methodology.

UNIFYING THE APPROACH

A manager applying the technical approach to pairs trading will go through several steps in order to identify the pairs he wishes to include in his portfolio. The feature that unifies the process is that underlying each step is some view to technical analysis. By combining the technicals of each stock and pair of stocks that he is considering, the manager brings together the market-neutral element and the arbitrage element with the key features of the technical analysis element. This process allows the manager to consider both the strength of the relationship and the likelihood that the relationship will persist, without losing sight of how his matched equity pairs relate over time. Furthermore, this approach provides a strong basis for determining appropriate entry and exit points, and is easily adaptable to a model or manual review.

In the following chapter, the last step prior to actual portfolio construction is examined in depth. This should give the reader the final tools needed in order to begin successfully trading matched equity pairs.

CHAPTER 12

The Overlays

After a manager has selected the matched equity pairs he wishes to include in his portfolio, the final step before trade execution is to perform two overlays to each pair: a fundamental overlay and a technical overlay. The goal of each of these steps is not to find further support for the manager's opinion about the pair, but rather to identify any arguments that the pair should be excluded. This step may seem painfully redundant to some readers, but performing each overlay will help the manager to eliminate potential blow-ups that would have a very negative affect on performance. It is impossible to completely avoid pairs in which the relationship between the two stocks quickly breaks down; however, performing this last level of analysis eliminates the obvious weaknesses and reduces the number of such occurrences.

THE FUNDAMENTAL OVERLAY

The primary function of the fundamental overlay is to determine whether there are any fundamentally driven factors that would cause a candidate pair to be excluded from the portfolio. Two of the most prominent reasons this type of analysis would exclude a pair are major news events and earnings announcements. Either of these can act as a catalyst for an unpredictable price shock, causing a pair to move very quickly. In some cases, such movement might work to the manager's advantage, but there is no way to predict in which direction the shock will drive either stock in the pair to move. Therefore the manager is better off excluding the pair from the portfolio and selecting a different pair for inclusion.

The most successful pairs that a manager may include in his portfolio are those that have diverged from their average historical relationship to extreme entry points. This type of extreme divergence increases both the likelihood that the pair will begin mean reversion after the pair is opened and the amount of potential profit the manager can expect the pair to yield. Under normal circumstances, this type of extreme is reached through gradual divergence when one stock outperforms the other over a period of time. In certain instances, however, a highly correlated matched equity pair will reach an extreme entry point as the result of a price shock to one of the two companies being considered. In this situation, it is important for the manager to consider the catalyst for the price shock.

Figure 12.1 shows the price relationship between two companies being considered as a potential pairs trade. The pair has clearly moved to an extreme that presents an attractive entry point and should have a solid profit potential. In performing the fundamental overlay, however, the manager discovers that ABC just announced that it has failed to meet earnings expectations and is significantly lowering its projections of future earnings. Figures 12.2 and 12.3 represent the price action of ABC and XYZ respectively. One may observe from the graphs that while XYZ has displayed fairly stable price action, ABC has recently experienced a major price shock. This graphical information alone is not sufficient for the manager to determine whether the pair is appropriate. By performing the fundamental overlay, the manager discovered the reason for the price shock and may now determine whether he believes that the sell-off was justified.

In this case, if the manager views the sell-off as an overreaction, he may deem this an acceptable pair. If he believes that ABC will quickly re-

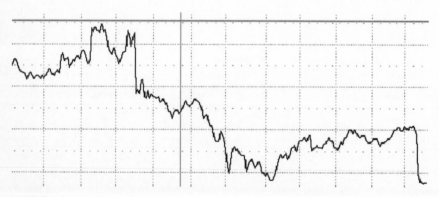

FIGURE 12.1 Price Relationship between ABC and XYZ Companies

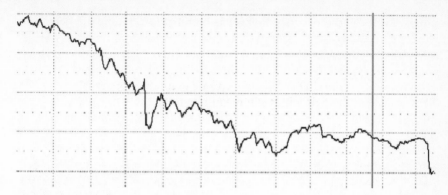

FIGURE 12.2   Price Action of ABC

cover, he has an opportunity to capitalize on it as the stock rises. Having made this judgment in the context of a pair, the manager is still somewhat protected if ABC does not recover and continues to decline. Under the same circumstances, if the manager believes that the sell-off was justified, he will likely pass on this pair, viewing the price action as the beginning of a new average relationship between ABC and XYZ, not the extreme divergence he is seeking.

A price shock like the one just described may be driven by either a major news release or by an earnings announcement and is not necessarily negative. A manager will be more suspicious of negative price shocks, however, because a stock is more likely to quickly lose gains than to quickly recover losses. In either case, when a manager observes a sharp change in the price of one side of a pair, he must determine whether the events that caused that stock to move so quickly are reasons to eliminate

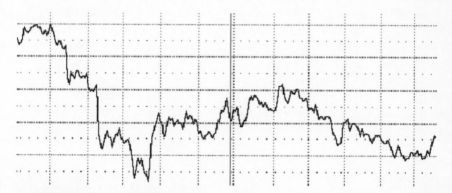

FIGURE 12.3   Price Action of XYZ

the pair from the portfolio. This choice, of course, involves a degree of judgment and experience, but if a manager is unsure, he should elect the safer choice—to skip the pair.

Price shocks are not the only type of fundamental event that may lead a manager to exclude a pair from his portfolio. In some cases, the manager may discover that the potentially high-impact news has not yet been released. Some examples of this include scheduled earnings announcements—the scheduled announcements of the results of an investigation into one of the companies, or the results of an FDA decision on approval for a new major drug. If a manager knows that this type of information is about to become public, he will often elect to eliminate a pair from consideration, at least until the news has been released and the market has had a chance to react to it. Eliminating such pairs is not an absolute rule, but a successful manager will need to develop a sense of when a pair is too risky to fit his particular style.

The fundamental overlay is not a purely scientific process that will perfectly protect the manager from investing in losing pairs. Its purpose is to prevent the manager from investing in a pair that has exhibited major warning signs. If this overlay is not performed, particularly by managers who are basing the majority of their process on a technical model, the manager will likely invest in some unprofitable pairs that could have been avoided with a simple review of readily available information. The overlay is not intended to replace a full fundamental analysis of each stock, but rather to catch blatant warning signs that are easy to detect.

THE TECHNICAL OVERLAY

The purpose of the technical overlay is the same as for the fundamental overlay: to eliminate pairs that have blatant, easily detectable flaws. To perform a technical overlay, a manager considers the technicals of each side of the pair individually to ensure that there are not forces likely to make one or both sides of the pair behave contrary to their expected directional bias. The need for this type of analysis is dependent on the method used for selecting pairs, but, as most sophisticated pairs traders focus on the characteristics of the pairs themselves, a cursory check of the technical factors affecting each side of the pair is a good idea.

There are two primary factors that a manager considers when performing the technical overlay: (1) momentum and (2) resistance or support levels. While it is unlikely that the technical factors that make a pair attractive will not translate to the technicals of the individual stocks that form the pair, it is possible and should be considered. Furthermore, by conducting this level of analysis, the manager is often able to improve the accuracy of his entry point at a reversal level.

When the manager considers momentum factors as a part of the technical overlay, he is confirming that the momentum of each stock individually does not contradict the analysis done on the pair. Figure 12.4 is the graph of a stock being considered as the long side of a potential pairs trade. From the graph it can be seen that the stock has a very high RSI reading, indicating that the stock is relatively overbought. This reading indicates to the manager that this stock is likely to reverse in the near future and is not a particularly good long candidate. The manager may decide to exclude the pair because he does not wish to be long this particular stock.

While the above example is rare, it does illustrate the type of information that can prove vital when performing a technical overlay. Despite the fact that the pair displayed all of the required characteristics, the manager does not wish to take a long position in a stock that he believes is on the verge of a reversal. One should note that the manager is not explicitly taking a long position (recall that pairs trading is a relative-value play and that its success is not dependent on either the positive performance of the long stock or the negative performance of the short stock; only the relative performance is critical). Therefore he need not exclude a pair based only on this type of analysis. With this in mind—coupled with the vast number of potential pairs candidates that exist—the manager may be hesitant to enter a pairs trade when he believes there is a high probability that one side of the trade will perform poorly.

The same considerations are made when evaluating the intended short side of a pair. Figure 12.5 is the graph of a stock that is being considered as the short side of a candidate pair for the portfolio. In this case, the stock shows strong signs of being oversold, and a manager may conclude that this stock is likely to reverse and run higher. Again, the manager must

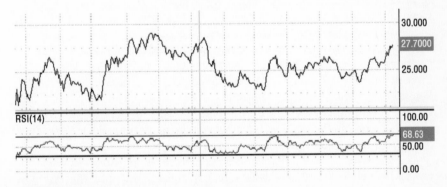

FIGURE 12.4 ABC Corporation with High RSI

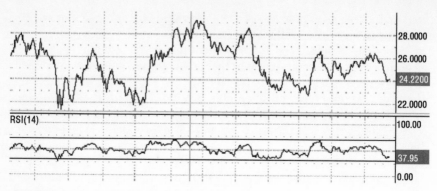

FIGURE 12.5   XYZ Corporation with Low RSI

determine whether this is a sufficient reason to exclude the pair from the portfolio, but given the probability that one side of the pair is likely to perform poorly, the wise manager will look for better candidates to include.

Resistance Levels

The other factor that the technical overlay is designed to reveal is any significant support or resistance levels that may exist for either of the individual stocks in a candidate pair. Finding these levels is useful because they can help the manager both identify potential issues with one side of the pair and more accurately identify optimal entry points. To do this requires a certain understanding of technical analysis and charting that may extend beyond some of the basics discussed Part Three, but the general concepts are relatively straightforward and can easily be applied with minimal additional research.

In order to illustrate some of the key elements of a resistance level review, consider the graph in Figure 12.6. To begin the analysis, assume that the graph is for the stock (ABC) that is being considered as the long side of a candidate pair. Two resistance levels are delineated in the chart and may be considered equally legitimate. If the manager considers level 1 to be the more significant resistance level, his opinion may be that the stock has broken this level and will likely continue to rise. In this case, the overlay supports the pairs analysis, and the manager will likely initiate the trade to include the pair in the portfolio. If, however, the manager believes resistance level 2 to be more significant, he may believe that ABC has limited upside potential and may choose to exclude the pair from the portfolio. In the latter case, ABC may continue up through the resistance level, but if this does not occur, the low potential maximum gain may cause the trader to skip the pair.

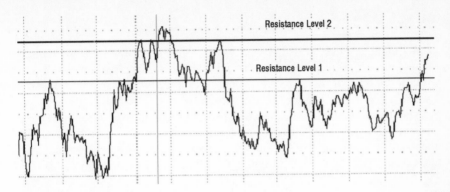

FIGURE 12.6 Resistance Levels for ABC Corporation

In order to understand other benefits of this type of analysis, now assume that ABC is being considered as the short side of the candidate pair. If the manager considers resistance level 1 to be the more significant of the two levels, this may indicate that the stock is likely to continue its run and be a poor short candidate. Under these circumstances, the manager may choose to exclude the pair because regardless of the characteristics of the pair as a whole, the short side has a strong probability of losing money. If the manager believes that resistance level 2 is the more significant level, he faces a different type of decision. He may view this analysis as supporting his opinion of the candidate pair and choose to initiate the pair for the portfolio. Alternately, he may decide that the pair should remain a strong candidate on a watch list awaiting determination as to whether the resistance level in question will hold. If the manager decides to delay entering the pair until the resistance level holds, assuming no major changes occur on the long side of the pair, the manager will have effectively improved his entry point. While it is unlikely that the long side of the pair would remain completely unchanged, by combining the results of the technical overlay for each side of the pair, the manager may be able to come closer to an entry point that represents the commencement of the mean reversion process.

The technical overlay is arguably the least important step in the pairs trading investment process. It requires a high degree of experience and expertise, and one is extremely unlikely to find a pair with strong technical characteristics that are not supported by the technicals of the individual sides of the pair. Despite the subtlety of this overlay, conducting it is advisable because of the potential problems it can eliminate. Traders who are less comfortable with this type of analysis should still perform the procedure but rely less heavily on it until an appropriate comfort level has been reached.

CONCLUSION

Some managers may consider the two overlays described in this chapter redundant and unnecessary, but the time involved is minimal when considered in the light of the potentially devastating trades that may be avoided by using these overlays in the investment process. Traders relying more heavily on a technical model will find the most benefit from these overlays, because often these traders are less familiar with the details of the individuals stocks in their investment universe than are those who manually match equity pairs of the individuals stocks in their investment universe.

CHAPTER 13

The Unified Pairs Trading Theory

The combination of each of the elements of pairs trading into the comprehensive investment process forms the Unified Theory of Pairs Trading. By applying this theory to practical trading, a manager should be able to create a balanced portfolio that has a low risk profile and produces steady returns. Under the weight of recent market conditions, the application of the principles of market neutrality, arbitrage, and technical analysis to various equity markets allows a manager to leverage the power of each strategy and minimize many of their weaknesses.

At the outset of this investigation, a definition of pairs trading was offered to help give the reader an idea of the goals to be accomplished in these pages:

Pairs trading: A nondirectional, relative value investment strategy that seeks to identify two companies with similar characteristics whose equity securities are currently trading at a price relationship that is out of their historical trading range. This investment strategy will entail buying the undervalued security while short-selling the overvalued security, all while maintaining market neutrality.

Now that each of the elements has been explored and several practical approaches to the theory have been outlined, the reader should have a sufficient understanding of the theory to begin trading. From selecting an investment universe and setting selection criteria to building a model and applying the appropriate overlays, the reader has been taken from initial desire to execute the strategy and given the tools to build a pairs portfolio. The ability to successfully put the theory into practice is not immediate, however, and requires the patience to become familiar with carrying out the required steps. To that end, the remainder of this chapter will cohesively retrace the steps and then point out some of the common pitfalls.

PUTTING IT ALL TOGETHER

Transforming the Unified Theory of Pairs Trading from a theoretical construct that exists on paper into a practical reality capable of generating profits is a six-step process:

1. Formulate the selection criteria.
2. Generate a list of candidate trades.
3. Perform the fundamental and technical overlays.
4. Execute the trade.
5. Manage the trade.
6. Close the trade.

The successful execution of each of the above steps is a critical element in the process of becoming a profitable pairs trader. As is the case with any trading methodology, the complexity and success of the final three steps, the actual trading, are integrally dependent on the care and skill that go into the first three. A manager who has carefully designed his approach, diligently completed his research, and been honest with himself about the risks will have relatively far less to do in terms of trading than if he is attempting to guide his trades by feel. This is not to suggest that many of the most successful traders do not jump into the market and trade on instinct; a trader's gut feeling is one of his most important tools and something that can be honed over time. For the layman or beginner, however, this approach tends to be a costly way to learn. Experienced traders use research, systems, and discipline because they work.

FORMULATE THE SELECTION CRITERIA

This is the most difficult and time consuming step in the process, but fortunately one that must only be completed once. This step includes selecting a trading universe; constructing and testing a model, if one is to be used; and creating general buy and sell guidelines. An individual trader's resources and expected trade duration will affect each of these factors, but the structure is functionally the same in all cases. In each case, a trader must determine the number of stocks that can be reasonably analyzed; for those who intend to use an automated model or screening tool, the universe can be much larger than for traders who intend to perform the majority of their research manually. Furthermore, those traders who intend to use an intermediate to long-term trade duration are more likely to have the time to devote to analyzing a greater universe of data.

Once the trading universe has been selected, the trader must decide the basis for analysis. If a model is to be used, the input factors must be selected and tested, both individually and then in tandem, to assure a satisfactory predictive ability. This process can be accomplished in a number of ways, each described in earlier chapters, but after the model has been built, it should be thoroughly back-tested. Back-testing is the process by which a trader turns back the clock and determines if his model would have been successful using historical data. Before back-testing can be accomplished, buy and sell criteria must be selected. For the pairs trader these decisions include each of the following:

- The level of divergence required for trade initiation.
- The stop-loss and profit objective levels.
- The maximum acceptable duration (how long will a trade be left open that has neither been stopped out nor hit its profit objective).
- Maximum number of pairs in the portfolio (when back-testing, one must know which trades would not have been executed due to capacity issues).
- Auxiliary factors (what level of RSI, MACD, etc., must be reached for a trade to be initiated).

After these criteria have been set, a model may be back-tested to determine if it has any value. This is accomplished by assuming a start date several years in the past and then determining what trades the model would have indicated on an ongoing basis. This process usually requires the aid of one of the various pieces of computer software available if the analysis is to be performed over a long period, but it yields performance figures that are invaluable in developing a successful model.

The results of a back-test not only provide the general level of success or failure of a model but also help a trader gain insight into the model through the analysis of different performance trends in different market environments. For example, if a trader were to run a 10-year back-test and determine that the model performed well in bull markets and poorly in bear markets, he could accurately conclude that his model was biased toward the long side of the portfolio. Because a trader's first attempt at creating a model is rarely without the need for improvement, analyzing back-tested results is critical. It is from these insights that a trader may adjust his model and hope to improve it, rather than employing a method of trial-and-error.

Back-testing, and the resulting model improvements, is associated with certain risks that should be understood. The process of making minor improvements to a back-tested model in hopes of gradually improving performance results is called optimization. This process is quite useful for making major changes to the model and developing a methodology in which a trader may have confidence. The problem with optimization, however, is that as the process is constantly repeated, the model becomes increasingly targeted on the specific period being tested and less applicable to general market conditions. As a corollary, recall the discussion of linear regression analysis. In linear regression, a best-fit line is chosen to represent a series of data points so that an equation can be determined. If this process were sufficiently optimized, and allowed to consider nonlinear equations, it would be possible to determine an equation whose graph intersected every available data point in the series. While this might seem beneficial, the problem is that the new complex equation, while perfectly modeling this set of data, may not adequately model a different set of data. Returning to the stock market, if a trading model is too specific (i.e., there has been too much optimization), it may produce superior results for a given five-year period but have little relevancy in the future. The ideal trading model is specific enough to capture the principles it is modeling while remaining general enough to be applicable under all types of market conditions.

The other concern about back-testing relative to a pairs trading model is that under the approach advocated here, certain external factors affecting trading decisions are not built into the model. Some traders, for this reason, favor black-box system approaches because they can be more accurately tested. System trading, however, as discussed earlier, often fails to account for some of the subtleties easily detected by the trader. Factors such as negative news events likely to change the nature of a given stock's price action are nearly impossible to program into a model; thus, a blended approach is advocated in these pages.

Given that only a portion of the expected trading criteria to be included are reflected in the model, a trader must take care when analyzing the results of a back-test. Because the goal of the human element is to eliminate price-shock-causing events from the portfolio, those trades in the back-test with extreme moves should usually be excluded. The proper way to analyze a back-test, given this methodology, is to review the results on a trade-by-trade basis. Any trade that appears to have a non-average performance result should be treated as an outlier and excluded from the net performance of the test.

The result of this condition is that it is difficult to get a dependable prediction from back-testing on expected performance results. While this would seem to place the trader in a somewhat untenable position relative to moving forward, if the general results of the test are positive, the trader may proceed confidently. A degree of optimization is appropriate, but only to the extent that it addresses major flaws in the system. The job of the trader now is to avoid those trades that can have cataclysmic results for the portfolio and to generally keep the portfolio functioning along the middle course. The combination of a solid model and thorough auxiliary research should keep one's portfolio performing to relative expectations.

DETERMINE THE CANDIDATES

After a selection process has been defined, a trader must use that process to generate a list of candidate trades. If relying on manual research, the results of this inquiry constitute the list; if relying on a model, the model's output serves as the list of candidates. The frequency of the procedure is directly dependent on the targeted trade duration with the portfolio. A trader or manager who intends to hold a given position for several hours to several days will need to generate candidate trade with far greater frequency than a manager whose average holding period is measured in months.

Opinions differ greatly as to whether this process should be conducted during times when no trades are anticipated (when the portfolio is fully invested at capacity). One school of thought argues that creating a list of candidate pairs for analysis that have no chance of being executed is a waste of the manager's time, and ultimately unnecessary. This school further argues that performing this step can weaken a trader's confidence in his existing portfolio and lead to impulsive and damaging decisions. The fear is that when a manager is faced with an untainted opportunity (any of the trades on the newly created list), he is likely to consider open positions that have moved against him more negatively. Forced to decide between a trade that appears not to be working and a trade that looks like an attractive opportunity, the trader may violate his discipline and replace the trade. Once a manager begins second-guessing his trades and violating the buy and sell rules that have been established, the likelihood of success diminishes sharply. Disciplined research without disciplined execution is as bad as no research at all.

The other school of thought argues that by performing this process on a regular basis, regardless of the portfolio's capacity, the manager is able to stay more in tune with the market environment in which he is trading. This argument implies that the performance of this process is a kind of discipline unto itself. Those subscribing to this school would further suggest that part of actively managing a portfolio involves evaluating whether open positions are performing to expectations. In cases where an open position is faltering, swapping in a potentially better trade is not only acceptable but also required. For example, if a week after a trade is initiated, unfavorable news breaks on one of the stocks in the trade, the manager does not necessarily need to wait for the trade to be stopped out before closing the position. Active management means evaluating one's portfolio on an ongoing basis.

THE OVERLAYS

As discussed in Chapter 12, the next step in the investment process is to perform both a fundamental and a technical overlay. These steps are taken to ensure that there is not some compelling reason, not accounted for in the selection process, why the trade should be rejected. The other function of this step is to customize the buy and sell rules for a particular trade. The performance of these steps constitutes the human element that can distinguish a blended approach to portfolio management from a straight system-based approach.

While the specifics factors for rejecting a trade have been thoroughly discussed, it is useful to consider how the technical overlay can assist a manager in customizing his buy and sells rules for a specific trade. Similar to the resistance level analysis described in Chapter 12, these levels can be used to adjust profit objectives and stop loss levels according to the specifics of a given trade. Consider the graph in Figure 13.1. This chart represents the recent price action for a candidate trade that a manager intends to execute. In this example, given the illustrated support level around 2.3, setting the stop-loss at or just below this level is appropriate. Figure 13.2 depicts the same pair relationship six weeks later. As can be seen from the graph, if the stop-loss had been set at a more standardized 8 to 10 percent, this trade would have ultimately been stopped out for a far greater loss than necessary. The same type of analysis can be performed in terms of profit objectives and resistance levels.

While this example is simplified for ease of explanation, it underlines the effectiveness of customizing the buy and sell rules according to technical factors. By making minor adjustments to standard buy and

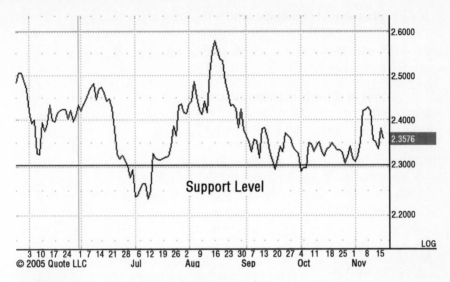

FIGURE 13.1   Price Action and Support Level

sell criteria, a manager may potentially avoid larger losses and protect profits. Despite the subtlety of this procedure, conducting it is advisable because of the potential problems it can eliminate. Traders who are less comfortable with this type of analysis should still perform the procedure but rely less heavily on it until an appropriate comfort level has been reached.

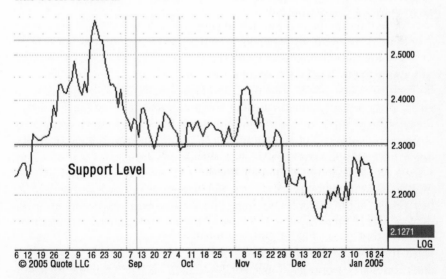

FIGURE 13.2   Price Action and Support Level—Six Weeks Later

EXECUTE THE TRADE

While this would seem to be the most straightforward step in the investment process, there a few subtleties that bear mentioning. As a result of
the uptick rule when shorting a stock, trading order can play an important
role in the process, particularly when dealing with more volatile or less
liquid stocks. Generally speaking, the short side of a trade should be executed and filled before the long order is placed. While share amounts are
commonly calculated before the process is begun, in cases where the
short stock moves dramatically before the order is filled, the share
amounts may be rebalanced for dollar neutrality before executing the long
position. In such cases, a spot check should be performed to assure that
there is still sufficient profit potential in the pair before initiating the long
position. If it is determined that a significant portion of the expected move
has taken place while waiting for a short order to be filled, the short
should be covered and the trade abandoned. This will likely result in a
small profit (the short was filled in the direction of the trend), but even in
the case of a small loss, this is preferable to initiating a trade that has already lost a significant portion of its profit potential.

In addition to the option of manually entering trades, there are a limited number of trading programs designed to handle pairs execution.
These programs are designed to simultaneously work each side of the
trade, particularly for larger orders, in an attempt to hit a prespecified
price ratio. For most traders, such programs are more of a convenience
than a necessity because the slippage that occurs during execution is minimal relative to the profit objective of the overall trade.

MANAGE THE TRADE

Once a trade has been initiated, it is the responsibility of the trader to
manage the position according not only to the predetermined buy and sell
rules, but also to the changing market environment. The trader must be
cognizant of unexpected news releases affecting either of the stocks in a
trade and be prepared to adjust his thinking accordingly. Likewise, he
must be mindful of the pair's price action and constantly adjust the risk/re-
turn profile of the trade. For example, if a trade with an expected duration
of three weeks were to achieve 50 percent of its profit objective in the first
day after execution, the trader would have to reevaluate the potential reward for keeping the trade open. In such a situation, the trader could
chose one of two options to prudently manage the trade moving forward.
First, the trade could be immediately closed with the view that the addi-

tional return does not warrant either the risk or the opportunity cost associated with inaction. This is sound logic because while the trade still has roughly its entire duration remaining, the potential profit has been halved. The second option is to initiate a trailing stop-loss level to lock in at least a portion of the profit. This is also a sound option because the additional profit potential is, in a sense, risk-free; the trade can no longer lose money and offers the remaining profit potential, therefore, free of charge. Over time, an individual trader will develop a feel for which of these options more suits his particular style, and may make different decisions for different pairs at different times.

CLOSE THE TRADE

For a manager who remains disciplined and follows the predetermined buy and sell rules as well as the signals received from the market, this is the easiest step in the process. The most difficult criterion for a trader to adhere to, and therefore one worth mention, is the duration limit. It is often difficult to close a trade that is losing a modest sum but has expired. The natural inclination is to opt to "give it a few days," in hopes that the break-even level can be restored. While rarely cataclysmic, and often rewarding, this behavior ignores opportunity cost and should be avoided. In the time that a trader waits to recover his losses (albeit small as the stop level has not been reached), other potentially profitable trades are being ignored. Clearly, closing losing trades can be an unpleasant experience, but traders who dedicate time and resources to avoiding closing losing trades are usually rewarded with larger losses or reduced profits.

CONCLUSION

While some traders may wish to augment their knowledge of various aspects of each individual element, anyone who has read carefully this far may now beginning trading equity pairs with an expectation of success. For those interested in exploring options, futures, and currencies, Part Five addresses each of these asset classes and then works through several examples from start to finish. The examples provided in Chapter 17 are recommended for all readers as they give insights from the author's personal experience.

Advanced Strategies and Examples

There is a tide in the affairs of men
Which taken at the flood, leads on to fortune;
Omitted, all the voyage of their life
Is bound in shallows and in miseries.
                                        —Shakespeare

CHAPTER 14

Options Basics: Terms and Strategies

The use of options within the framework of the Unified Theory of Pairs Trading gives a trader expanded flexibility when creating a portfolio. Whether using options as a substitute for equities or as an overlay for the purpose of risk management, a trader will seek to capture a distinct advantage by altering his basic pairs trading approach. The level of difficulty involved in deploying an options-based trade can range significantly but will always involve greater complexity than a straight equity pairs trade. This chapter is divided into two distinct sections: basic terms and basic strategies. In the terms sections, the reader will be introduced to some of the basic principles of options theory and the associated jargon. In the strategies section, the reader will be presented with a description of some of the most common options theories. Neither of these sections should be considered a complete tutorial on options theory; they are presented to lay the foundation for subsequent discussions on integrating options into the unified theory.

BASIC TERMS

As a basis for our exploration of options theory, let's begin with a working definition of an options contract:

Option: The right, but not the obligation, to buy or sell a stock (or other security) for a specified price, on or before a specific date.

179

Intrinsic value and time value are two of the main determinants of an option's price and are driven by both the price and volatility of the underlying stock or security.

From this definition, it should become immediately evident that when constructing a matched equity pair using options, one must not only consider the elements of the pair but also the factors that drive the associated options. There are four key factors when considering an option, each of which must be assessed prior to executing a trade: relative value, timing, volatility, and changes in the relationship between the option and the underlying stock. Each of these will affect how the option is priced as well as how the option is likely to react to various changes in the underlying stock and in the general market. Comprehension of these terms will aid in both understanding how options may be applied to pairs trading and defining the scope of the current investigation. Some of the subtleties of options theory are purposefully excluded from these pages because they do little to advance our understanding with the framework of the unified theory.

Relative Value

While this term has been defined within the equity sections of this book as the basis from which performance is derived in pairs trading, in the case of options it refers to the strike price of the option contract relative to the price of the underlying stock. Options are classified into three groups of relative value that carry the following definitions:

At-the-money: At-the-money (ATM) means that the strike price of the option is the same as the market price of the underlying stock. In such case, the price of the options contract represents time premium only and is neutral relative to the underlying stock.

In-the-money: In-the-money (ITM) means that the option is carrying a degree of intrinsic value. For call options, this means that the strike price of the option is below the current market price of the underlying stock. If the option were to be exercised (the stock called and purchased at the strike price), an automatic profit could be generated by immediately selling the newly purchased shares at the higher market price. For put options, ITM options carry a strike price that is above the current market value of the underlying stock. If the option were to be exercised (the stock put and sold at the strike price), an automatic profit could be generated by purchasing the newly sold shares at a lower market price.

Out-of-the-money: Out-of-the-money (OTM) means that the option is carrying no intrinsic value (time premium only) and would result in an immediate loss if exercised. For call options, this means that the strike price of the option is above the current market price of the underlying stock. If the option were exercised (the stock called and purchased at the strike price), an automatic loss would be generated because the stock was purchased at a price above that which was available in the market. The reverse mechanics apply to put options.

Each of these three levels is of significant importance when discussing pairs trading because each carries different advantages and disadvantages when considering the execution of various strategies. In terms of the basic strategies that will be highlighted in the second half of this chapter, it is most common to use ITM options because their price action is most similar to that of their underlying securities. When considering any strategy, however, particularly more advanced approaches, a solid understanding of how each of these types of options behave under different conditions will provide a trader with a distinct advantage in executing a successful trade.

These three definitions highlight two other terms that should be clearly defined: *intrinsic value* and *time premium value*. Intrinsic value can be defined as the dollar value of the options contract were it be exercised. It is only found in the price of an ITM option because this is the only type of option that carries a built-in cash value. In most cases, an option's price is based on the value of the right to buy or sell the security in the future in the hope of realizing some intrinsic value. Only options that would result in a dollar return if exercised carry intrinsic value. The other type of value that affects the price of an option is time premium value. This is the value placed on the right to exercise the option. This value is directly correlated to the amount of time remaining until the expiration of the option, and thus it decreases over time; at expiration, time value falls to zero and the option's price is equal to its intrinsic value. ATM and OTM options are priced purely based on time premium.

Timing

Timing, when referring to an options-based pairs trade, refers to both the time premium built into the price of the option and the appropriate expiration date of the option. The trader must consider the expected duration of the trade and select his options carefully. If all other factors are held constant, using options that carry the lowest possible time premium is preferred. Time premium erodes over time and should be minimized to whatever extent possible. While in most cases a higher time premium signals that the volatility of the underlying stock is higher, the effects of time premium on the expected return of the trade should be considered.

Selecting the appropriate expiration month is equally important and directly tied to time premium. Options contracts that have longer until expiration will always carry a higher time premium than those with shorter expirations. A trader must allow sufficient time for the expected mean reversion to occur but does not want to overpay for additional time premium that is not needed. If the trader selects options that expire too quickly, the benefits of his original analysis are lost as the mean reversion has not been given sufficient time to be completed. Similarly, if the trader selects options that expire too far in the future, he will likely significantly overpay for the options and decrease the overall profitability of a successful trade. It should be evident that of the two choices, selecting options that carry unneeded time until expiration is preferable, as this choice still allows the trade to successfully run its course, but careful analysis should be performed to determine what duration is reasonable.

Volatility

Volatility is the single most important concept in options theory because it differentiates options theory from stock trading. While stock traders do measure the volatility of a given issue, beta, it is not built into the price of the stock; high beta stocks do not cost more than low beta stocks. When dealing with options, however, volatility is a key factor in determining the price of an option; the options on high-volatility stocks do cost more than those on low-volatility stocks. This relationship exists because a higher volatility underlying stock provides more return potential and thus a higher price. While this relationship is somewhat intuitive, consider the example of two stocks, A and B. Stock A is very volatile and stock B is not. A call option on stock A will be priced higher than a call option on stock B with the same expiration. During the period until expiration, stock A may rise by 10 percent, given its high volatility, while stock B is unlikely to rise more than 2 percent. As the holder of a call option profits as the underlying stock rises, the call on stock A has more profit potential and is thus priced higher to reflect this increased potential.

When constructing a pairs trade, a trader must consider not only the volatility of each of the stocks being considered for pairing, as this will affect time premium and options price, but also the relative volatilities of the two stocks. Similar to beta neutrality, this can have a significant impact on the degree to which systematic risk is controlled in a given trade. While certain strategies are designed around pairing options with different volatilities in order to capture pricing discrepancies, a discussion of these is reserved for a later chapter.

Directly tied to the concept of volatility is the options-specific term *implied volatility*. This is a measure of volatility that depends on current market conditions rather than on an analysis of historical price action. It is often considered to be a more accurate measure of volatility because it factors in current market events such as takeover rumors or earnings expectations. Historical volatilities cannot properly account for news-driven upticks in volatility; as volatility is a key factor in most options pricing models, the deficiencies in historical volatility measures can cause these models to give the false impression that an option is mispriced. Implied volatility often differs over time from real volatility. This discrepancy, besides giving a trader a more accurate measurement for use in an option-pricing model, can give the trader an insight into the expected behavior of the option. Certain strategies highlight implied volatility, making it an important term to understand.

Changes in the Option-to-Stock Relationship

In addition to considering the relationship of an options contract to its underlying security, a trader must also consider how that relationship changes. Over the expected duration of a given trade, changes in this relationship can have a significant impact on the success of the trade. For example, if during the duration of a given trade the volatilities of the two stocks decrease significantly, this will likely cause the relationship between an option's price and the price of the underlying stock to change. In this case, one would expect the option to decrease in price more rapidly than initially expected because the market will no longer require the buyer of the option to pay as much time premium for a contract on the now less volatile underlying stock; the relationship between an option and its underlying stock changes over time and must be taken into account when considering initiating a trade.

The rate at which this relationship changes is quantified in options theory and referred to as *gamma*, one of four relationships labeled with

Greek letters; these four statistics are commonly referred to as "the Greeks." Gamma is the first derivative, or the rate of change of *delta*, which measures the relationship between the price of an option and the price of its underlying security. The definitions are as follows:

Theta: The amount of time decay for a given option relative to each day that passes. Because time decay is not a linear relationship, theta tends to increase as the option moves to expiration.

Delta: The amount by which an option's price changes relative to a 1-point move in the underlying security. This number ranges from 0.0 to 1.0 for call options and from 0.0 to –1.0 for put options.

Gamma: The rate of change of delta. Stated another way, the amount by which an option's prices changes relative to a 1-point move in the delta of the underlying security.

Vega: The relationship between the price of an option and the implied volatility of that option; how much does the option's price changes relative to a 1 percent change in volatility.

Each of the Greeks is used as a risk management tool in different situations, and each is significantly impacted by volatility. They are considered some of the most subtle and complex material in options theory but are very useful in pairs trading and will be addressed, as appropriate, with each of the strategies presented.

By understanding each of the key factors of options theory described here, a trader will be able to make an informed decision on how to incorporate options into the construction and management of his portfolio. These factors form the basis of all options trading and should provide a sufficient foundation to begin a discussion of specific applications and strategies. Once these basic strategies have been understood, it will be appropriate to relate both the theory and the application to pairs trading so as to determine how a manager may use options to augment his trading arsenal.

BASIC STRATEGIES

Options are a very powerful tool by which a manager may both improve returns and manage risk within his portfolio. In order to lay the foundation for relating pairs trading to options trading, it will be helpful to understand several basic options strategies. Each options strategy presented will be specifically applicable to pairs, will provide the reader with some insight into how the two relate, and will help solidify the necessary foundation required to begin trading successfully. Many of the strategies presented will be familiar or redundant to individuals with experience trading options; such readers may wish to skip ahead to Chapter 15. At the conclusion of this chapter, the reader should have a functional understanding of basic options strategies sufficient to begin integrating options into the unified theory.

Call Options

The purchase of a call option is the most basic strategy in options trading. A call gives the buyer the right, but not the obligation, to purchase 100 shares of the underlying stock at the strike price at any time until expiration. This is considered a bullish strategy because the value of the option will increase as the price of the underlying security rises. The maximum loss on such a position is the price paid for the option because there is no obligation to exercise the contract; in this case it will expire worthless. The maximum gain on a call option is unlimited. As the price of the underlying security continues to climb, so will the value of the option.

Options are derivative instruments and, therefore, for every option that is purchased there must be a counterparty to write or sell the contract. Selling call options is a bearish strategy because the maximum gain occurs for the seller if the price of the underlying security decreases and the contract expires worthless. In such a case, the seller's gain is the amount for which the contract was sold, also called the premium. The maximum loss on a call selling strategy is dependent of whether the call is *covered* or *naked*. When a call is exercised, the seller of the contract must deliver 100 shares of the underlying stock to the buyer who is exercising his option. If the call is covered, the seller has already purchased the stock and simply delivers the 100 shares from his inventory. In this case, the maximum loss is the price paid for the 100 shares minus the premium collected when the option was sold. If the option is naked, the seller has not purchased the 100 shares prior to selling the option. When the option is exercised, the call option seller must purchase the 100 shares at its current market price; the loss in this situation, therefore, is unlimited.

Put Options

The mechanics of put options are very similar to those of call options, but put options give the buyer the right to sell, rather than buy, a given stock at a given price at any time prior to expiration. Selling a put option is bearish because as the price of the underlying security falls, the price of the option will increase. The risk in buying a put is the premium paid for the option, while the maximum gain is unlimited. Selling, or writing, puts is just the opposite of selling call options. The maximum gain for a put seller is the premium collected on the sale, while the risk is unlimited.

Vertical Spreads

Vertical spreads are the most basic limited-risk options strategies. These simple hedging strategies enable traders to take advantage of the way options premiums change in relation to movement in the underlying asset. Vertical spreads combine long and short options with different strike prices and the same expiration date in order to profit from a directional move in the price of the underlying security. While the profit potential on such a strategy is limited, the risk is limited as well. One of the keys to understanding these managed risk spreads comes from grasping the concepts of intrinsic value and time value, variables that contribute greatly to the fluctuating price of an option. Vertical spreads are classified into the following four categories: a bull call spread, a bull put spread, a bear put spread, and a bear call spread.

Bull Call Spread   A bull call spread is a debit spread (debit spreads have a net cost, while credit spreads have a net profit) created by purchasing a call with a lower strike price and selling a call with a higher strike price, both with the same expiration date. The setup procedure for opening a bull call spread can be summarized in ten steps:

1. Look for a moderately bullish market in which a modest move is expected in the underlying security.
2. Review call options premiums per expiration dates and strike prices.
3. Investigate implied volatility values to determine if the considered options are overpriced or undervalued.
4. Explore past price trends and liquidity by reviewing price and volume charts for the past year's market activity.
5. Choose a lower strike price call option to buy and a higher strike price call option to sell with the same expiration dates.

6. Calculate the maximum profit potential of the spread by multiplying the value per point (if other than 1, based on delta) by the differences in the strike prices and subtracting the net premium paid.
7. Calculate the maximum potential risk by determining the net premium paid for the two options contracts.
8. Calculate the break-even level by adding the lower strike price to the net premium paid for the two options contracts.
9. Create a risk profile for the trade to graphically determine the trade's feasibility.
10. Initiate the trade by placing the two trade orders.

The maximum profit is achieved when the price of the underlying stock rises above the strike price of the short call. If the short call is exercised, the trader will exercise the option that was purchased at the lower strike price. The profit is the difference between the proceeds generated by the sale of the stock at the higher strike price, and the expense of the purchase at the lower strike price, plus the net premium paid. The profit potential on this strategy is limited and, therefore, should not be used if a large move in the underlying stock is predicted.

Consider the following example, with XYZ selling for $42:

Buy 1 July 45 call at $3 $3 debit
Sell 1 July 50 call at $1 $1 credit
Net $2 debit

The maximum profit for this example will be achieved if XYZ trades above $50 before expiration. In this case, a profit of $3 ($50 minus $45, less $2) is generated. The maximum loss occurs if XYZ is below $45 at expiration; this leads to a loss of the net premium paid, $2. This is a particularly aggressive example because all of the involved calls are out-of-the-money. This is a way to keep the cost of the spread low, but it requires a more significant move to be profitable.

Bull Put Spread   A bull put spread is a credit spread created by purchasing a put with a lower strike price and selling a put with a higher strike price, both with the same expiration date. The setup procedure for opening a bull put spread can be summarized in these 10 steps:

1. Look for a moderately bullish market in which a modest move is expected in the underlying security.
2. Review put options premiums per expiration dates and strike prices.

3. Investigate implied volatility values to determine if the considered options are overpriced or undervalued.

4. Explore past price trends and liquidity by reviewing price and volume charts for the past year's market activity.

5. Choose a lower strike price put option to buy and a higher strike price put option to sell with the same expiration dates.

6. Calculate the maximum profit potential of the spread by determining the net premium received for the two options contracts.

7. Calculate the maximum potential risk by multiplying the value per point (if other than 1, based on delta) by the difference in the strike prices and subtracting the net premium received.

8. Calculate the break-even level by subtracting the net premium received for the two options contracts from the higher strike price.

9. Create a risk profile for the trade to graphically determine the trade's feasibility.

10. Initiate the trade by placing the two trade orders.

In this type of spread, the maximum profit potential is achieved when both options expire worthless and the net premium received is captured. Similar to selling puts or calls, as described earlier, a trader using this type of strategy is said to be "selling premium." These types of strategies differ from others in the fact that when a trader sells premium, he realizes his maximum profit at the beginning of the trade and then hopes that the market does not take it away. While this seems counterintuitive, premium-selling strategies can give a disciplined trader a tool to consistently mine small profits from the market.

Consider the following example, with XYZ selling for $42:

Buy 1 July 40 put at $2	$2 debit
Sell 1 July 45 put at $4	$4 credit
Net	$2 credit

The maximum profit for this example will be achieved if XYZ trades above $45 before expiration, and is equal to the net credit received, $2. The maximum loss occurs if XYZ is below $40 at expiration. In this case, the loss is $3 ($45 minus $40, less $2). This is not a particularly attractive example because the maximum potential loss is greater than the maximum potential gain.

Bear Put Spread   A bear put spread is a debit spread created by purchasing a put with a higher strike price and selling a put with a lower strike price, both with the same expiration date. The setup procedure for opening a bear put spread can be summarized in 10 steps:

1. Look for a moderately bearish market in which a modest move is expected in the underlying security.
2. Review put options premiums per expiration dates and strike prices.
3. Investigate implied volatility values to determine if the considered options are overpriced or undervalued.
4. Explore past price trends and liquidity by reviewing price and volume charts for the past year's market activity.
5. Choose a higher strike price put option to buy and a lower strike price put option to sell with the same expiration dates.
6. Calculate the maximum profit potential of the spread by multiplying the value per point (if other than 1, based on delta) by the difference in the strike prices and subtracting the net premium paid.
7. Calculate the maximum potential risk by determining the net premium paid for the two options contracts.
8. Calculate the break-even level by subtracting the net premium paid for the two options contracts from the higher strike price.
9. Create a risk profile for the trade to graphically determine the trade's feasibility.
10. Initiate the trade by placing the two trade orders.

The maximum profit is achieved when the price of the underlying stock falls below the strike price of the short put. If the short put is exercised, the trader will exercise the option that was purchased at the higher strike price. The profit is the difference between the proceeds generated by the sale of the stock at the higher strike price, the expense of the purchase at the lower strike price, plus the net premium paid. The profit potential on this strategy is limited and, therefore, should not be used if a large move in the underlying stock is predicted.

Consider the following example, with XYZ selling for $63:

Buy 1 July 65 put at $3	$3 debit
Sell 1 July 60 Call at $1	$1 credit
Net	$2 debit

The maximum profit for this example will be achieved if XYZ trades below $60 before expiration. In this case, a profit of $3 ($65 minus $60, less $2) is generated. The maximum loss occurs if XYZ is above $65 at expiration; this leads to a loss of the net premium paid, $2.

Bear Call Spread   A bear call spread is a credit spread created by purchasing a call with a higher strike price and selling a call with a lower strike price, both with the same expiration date. The setup procedure for opening a bear call spread can be summarized in 10 steps:

1. Look for a moderately bearish market in which a modest move is expected in the underlying security.
2. Review call options premiums per expiration dates and strike prices.
3. Investigate implied volatility values to determine if the considered options are overpriced or undervalued.
4. Explore past price trends and liquidity by reviewing price and volume charts for the past year's market activity.
5. Choose a higher strike price call option to buy and a lower strike price call option to sell with the same expiration dates.
6. Calculate the maximum profit potential of the spread by determining the net premium received for the two options contracts.
7. Calculate the maximum potential risk by multiplying the value per point (if other than 1, based on delta) by the difference in the strike prices and subtracting the net premium received.
8. Calculate the break-even level by adding the lower strike price to the net premium paid for the two options contracts.
9. Create a risk profile for the trade to graphically determine the trade's feasibility.
10. Initiate the trade by placing the two trade orders.

In this type of spread, the maximum profit potential is achieved when both options expire worthless and the net premium received is captured. This is another example of a premium-selling strategy.

Consider the following example, with XYZ selling for $33:

Buy 1 December 35 call at $1	$1 debit
Sell 1 December 30 call at $4	$4 credit
Net	$3 credit

The maximum profit for this example will be achieved if XYZ trades above $35 before expiration and is equal to the net credit received, $3. The maximum loss occurs if XYZ is below $30 at expiration. In this case, the loss is $2 ($35 minus $30, less $3).

Each of these vertical spreads is attractive in varying market conditions because they give the manager a means to realize profits while still strictly controlling for risk. They require the manager to take a directional bias, but they offer controls that are not available in the equity market. Additionally, because options have a built-in leverage feature, these strategies allow the trader to realize the profits described using substantially less capital than would be required for an equity investment. As with most options strategies, vertical spreads offer leveraged, limited-risk opportunities that, if carefully crafted, place minimal limits on profit potential.

Back Spreads   The back spread is an options spread strategy in which one buys more options than are sold and it is executed within the same expiration month; this usually occurs in a 1:2 or a 2:3 ratio. This strategy is used when a large move is expected in the underlying security and can be done on either the long or the short side of the market using calls or puts, respectively. In either case, this strategy should always be initiated for a credit, which is accomplished by buying OTM options and selling a lesser amount of ITM options. The strategy offers limited downside risk and unlimited return potential.

Consider the following example, with XYZ selling for $53:

Buy 2 September 55 calls at $1 each $2 debit
Sell 1 September 50 call at $4 $4 credit
Net $2 credit

If the underlying security drops below $50 at expiration, all of the options in the spread will expire worthless and a $2 profit will be realized. If the stock rallies, however, the profit potential is unlimited because the trader owns extra calls on the long side. The maximum loss for this strategy occurs when XYZ is trading at $55 at expiration; in this case the long calls are worthless, while the short call results in a loss of the difference between the strike prices. Back spreads are appropriate only when a substantial move is expected in the stock.

CONCLUSION

Each of the preceding terms and strategies is pertinent to pairs trading and directly relates to applying options trading to the methodology. Used correctly, the inclusion of options contracts as either a substitute or an overlay can help a trader both increase returns and manage risk. The reader should now have a functional understanding of options basics sufficient to begin an investigation into practical applications.

CHAPTER 15

Pairs Trading with Options

The use of options in pairs trading, while usually reserved for more sophisticated managers, can be a powerful tool for increasing returns and managing risk. Options may either be applied as an overlay to an underlying pair or used as a substitute for the equity positions. When using them as an overlay, the manager must determine that the risk he is trying to mitigate is sufficient to warrant the additional expense, as it serves as a drag on performance. When used as a substitute, the manager must again factor for performance drag, but must also determine which strategy is most appropriate. The particular options strategy selected will often vary from trade to trade and will be a direct function of the combined characteristics of the underlying securities being considered.

THE OPTIONS OVERLAY

When a manager identifies an unexpected risk factor within a given pair in his portfolio, he may wish to use an options overlay. In pairs trading, an options overlay most commonly involves the purchase of options contracts against one side of the trade to fully or partially hedge against sharp swings in the price of that stock. In such cases, the options are being used as a risk management tool and are not intended to generate a profit on their own; rather, they are intended to protect one side of the trade from losses that the manager believes are both significant and imminent. Situations such as earnings announcements, FDA approvals, management

193

changes, mergers, and competitor news are all events that could lead a manager to believe that an option overlay is appropriate. In such cases, the manager maintains his longer-term view of the pair but initiates the hedge to cover the short-term negative impact of the perceived risk factor.

In order to flesh out both the specific logic and procedure for initiating an options overlay, consider the following example of ABC versus XYZ, opened on April 3:

Bought 1,000 ABC @ $60 = $60,000

Sold 1,500 XYZ @ $40 = $60,000

ABC is scheduled to announce earnings on April 15 and, while the stock has not fluctuated significantly, the manager is concerned that given the market's recent reaction to negative earnings announcements, negative earnings from ABC could cause a sharp drop in the stock. The manager also believes that if ABC announces earnings that are in line with or better than expectations, the expected mean reversion within the pair will occur. Under normal circumstances, a prudent manager would simply close the trade so as not to expose the portfolio to this potential price shock. Through the use of options, however, the manager is able to hedge this risk temporarily and readdress the trade after the earnings announcement has been made.

At the time the options overlay is being considered, April 9, the following prices are present in the market:

ABC	$62.40
XYZ	$40.60
ABC May $65 put	$ 3.10
ABC May $60 put	$ 1.10
ABC May $55 put	$ 0.20

During the first six days of the trade, the manager has made 4 percent on the rise in ABC and has lost 1.5 percent on the rise in XYZ, for a net gain of 2.5 percent or $1,500. In order to fully hedge his exposure to ABC, the manager must buy 10 puts (puts are used to hedge on the long side of the portfolio, while calls are used to hedge on the short side). Each of the puts listed at the three respective strike prices has a different advantage and each should be considered; for ease of explanation, the relative position of each choice is considered at expiration. Purchasing in-the-money (ITM) puts (the ABC May $65 put) has the advantage of most fully covering any decline in the price of ABC; the deeper in-the-money an option is, the closer that option's delta moves to 1. The ITM put will rise by nearly $1 for every dollar ABC declines. The downside to using the strike price is that ITM options are more expensive; creating this hedge will cost the manager $3,100. Purchasing the ABC May $60 put, slightly out-of-the-money (OTM), will be far less expensive but will not provide the same dollar-for-dollar protection as the ITM put until ABC trades below $60. The ABC May $55 put, which is deeply OTM, sometimes called a "crash put," is by far the cheapest solution but requires a precipitous fall in ABC before it provides any real protection.

In this example, the ITM puts are likely prohibitively expensive. If one assumes that the profit objective of this trade was 10 percent or $6,000, initiating the overlay with the ITM puts would cannibalize over half of the targeted profit if the trade were perfectly successful. Likewise, the deeply OTM puts provide so little protection that they may also be dismissed; the trade would likely be stopped out long before these options began to mitigate the losses. The slightly OTM puts, as is typically the case, provide the best balance between protection and expense. Fully hedging ABC will cost the manager $1,100, less than a quarter of the expected profit, and, should the stock begin to fall as the result of a negative earnings announcement, these puts will provide significant protection below the entry price.

The manager must consider a number of factors when selecting the strike price of the options to be used when creating an overlay. In addition to seeking a favorable balance between protection and expense, the volatility of the underlying security and the timing of the risk factor must also be considered. The manager should be aware of the volatility of the underlying security, not only because it directly affects the price of the options being considered, but also because it will help to define how far out-of-the-money the options he uses to hedge can be and still maintain effectiveness. When analyzing a more volatile stock, deeper OTM options are acceptable because the stock is more likely to reach these levels during a price shock. In the case of a less volatile stock, the option selected must be nearly at-the-money in order to provide protection.

The timing of the risk factor must also be considered when constructing an options overlay. In the preceding example, the exact date and time of the announcement was known and, therefore, very easy to account for in the analysis. The timing of a risk factor is not always as certain. In the cases of management changes or FDA announcements, for example, the timing may be vague. The options being used to create the overlay must not expire before the event occurs if the overlay is to be of any use. The manager must decide, therefore, in relation to both when the event is expected and when, relative to expiration, the overlay is being created, what expiration month is most appropriate.

Unbalanced Hedges

An options overlay need not perfectly hedge one side of the trade on a share-for-share basis. In the preceding example, it was assumed that the overlay hedge would be constructed using 10 contracts to represent the 1,000 shares of ABC held in the pair. The manager may make the determination that there is an advantage, on a risk/return basis, to purchasing fewer or more than 10 contracts to build the overlay. If the manager believes there is a low probability that the stock will experience a price shock and yet wishes to take some precautions, he may choose to hedge only a fraction of his position. This approach is a bit of a gamble because if he is correct and the hedge is not needed, he will have saved a portion of the option premium and bettered his performance. If, however, his guess is wrong and the price shock occurs, the position will not be fully protected. In making this decision, a manager may consider the expected worst-case scenario as a basis for selecting the degree of the hedge.

Staying with the previous example, if the manager believes that ABC will not trade below $58 on a negative earnings announcement, he may choose to hedge only 60 percent of his position using ABC May $60 puts. At $58, the puts will have only provided the manager with $0.90 of downside protection (the break-even level is the strike price minus the premium, $60 − $1.10 = $58.90). At $1.10, the premium paid for the options is greater than the protection provided; the hedge would have actually been a larger performance drag than if no hedge were taken. The manager initiates this hedge, however, because if the estimated worst-case is wrong and the stock continues to fall, a portion of the position is protected. A manager's decision to hedge a position, whether in part or in whole, is an important one that requires both skill and experience.

In another type of unbalanced hedge, a manager may buy more options than are needed on a share basis, if he determines that there is a mathematically driven reason to do so. Recall from this example that puts with a $55 strike price were trading at roughly a five-to-one ratio with those at the $60 strike price ($0.20 and $1.10 respectively). In this case the manager may decide to hedge his position in ABC by purchasing 50 ABC May $55 puts. This is still less costly that buying 10 ABC May $60 puts and may provide a better hedge. It is important to note that in unbalanced hedges of this nature, one can no longer assume that the options are held until expiration. In order for this type of approach to work, the option must have retained some time value when the hedge is closed.

To determine whether the deeper OTM options provide a better hedge if purchased in a larger quantity, the manager must consider the delta of each option. Recall that delta is the change in an option's price resulting from a $1 move in the price of the underlying security. In this case, if the delta of the lower-priced option is greater than one-fifth of the delta for the higher-priced option, there is an advantage to using the cheaper contracts. Using the same setup from the preceding example, assume the following:

ΔABC May $60 put = 0.30

ΔABC May $55 put = 0.07

Under these circumstances, using the ABC May $55 puts provides a better short-term hedge. For every dollar that ABC drops in price, the May $60 put rises by $0.30 and the May $55 put rises by $0.07; the hedge was constructed using five times more May $55 puts, so the resulting gain is $0.35. The puts with the lower strike price both cost less and will appreciate more rapidly if there is a decline in ABC stock. This example assumes that theta, time decay, is held constant and that the hedge is closed as soon as ABC announces earnings. If these contracts were held until expiration, the options with the higher strike price would always provide the better hedge.

The additional advantage of the May $55 puts is that should there be a crash in ABC, because the manager is holding a greater number of puts, a profit may be realized. If the stock dropped to $50, for example, the 10 May $60 puts would be worth $10,000 and the 50 May $55 puts would be worth $25,000. Each of these gains would be offset by a $10,000 loss in the underlying security. Each of these hedges would protect against the loss, but the latter provides profit potential if there is a significant downward move in the stock.

In addition to considering the relative deltas of the two options, a manager may consider gamma if the delta relationship is not favorable. Recall that gamma is the rate of change of delta. The manager may discover that simply because the delta relationship between the two options is not attractive under the current conditions, minor shifts in the price of ABC could lead to a favorable relationship. If one assumes that the relationship between the two options in this example were delta neutral (0.30 and 0.06 respectively), but that the May $55 put had a higher gamma, the manager could conclude that although there is not currently a delta argument for using the lower strike options, any move down in the stock will create a favorable delta relationship. Because the May $55 put has a higher gamma, as the price of ABC declines, the delta of this option will rise more quickly than the delta of the May $60 put. As this occurs, the delta relationship between the two options begins to favor the use of the lower strike options as was demonstrated before. This example, again, assumes that theta and vega are held constant, but demonstrates the relevance of the Greeks when analyzing options. There are countless numbers of options calculators available online that can aid in any of this analysis.

Risk Factors of Options Overlay

When creating an options overlay, there are two main risk factors of which a manager must be aware. The first, as was briefly touched on already, is performance drag. It is not uncommon for a manager to undo a significant portion of his analysis by complicating it with options theory. Pairs trading is a low-volatility market-neutral strategy that incorporates several risk controls without the use of options; an options overlay should only be used when there is a clear and significant reason for the manager to believe one side of his trade is in peril. In many cases, a negative event for one side of the trade will have a similar impact on the other side of the trade and leave the initial analysis intact. A negative earnings announcement from ABC in our example will likely put downward pressure on XYZ as well. If both stocks decline by an equal amount, the pair remains intact and mean reversion will likely proceed on course. The use of options in this case would not benefit the strategy but simply add an expense that would directly impact the profit potential of the trade and, with it, the performance of the portfolio.

The second and perhaps more important risk factor is that of directional bias. When one side of the trade is hedged, the manager has created a directional bias within the trade, which is specifically what pairs trading seeks to avoid. While the trade in our example maintains some of its profit potential after the hedge has been initiated, there is a clear bias to the short side of the market. If the market falls, ABC is hedged and the short of XYZ will be profitable; if the market rises, ABC will be profitable, after the hedge has been paid for, and XYZ will lose money. This is not an argument against using an options overlay to hedge when one is called for, but a manager must be careful not to hedge every position.

PAIRS OPTIONS STRATEGIES

In some cases a manager may wish to use options as a substitute for equities when initiating a pairs trade. Options provide built-in leverage, built-in protection, and some elegant combinations not available in an equity trade. On the downside, options may be less liquid, are far more complex, and have an associated cost not found in an equity trade. Prior to embarking on an options-based pairs trade, it is important to understand each of these factors as well as the specifics of how a pairs trade should be constructed when substituting options for equities.

The first advantage of using options is that they provide a built-in degree of leverage not available in the stock market. With a relatively small investment, a trader can control a significant amount of stock. A $2 option on a $50 stock will cost a trader $200 rather than $5,000 to own the same 100 shares of stock. This has the appeal of allowing a small manager to build a large portfolio with a limited budget. If a manager is prudent in his decisions, the leverage feature of options can provide a significant advantage.

The second advantage of using options is that in a carefully constructed trade, the manager has a built-in level of protection or stop-loss. Most options trades provide for an analysis of a worst-case event, which usually requires no action on the part of the trader. This can be invaluable because it is usually the unexpected disastrous trades that cause the most harm to a matched equity pairs trader. For example, if a manager buys calls on ABC rather than investing in the stock, an automatic worst-case stop-loss is in place—the premium paid for the options. If ABC drops by 2 percent or 20 percent, the most the options trader can lose is the premium paid. This is useful in cases where unexpected news causes a price shock to the stock before the equity trader has a chance to protect himself.

The disadvantages of using options include their complexity, liquidity, and expense. Using options theory in pairs trading adds an entire level of complexity that may be insurmountable for some managers. While options theory is not horribly difficult, the options-based pairs trader must complete his pairs analysis and then perform an options analysis before a trade can be executed. For some managers, this is simply too involved a process to be reasonably undertaken. In addition to complexity, a manager has to be aware that certain options, even when the underlying stock is very liquid, have liquidity constraints. A lack of liquidity can cause the manager difficulty in capturing profits, particularly when exiting a trade. Prior to executing a trade, a manager must check to be sure that the options of the securities being considered have adequate liquidity relative to the expected size of the trade to allow for easy entry and exit.

The final drawback of using options as a substitute is that of cost; options contracts have a cost beyond a simple investment in the stock. Because the manager must be certain that a trade both has time to complete the mean-reversion process and results in a sufficient gain if successful, deeply ITM options are usually the best choice. These options trade near parity and have the least time premium reflected in their price but tend to be more costly than other options. The ability to balance between appropriate cost and sufficient safety is a skill that may take a manager significant time to develop.

CALLS AND PUTS

The first options-based pairs trading strategy that will be investigated is the substitution of long calls and puts for the underlying equities. This is the most straightforward approach to using options in a pairs portfolio and will provide a solid foundation on which to build. In this approach, the manager simply buys call options as a substitute for the stock he wishes to go long on, and buys put options as a substitute for the stock that he wishes to go short. This creates both long and short exposure to the respective sides of the trade, but builds in both a dollar stop-loss and a duration limit when the options expire. The manager always purchases options because this provides unlimited profit potential on each side of the trade and limited risk; selling options would provide limited profit potential and unlimited risk.

There are a number of factors to be considered when selecting both the strike price and the expiration month of the options to be used. Generally, using options that are deep ITM provides the best proxy for the behavior of the underlying security because these options trade near a delta of 1.0. As delta approaches 1.0, the manager will see a $1 change in the price of the option for a corresponding move of $1 in the underlying security. In-the-money options tend to be more expensive, but relative to the capital required to buy the stock outright, the use of options requires significantly less capital and, therefore, price should be less important. The other reason to select deep ITM options is that they have very little time premium built into their prices. While the manager waits for a trade to mean-revert, the less drag on performance that is created by time decay, the more successful the trade will be. This sensitivity to time decay, however, must be tempered against the expected duration of the trade.

Selecting the appropriate expiration month is a direct function of the expected duration of the trade. A manager should select options that are sufficiently far from expiration to both allow the mean-reversion process to occur and to keep time decay at a minimum. Longer-term options are more expensive, even those deeply ITM, because they allow more time for the option to move in favor of the owner. It is important to note, however, that these options also have much lower theta values. Recall that theta is the amount by which an option's price will decline for each day that passes. As an option moves toward expiration, theta will increase. This relationship is not linear, however, so the pairs trader will not be punished for using longer-term options; the longer an option has until expiration, the less it will be affected by time decay over the same number of days held. Thus, a manager will wish to pick options that have substantially longer until expiration than the expected duration of the trade. The extra time will allow the trade to be closed with minimum time decay if the trade is successful, and builds in a cushion on duration if the trade moves more slowly than expected. In the latter case, time decay will be a factor and the manager will have to determine whether the trade should be given until expiration to mean-revert or should be closed at the expected duration.

To illustrate these principles, consider the following set of factors for both the underlying stocks and the associated options on May 12:

Stock ABC	$43.84
Stock XYZ	$65.76
ABC July $40 call	$ 5.20
XYZ July $70 put	$ 5.80

The manager has determined that buying ABC and selling short XYZ meets with all of his pairs trading criteria, but he wishes to execute the trade by substituting the referenced options. If this trade were to be executed with equities, the manager would buy 1,500 shares of ABC and sell short 1,000 shares of XYZ; this would create a dollar-neutral pair with $65,760 of exposure on each side of the trade. The equity trade has a profit objective of 10 percent and a stop-loss of 5 percent. To execute this trade using options, the manager will buy 15 ABC July $40 calls and buy 10 XYZ July $70 puts. The expected duration of the trade is three weeks, so the manager does not expect that time decay will play a major factor. Both the calls and the puts are ITM with deltas near 1.0, so the behavior of the options should be similar to that of the underlying stocks.

The first observation that a typical pairs trader will make is that long and short exposure are no longer dollar-neutral; the calls cost the manager $7,800 while the puts only cost $5,800. This is one of the by-products of using derivatives as a proxy for the underlying securities. The manager wishes to keep his exposure to the underlying stocks dollar-neutral so that similar percentage changes in those stocks will be neutralized. Were the manager to build an options trade that was dollar-neutral and both stocks should rise by 10 percent ($4.38 and $6.57, respectively), a loss would be recorded in the options trade even though the price relationship of the stocks remained constant. This logic is similar to why pairs should be considered from a ratio perspective rather than a spread perspective, or why dollar neutrality is used rather than share neutrality.

The second observation that can be made about this example is that the degree to which the selected options are ITM is not balanced in the trade. This is the case because options are not available at every strike price. XYZ was trading very near to the $65 strike price, so the next available strike was at $70, further away than the options used on the long side of the trade. This is both the nature of options trading and irrelevant to the pairs trader. As long as both options selected are sufficiently ITM to protect against time decay, the precise degree is of little importance.

It will now be useful to consider how the substitution of options affects the trade when it is closed. Assume that the trade mean-reverts as expected and that the following conditions exist three weeks after the trade was opened:

Stock ABC	$49.10
Stock XYZ	$67.08
ABC July $40 call	$ 9.60
XYZ July $70 put	$ 3.80

From the equity perspective the trade has moved to its profit objective and should be closed; ABC has risen 12 percent and XYZ has risen 2 percent (a loss on the short side) for a net gain of 10 percent. (This assumes that performance is measured relative to only one side of the trade, a profit of $6,576 relative to $65,760 invested; this assumption is based on using the proceeds of the short sale to pay for the purchase of the long shares and a 50 percent margin requirement. If these assumptions are not made, the trade results in a 5 percent gain of net market exposure.) In terms of the options trade, the ABC July $40 calls have risen $4.40 and the XYZ July $70 puts have fallen by $2.00; the net gain on this trade is $4,600: (15 × $4.40 × 100) – (10 × $2.00 × 100). It is important to realize that there was not a perfect correlation between the change in the stock prices and the change in the options prices. These differences are driven by both time decay and delta values that are below 1.0. While the gain in the options trade is smaller on an absolute dollar basis, the manager was only required to invest $13,600; the net gain on the options trade was, therefore, 33.8 percent. Had this trade lost money, the percent lost would have been far greater as well.

The conclusions that can be drawn from this example provide the basis by which a manager can determine if substituting options is appropriate. The use of options allows a manager to control the same amount of stock for a far smaller outlay of capital but will result in greater volatility on a trade-by-trade basis. If the manager has only a minimal amount of capital available, and is comfortable with this increased level of volatility, options may be a viable solution. If, however, a manager is seeking to control volatility, as is the case with most pairs traders, the use of options should be considered from a different perspective. Assume, for example, that a manager has $2 million in his portfolio. In the current example, despite the fact that the options trade was more volatile in terms of the trade itself, it resulted in a smaller and more stable dollar gain in terms of the overall portfolio. When considering the use of options, a manager must make the distinction between losses and gains in terms of the trades and those in terms of the portfolio.

Risk Factors of Using Calls and Puts

The primary risk factor for this strategy, as with any options-based strategy, is that if the pair is stagnant, a loss will result. When using equities, if neither of the stocks in the pair moves significantly during the expected duration of the trade, the trade can be closed for practically no loss; only the cost of commissions will affect the net return of the trade. Due to the nature of options, a manager is always working against time. If neither stock moves over the expected holding period, closing the trade will result in a loss of both time decay and commissions. Time decay can be minimized if the options to be used are carefully selected, but it cannot be avoided completely. Managers who use options are forced to follow much more stringent guidelines about time than are those who stick with equities. While an equity manager may decide to simply extend the time horizon on a given trade, at no cost to the portfolio, an options manager must close the trade, accept the loss, and look for a new opportunity.

PAIRS TRADING WITH VERTICAL SPREADS

In addition to using the simple substitution of calls and puts as described above, a pairs trader may wish to use a vertical spread as a substitute for one or both sides of his trade. This can be accomplished when the manager is expecting a modest move in either of the stocks being considered and wishes to exert further control over the risk. Recall that a vertical spread allows for limited risk and limited profit, so the selection of this strategy is considered more conservative than a simple substitution. By using a vertical spread, the manager is not limited to considering deeply ITM options, so the equity proxy may be accomplished for a lower cost than a simple substitution, but the profit potential is also limited.

To illustrate this strategy, the following example uses a bull call spread as a proxy for the long equity and a bear put spread as a proxy for the short equity. It is not necessary to use spreads on both sides of the trade, but is uncommon to use either a bull put or a bear call spread; these are both credit spreads in which the maximum potential of the trade is derived from the premium received. Credit spreads tend to be poor choices because they have greater risk potential; a pairs trader often expects one side of his trade to lose money, so the risk profile of a credit spread is unattractive. The conditions for this example are as follows on April 9:

Stock ABC	$34.80
Stock XYZ	$69.60
ABC June $35 call	$ 2.10

ABC June $40 call $ 0.60
XYZ June $70 put $ 2.80
XYZ June $65 put $ 0.90

The manager has determined that buying ABC and selling short XYZ meets with all of his pairs trading criteria, but he wishes to execute the trade by substituting the referenced options in vertical spreads. If this trade were to be executed with equities, the manager would buy 2,000 shares of ABC and sell short 1,000 shares of XYZ; this would create a dollar-neutral pair with $69,600 of exposure on each side of the trade. The equity trade has a profit objective of 10 percent and a stop-loss of 5 percent. To execute this trade using vertical spreads, the manager will buy 20 ABC June $35 calls and sell 20 ABC June $40 calls on the long side of the trade, and he will buy 10 XYZ June $70 puts and sell 10 XYZ June $65 puts on the short side of the trade. The expected duration of the trade is three weeks, so the manager does not expect that time decay will play a major factor.

The long side of the trade is created using a bull call spread and is initiated for a debit of $1.50 per spread for a net investment of $3,000 ($1.50 × 20 × 100). The maximum profit potential is $7,000 and occurs when ABC trades at or above $40. The short side of the trade is created using a bear put spread and is initiated for a debit of $1.90 per spread for a net investment of $1,900 ($1.90 × 10 × 100). The maximum profit potential is $3,100 and occurs when XYZ trades at or below $65. The pairs trader will again notice that the combination of these two investments is not dollar-neutral at the options level, but does properly represent the desired exposure to the underlying securities.

It will now be useful to consider how the substitution of vertical spreads affects the trade when it is closed. Assume that the trade mean-reverts as expected and that the following conditions exist three weeks after the trade was opened:

Stock ABC $40.05
Stock XYZ $72.40
ABC June $35 call $ 6.10
ABC June $40 call $ 1.20
XYZ June $70 put $ 0.80
XYZ June $65 put $ 0.10

From the equity perspective the trade has moved to its profit objective and should be closed; ABC has risen 14 percent and XYZ has risen 4 percent (a loss on the short side) for a net gain of 10 percent. In terms of the options trade on the long side, the ABC June $35 calls can be sold for $12,200 while the ABC June $40 calls must be covered for $2,400; the net gain on the spread is $6,800 (($12,200 – $2,400) – $3,000). On the short side of the trade, the XYZ $70 puts can be sold for $800 while the XYZ $65 puts must be covered for $100; the net loss on the spread is $1,200 (($1,900 – $800) + $100). The result for the pair of spreads is a gain of $5,600, compared to a gain of $6,960 if the trade had been done using equities.

These results again highlight both the benefits and drawbacks of using options. The trade returned a far greater percentage based on the capital invested than the same trade in the equity market would have. However, the absolute dollar return was lower for the options trade. These results must be interpreted within the proper context to determine their relative benefit. Additionally, while time decay was minimal, a careful review of the options' prices reveals another feature of options that can be detrimental to return. If one considers the ABC June $35 call, for example, it can be seen that a move in the price of the underlying security of over $5 resulted in a move in the option of less than $4. Part of this can be explained by the option's delta being below 1.0, but part of it is explained by the fact that the deeper ITM the option becomes, the greater theta becomes on the time value piece of the price. Very deep ITM options always trade near their pure intrinsic value; the time decay is not as much the result of the number of days that passed as mean reversion occurred, but rather a function of increasing theta.

In order to highlight another potential drawback to using options, consider the preceding example under a different set of circumstances when the trade is closed:

Stock ABC	$34.10
Stock XYZ	$61.25
ABC June $35 call	$ 0.20
ABC June $40 call	$ 0.05
XYZ June $70 put	$ 9.20
XYZ June $65 put	$ 4.80

From the equity perspective the trade has still moved to its profit objective and should be closed; ABC has fallen 2 percent and XYZ has fallen 12 percent (a gain on the short side) for a net gain of 10 percent. The options side of the trade presents a quite different picture in this case, however, than it did previously. On the long side, the ABC June $35 calls can be sold for $400 while the ABC June $40 calls must be covered for $100; the net loss on the spread is $2,700 (($3,000 – $400) + $100). On the short side of the trade, the XYZ $70 puts can be sold for $9,200 while the XYZ $65 puts must be covered for $4,800; the net gain on the spread is $2,500 (($9,200 – $4,800) – $1,900). The result for the pair of spreads is a loss of $200 compared to a gain of $6,960 if the trade had been done using equities. The resulting loss from the combination of spreads is caused by the fact that twice as many spreads were required to act as a proxy for the long side of the equity trade. Furthermore, the XYZ $70 Puts are trading closer to parity than the XYZ $65 puts because they are trading more deeply ITM.

This most recent example demonstrates one of the drawbacks of using vertical spreads and of using options in general. Vertical spreads limit the profit potential of the equity trade for which they serve as a proxy in ways simple substitutions do not. The fall in XYZ below $65 was not captured by the spread because of the limitations in this type of strategy. While a wider spread could have been used, selling XYZ June $60 puts rather than those with a $65 strike, the initiation of this spread would have cost more. In the example where both stocks fell, this would have provided greater profit to the manager, but in the case where both stocks rose, this would have served to decrease performance. In this example, the additional cost of using a wider spread would have been minimal and therefore advisable, but this is not always the case. A manager should determine the necessary width of a spread based upon the maximum expected move in the stock; in this case, as the trade had a 10 percent profit objective, a spread that could capture a minimum of that 10 percent, or $6.96, should have been used.

This example also highlights the dangers of options strategies that have an unequal number of contracts on each side of the trade. This imbalance is necessary to properly mirror a dollar-neutral equity trade, but it creates complications within the options strategy. If the more heavily invested side of the options trade is the losing side (recall that the majority of successful pairs trades are not profitable on both sides of the trade), proper analysis and trade construction can still lead to a loss. Before initiating a pairs trade using options, a manager should consider various trade scenarios and determine if there is a sufficient advantage to substituting an options strategy. If no distinct advantage can be identified, the trade should be executed in the equity market.

Risk Factors of Vertical Spreads

As with the simple substitution strategy, the primary risk factor for this strategy is that if the pair is stagnant, a loss will result. If a trade is constructed using equities and during the expected duration of the trade neither stock's price changes significantly, the trade can be closed for practically no loss; only the cost of commissions will affect the net return of the trade. Due to the nature of options, a manager is always working against time. Both time decay and commission cost will be lost in a stagnant options strategy. Time decay can be minimized if the options to be used are carefully selected, but it cannot be avoided completely. As was stated previously, managers who use options are forced to follow much more stringent guidelines about time than those who stick with equities. While an equity manager may decide to simply extend the time horizon on a given trade, at no cost to the portfolio, an options manager must close the trade, accept the loss, and look for a new opportunity.

BACK SPREADS

Back spreads are specifically designed to avoid some of the problems that are found in vertical spreads. Where a vertical spread provides a profit if closed when the underlying security is trading within a given range, the width of the spread, a backspread provides a profit if closed when the underlying security is trading anywhere outside of the width of the spread. A backspread is used when a manager expects that one or both of the stocks being considered is likely to experience a significant move. It is one of the only credit spreads used in pairs trading and provides both limited risk and unlimited return potential. The worst-case and maximum loss occurs in a back spread when the underlying security closes near one extreme of the spread range (the top for calls and the bottom for puts).

To illustrate this strategy, the following example uses one back spread as a proxy for the long equity and another as a proxy for the short equity. It is not necessary to use spreads on both sides of the trade, but doing so in this example will help to highlight some of the strengths and weaknesses of the strategy. The conditions for this example are as follows on January 16:

Stock ABC	$34.10
Stock XYZ	$68.20
ABC March $30 call	$ 4.80
ABC March $35 call	$ 1.40
XYZ March $70 put	$ 2.40
XYZ March $65 put	$ 0.80

The manager has determined that buying ABC and selling short XYZ meets with all of his pairs trading criteria, but he wishes to execute the trade by substituting the referenced options in back spreads. If this trade were to be executed with equities, the manager would buy 2,000 shares of ABC and sell short 1,000 shares of XYZ; this would create a dollar-neutral pair with $68,200 of exposure on each side of the trade. The equity trade has a profit objective of 10 percent and a stop-loss of 5 percent. To execute this trade using back spreads, the manager will buy 40 ABC March

$35 calls and sell 20 ABC March $40 calls on the long side of the trade, and he will buy 20 XYZ March $70 puts and sell 10 XYZ March $65 puts on the short side of the trade.

The long side of the trade is created using a back spread and is initiated for a credit of $2.00 per spread, for net proceeds of $4,000 ($2.00 × 20 × 100). The maximum profit potential is unlimited when ABC trades above $40; if ABC trades below $30 at expiration, all of the calls will expire worthless and a $4,000 profit is realized. The maximum loss for this spread is $6,000 and occurs if ABC is trading at $35 at expiration. In this case, the long calls are worthless and the short calls will result in a loss of $5 per contract, the difference between the strike prices. This loss is somewhat offset by the proceeds that were collected when the spread was initiated. The short side of the trade is created using a back spread and is initiated for a credit of $0.80 per spread for net proceeds of $800 ($0.80 × 10 × 100). The maximum profit potential is unlimited when XYZ trades below $60; if XYZ trades above $70 at expiration, all of the puts will expire worthless and an $800 profit is realized. The maximum loss for this spread is $4,200 and occurs if XYZ is trading at $65 at expiration. In this case the long puts are worthless and the short puts will result in a loss of $5 per contract, the difference between the strike prices. This loss is somewhat offset by the proceeds that were collected when the spread was initiated.

The first observation that can be made about this setup is that when using back spreads, unlike either vertical spreads or simple substitution, a profit can be achieved if either side of the trade moves sharply against its intended direction. If, for example, ABC, which is the long side of the trade, experiences a significant decline, the use of a back spread will result in a $4,000 gain. This is particularly appealing to a pairs trader because he expects that one side of the trade will likely lose money. If that decline is sharp enough, the side of the trade that loses from the equity perspective may provide an additional gain. Furthermore, if the manager is wrong on both sides of the trade, he may still be able to realize a gain or perhaps break even.

The second observation that an astute manager can make from the preceding information is that this type of strategy is particularly susceptible to the risk factors described in the previous two. A stagnant trade when using back spreads can lead to the maximum loss for this strategy. The result is that while a back spread presents several appealing features to a pairs trader, it will often be reserved for use with particularly volatile stocks, such as those in the technology or biotechnology sectors. Using back spreads when constructing trades involving bellwethers is inadvisable as these stocks are not prone to swings of sufficient size to realize the profit potential of this approach.

It will now be useful to consider how the substitution of vertical spreads affects the trade when it is closed. Assume that the trade mean-reverts as expected and that the following conditions exist three weeks after the trade was opened:

Stock ABC	$41.60
Stock XYZ	$76.38
ABC March $30 call	$12.10
ABC March $35 call	$ 7.20
XYZ March $70 put	$ 0.15
XYZ March $65 put	$ 0.05

From the equity perspective the trade has moved to its profit objective and should be closed; ABC has risen 22 percent and XYZ has risen 12 percent (a loss on the short side) for a net gain of 10 percent. In terms of the options trade on the long side, the ABC March $35 calls can be sold for $28,800 ($7.20 × 40 × 100) while the ABC March $40 calls must be covered for $24,200; the net gain on the spread is $8,600 (($28,800 − $24,200) + $4,000). On the short side of the trade, the XYZ March $65 puts can be sold for $100 while the XYZ March $70 puts must be covered for $150; the net gain on the spread is $750 (($800 − $150) + $100). The result for the pair of spreads is a gain of $9,350 compared to a gain of $6,960 if the trade had been done using equities.

In this case, as a result of the significant swing in both stocks, the use of options proved superior on both a percentage and absolute dollar basis. When dealing with particularly volatile stocks, a back spread can provide a better return than the underlying security because the spread is initiated for a credit and because a back spread gives the owner double exposure to the upside beyond a given point. By capitalizing on this volatility, a manager can provide himself with unlimited profit potential while still limiting risk within a given trade. It is important to note that success of this kind is dependent on large moves in the stocks being considered in the pair.

In order to highlight a potential drawback to using this strategy, consider the preceding example under a different set of circumstances when the trade is closed:

Stock ABC	$37.85
Stock XYZ	$68.88
ABC March $30 call	$ 8.20
ABC March $35 call	$ 3.40
XYZ March $70 put	$ 2.60
XYZ March $65 put	$ 0.40

From the equity perspective the trade has still moved to its profit objective and should be closed; ABC has risen 11 percent and XYZ has risen 1 percent (a loss on the short side) for a net gain of 10 percent. The options side of the trade presents a quite different picture in this case, however, than it did previously. On the long side, the ABC March $35 calls can be sold for $13,600 ($3.40 × 40 × 100) while the ABC March $40 calls must be covered for $16,400; the net gain on the spread is $1,200 (($13,600 − $16,400) + $4,000). On the short side of the trade, the XYZ March $65 puts can be sold for $800 while the XYZ March $70 puts must be covered for $2,600; the net loss on the spread is $1,000 (($800 − $2,600) + $800). The result for the pair of spreads is a gain of $200 compared to a gain of $6,960 if the trade had been done using equities.

This most recent example demonstrates one of the drawbacks to using back spreads. Despite the fact that the underlying securities behaved as expected on a pairs trading basis, the use of back spreads to initiate the trade resulted in practically no profit. Had this trade moved down by equal percentages, away from the more heavily weighted side of the options trade, it would have resulted in a loss. Back spreads require that the underlying securities on which they are placed experience very significant price swings in order to be effective. While they can be a useful tool for a pairs trader in certain sectors, they should be used with caution. As was the case with other types of options strategies, there is a significant risk, even more so when using back spreads, if the underlying securities are stagnant.

COMBINING THE STRATEGIES

A pairs trader will often choose to use these strategies in different combinations depending on both his particular view of the underlying securities and his analysis of the available options. In some cases, a pairs trade may be constructed by pairing an equity on one side of the trade with a simple substitution or a spread on the other. The goal of the manager is to create a trade that both maximizes profit potential and minimizes risk. Options can be a powerful tool for achieving that end, but should not be used unless a clear advantage can be identified.

One case in which a manager may choose to combine strategies is when he has a clear bias toward one side of the trade. If, for example, he believes that stock ABC is an excellent value but, as a risk management procedure, wishes to pair it with stock XYZ, he may favor the combination of strategies. His view of the long side of the trade is favorable, while his view of the short side is mixed; there is a clear bias to the long side of this trade, despite the fact that the trade meets all other pairs criteria. The manager may choose to either buy the equity of ABC or use a simple substitution of call options as a proxy, and construct a vertical spread on XYZ to complete the pair. These steps are taken because the manager does not wish to limit his profit potential on ABC, yet wishes to keep the short side of the trade as inexpensive and low risk as possible. On the long side of the trade, the manager has given himself unlimited profit potential, while on the short side, both his risk and profit potential are limited.

Other common scenarios in which the combined use of strategies might appear include cross-sector trades, trades in which there is a large beta discrepancy, and those in which there is a large discrepancy in options pricing from one side of the trade to the other. In both cross-sector trades and those in which the matched equities have significantly different betas, a manager may wish to use a back spread on the high-volatility side of the trade and another strategy to fill the more stable side. In the case of notable pricing discrepancies, the manager may choose a vertical spread to capitalize on the expensive options, while using a simple substitution for the cheaper options. In each of these cases, the manager is able to identify a specific factor that favors the use of one strategy over the other and, as a result, tailors his trades appropriately.

These strategies may be combined in any number of ways, each tailored to the specifics of the given situation. By understanding each of these strategies the manager gives himself the greatest possible number of tools with which to construct his trade. Over time, a manager will develop a sense for which of these strategies is most appropriate to a given situation, and will learn to take care when adding an options element to his portfolio.

CHAPTER 16

Futures and Currencies

Futures contracts are similar to options contracts but, much as the name implies, there is no option feature; upon expiration, a futures contract is executed either for cash or for physical delivery. The principles, however, that drive the use of futures within the context of pairs trading are similar to those discussed in the preceding chapters on options, with other principles borrowed from the earlier discussion on equities. The decision by a pairs trader to place trades in the futures markets tends to be based on the identification of an expanded number of trading opportunities, the trader's comfort with futures, and a positive fit between the trader's style and the price action found in futures. As was the case with options, the use of futures can be advantageous to a pairs trader, but only when the inherent differences between the two markets are understood.

Futures contracts are most commonly associated with commodities, but the futures markets for financial indexes, bonds, and currencies are among the most liquid in the United States. The primary focus here will be on commodity futures; in this limited context, the principal difference between equity and futures pairs trading will become readily apparent. After a sufficient foundation comprised of these principles has been laid, the unique attributes of different types of futures will be explored. It will be assumed that the reader is already familiar with the unified theory of pairs trading, so many of these principals will not be explained.

Delineating futures pairs trades from equity and options trades are their dependence on extrinsic events, the inclusion of natural correlations, and the speed with which they change. These features can of course exist outside of the futures markets, but they are more likely to play a central role in futures. The effect of each of these features adds a level of complexity that a manager must be both aware of and prepared to control for. The inclusion of futures in a pairs portfolio offers different advantages and drawbacks than the simple use of equities. By understanding these differences, a manager can make an informed decision as to whether they should be included in his portfolio.

EXTRINSIC EVENTS

Climatic, geopolitical, and governmental forces tend to have more a direct and therefore significant impact on the price of commodities. As a result, futures prices are highly dependent on the same factors: A drought may send wheat prices soaring, unrest in the Middle East may drive up gas prices, and a new government subsidy on cotton may increase demand and therefore the price of the associated futures contract. In each of these cases, some extrinsic force is responsible for driving the price of a commodity in a much more direct and uncontrollable way than a news event in the stock market. While the announcement that ABC Corporation may fall short of earnings expectations can be planned for and kept in context, a month-long drought that cuts the yield of wheat in half can be neither anticipated nor overlooked.

The effect of extrinsic events on pairs trading in the commodity markets is critical because it violates many of the principles already discussed. When a trader observes a significant divergence in two correlated commodities that are statistically likely to mean-revert, an understanding of the external factors affecting the trade is critical. The divergence may be caused by an outside force that will not sway under the pressure of statistical analysis; a two standard deviation divergence implying a 97 percent chance of mean reversion cannot make it rain. Furthermore, there are often conflicting forces, the effects of which are difficult to determine. For example, while a drought may push wheat prices up, the low-carb craze may help to keep prices down. Predicting the power of these individual trends and how they interact can be a serious challenge.

A matched equity pairs trader, particularly one who relies heavily on trade technicals, is often unconcerned with the fundamental news driving a given stock. The mantra of the technician is that all relevant events are reflected in the price action of that stock. While the futures markets tend to be even more technically driven than the equity markets, the result of there being a greater percentage of professionals in these markets, extrinsic events are inescapable. A technical futures trader might argue that the drought responsible for driving wheat prices is reflected in the continuously rising price of wheat, but many of the technical indicators that the pairs trader relies on, such as those describing overbought and oversold conditions, may cease to have good predictive ability under extreme circumstances. Compounding this problem is the fact that a pairs trader tends to consider a trade from the overall pair perspective before considering the price action of the individual legs of the trade. This practice, while advantageous in the equity markets, can often mask the effects of an extrinsic event in the futures markets.

The simplified result of such events, as they relate to a pairs trader's approach to the markets, is that fundamental trends should be more closely monitored. Some of these trends can be controlled for through increased care in the pairing process, but the general trends should be known before a trade is executed. For example, if a pairs trader is planning to match soybeans and soybean oil, it is reasonable to assume that a shortage in soybeans will likely cause a shortage in any derivative product. While this logic is generally sound, it does not apply in all cases and the underlying trends should be monitored. Soybean prices may have risen based on projections that upcoming crops will have lower than expected yields; soybean oil producers may have predicted this condition and overstocked their inventories ahead of time. In this case, the rise in soybean prices is the result of a perceived shortage and, due to appropriate planning by the oil producers, no short-term rise in soybean oil results. It is certainly possible to create any combination of events with hugely varying results, but, generally speaking, the futures pairs trader should pay attention to fundamental trends in the commodities he is trading.

NATURAL CORRELATION

Throughout the commodity universe, there are many natural correlations that can affect how a pairs trader approaches the market. Crude oil relative to heating oil relative to gasoline is one such example. Many of these spreads have been traded by futures traders for years, which aids in the probability that they can continue to be successful. While it can be argued that two semiconductor producers share a type of natural correlation, their products are similar but neither interchangeable nor dependent on each other. On the other hand, a rise in oil prices must result in an increase in gasoline prices, as one is derived from the other. Generally, these natural relationships tend to follow exactly as one would expect. While paradigm shifts may occasionally occur (e.g., the development of a cheaper refining process), these will only serve to adjust rather than sever the relationship.

In contrast, in the example of the semiconductor producers, one may miss earnings or go out of business without destroying the other.

To illustrate the power of natural correlation, consider the relationship between soybeans and soybean oil. Despite some of the intrinsic factors that may affect this relationship, the derivative nature of this combination makes it a natural pair. Figure 16.1 is the chart of May 2005 soybeans for the past 12 months and Figure 16.2 is the chart of May 2005 soybeans oil for the same period. An initial investigation of these two charts reveals the expected high level of similarity. When considered as a pair (see Figure 16.3), the chart reveals that while there are trends and fluctuations, as one would expect with any pair, the relationship is very stable. The existence of these fluctuations is what allows the trader to successfully apply the pairs trading methodology to the relationship.

Soybeans and soybean oil offer just one example of the natural correlations that exist in the commodities markets. Many of these relationships are so common that the various exchanges track the spread between them and give traders margin discounts when executing trades in these spreads. While many futures traders rely on these spreads as the basis for their own trading systems, the mechanics of a spread trade and those for a pairs trade are often different. Recall the discussion of the difference in these two approaches from Chapter 2; a spread trade dealing in differently priced securities takes a market direction bias, while a pairs trade is designed to avoid such a bias.

Natural correlations exist, not only between similar types of commodities but also between the futures contracts for the same commodity in dif-

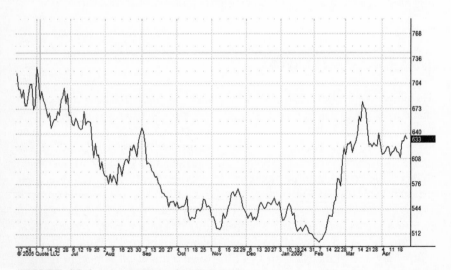

FIGURE 16.1 May 2005 Soybeans Futures

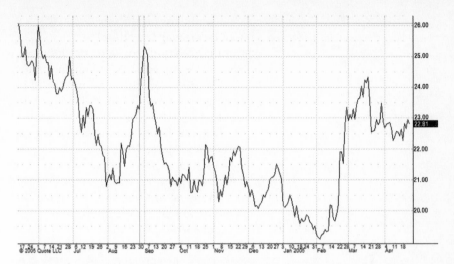

FIGURE 16.2   May 2005 Soybean Oil Futures

ferent expiration months. This type of relationship is more explicit because the forces affecting different contract months are even more subtle than those affecting different yet related commodities. Consider the chart of the May 2005 soybeans contract in Figure 16.4 and the chart of the August 2005 soybeans contract in Figure 16.5. Upon simple observation, these contracts appear to be nearly identical. The differences between the two contracts

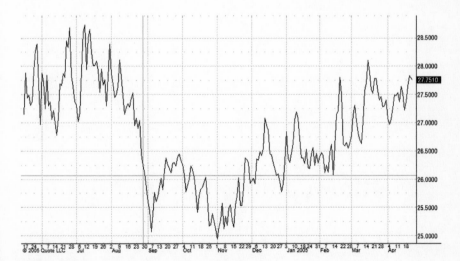

FIGURE 16.3   Price Relationship, Soybeans and Soybean Oil Futures

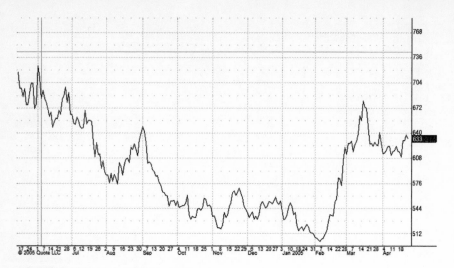

FIGURE 16.4 May 2005 Soybeans Contract

are driven by cost-of-carry considerations and minor differences in expected supply at the time of expiration. The chart in Figure 16.6 represents the pair relationship of these two contracts. Again, making note of the small fluctuations in the relationship, the pair demonstrates remarkable stability.

The effect of natural correlation on pairs trading is that in many cases the trader may be more confident that a particular trade will ultimately

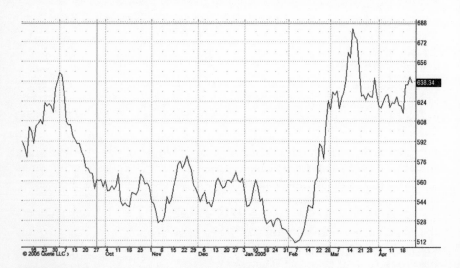

FIGURE 16.5 August 2005 Soybeans Contract

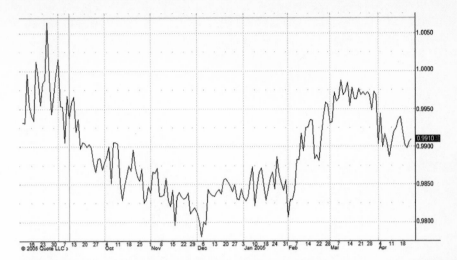

FIGURE 16.6 Pair Relationship, May and August 2005 Soybeans

mean-revert; this increased confidence is the result of both the fact that the relationship is so stable and the fact that the trade may be tracked and traded as a spread by a major exchange. In many cases the corresponding moves with a naturally correlated pair are very small and difficult to capture. A relative-value strategy depends on the trader's ability not only to identify but to capture the divergence and mean-reversion movement. In stable markets, certain opportunities may be lost because there is insufficient volatility in the relationship between the two related commodities to make a trade profitable.

SPEED

The final significant difference between a commodity futures pairs trade and one in the equity or options markets is that of speed. The intraday fluctuations in a given futures pair may be sufficiently large to affect the trade's duration. The futures markets employ large degrees of margin, and, as a result, small moves in a trade create very significant changes in the dollar value of that trade. A single point move in certain futures trades can result in tens of thousands of dollars gained or lost very quickly. The result is that a commodity futures pairs trader may be in and out of the market very quickly, picking up and losing fractional points in each trade toward the end of net profit. This often means that analysis must be purely technical and that execution becomes of supreme importance.

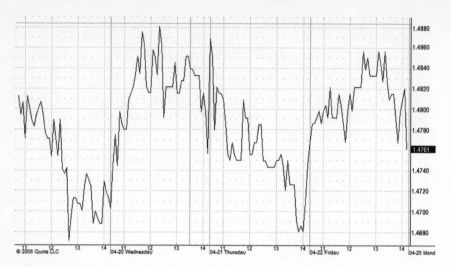

FIGURE 16.7   Intraday Price Fluctuation, May 2005 Wheat and Corn Contracts

If one considers the chart in Figure 16.7, which represents the intra-day price fluctuation for several days between the May 2005 wheat contract and the May 2005 corn contract, the speed of the futures market becomes clear. Within the course of a given trading day, this relationship goes through several peaks and valleys, each representing a potential entry or exit point. While this relationship is tradable, each of these fluctua-

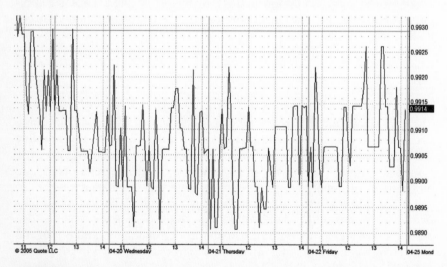

FIGURE 16.8   Intraday Price Fluctuation, May and August 2005 Soybeans Contracts

tions can represent significant dollar moves after leverage is considered. The chart in Figure 16.8, which represents the intraday price action for the May 2005 soybeans contract and the August 2005 soybeans contract, demonstrates that each of these bounces may represent only a few minutes. Before deciding on a pairs trading approach within the futures market, a manager must determine that he is prepared to carefully monitor the market on a minute-by-minute basis and that he is willing to accept a higher level of volatility than was present in the equity markets.

CURRENCIES

Currencies are a specialized form of futures contract that trade globally and are highly liquid. These are the only pairs relationships that are tracked and reported as pairs (exchange rates). The result of such high visibility is that these pairs tend to offer a plethora of resources and opinions as to their likely behavior. They are more deeply influenced by macroeconomic events than any other security type and, as such, require a degree of awareness that may be troubling to beginning traders. Furthermore, with the 24-hour availability of an open market, currency trading may require a greater commitment of resources than is practical for the average trader.

Currency pairs trading follows all of the same principles described in the discussion of futures, but considering an example may be useful. Figures 16.9 and 16.10 represent the daily price action of the June 2005 Swiss franc contract and the June 2005 British pound contract, respectively, over

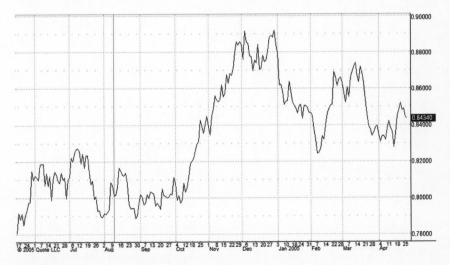

FIGURE 16.9 Daily Price Action, June 2005 Swiss Franc Contract

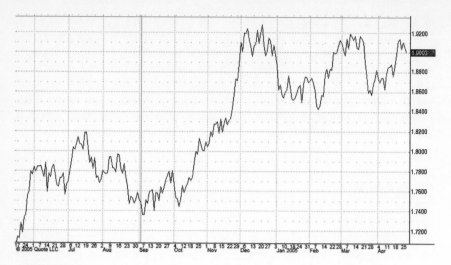

FIGURE 16.10 Daily Price Action, June 2005 British Pound Contract

a 12-month period. Note that each of these contracts is initiated in U.S. dollars (USD), so there is an implied pair in each of these contracts already. While the two charts appear similar, there are some clear differences. This is to be expected, as the global events that affect one currency are likely to differ from those affecting another, particularly when both are considered relative to the economy of the United States.

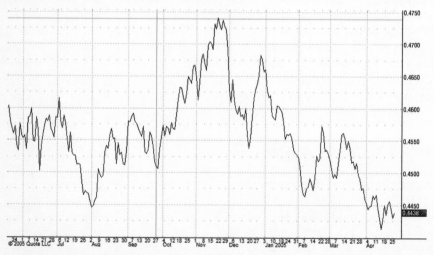

FIGURE 16.11 Eleven-Month Price Relationship between Swiss Franc and British Pound Contracts

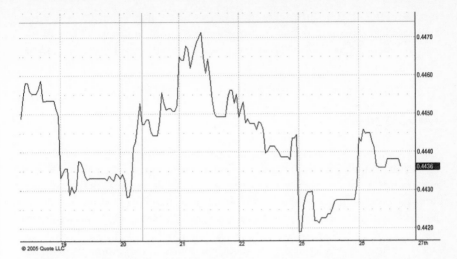

FIGURE 16.12 Seven-Day Price Relationship between Swiss Franc and British Pound Contracts

When considered as a pair, however, as in Figure 16.11, a clear and tradable relationship is observed between the two currencies. The pairs trading principles of the Unified Theory, adopted for the futures markets, can be applied to this relationship as to any other. Figure 16.12 shows the same relationship, the Swiss franc versus the British pound, on a much shorter time frame. This chart is included to demonstrate that the speed with which currencies trade follows the guidelines established for futures. When considered on this time scale, relative moves in the relationship are less likely to be the result of macroeconomic events; there is insufficient time for the market to assimilate the information and create a larger scale trend. The result of this is that short-term currency trading is highly technical and a potential area of concentration for any pairs trader.

OPTIONS ON FUTURES

Similar to stocks, the majority of futures contracts are optionable and, while the principles and strategies presented in previous chapters are applicable, the principles of futures are still at work. The use of options is one way for a pairs trader both to become comfortable with futures and to slow down the velocity with which they trade (a function of delta). Options strategies can be built with strict risk parameters that can prevent a novice trader from losing significant sums while he is learning. Recall that futures contracts use large degrees of leverage and that small moves can cause mounting losses quite quickly. Through the use of a protected options strategy, some of the risks inherent in futures trading can be controlled.

CONCLUSION

The use of futures can provide a pairs trader with additional opportunities to identify quality trades. Due to the low correlation between equities and commodities, the experienced trader may be able to shift between markets as conditions fluctuate. Pairs trading is dependent on a minimum level of market volatility, and while static market conditions may exist in one market, more favorable conditions may exist in the other. Pairs trading with futures, while similar to matched equity pairs trading in most aspects, has certain unique features that must be understood by a manager before endeavoring to add these instruments to his portfolio.

CHAPTER 17

Trade Examples

The purpose of this chapter is to provide the reader with a step-by-step illustration of how a pairs trade is researched, executed, managed, and closed from a variety of perspectives, using three equity trade examples: a fundamentally driven trade, a technically driven trade, and a blended trade. Although the latter is most specifically parallel to the approach advocated throughout this text, the exploration of each should provide some important insight to those traders wishing to pursue alternate approaches. The existence of some selection criteria through which candidate pairs are identified is assumed, but the specifics are not discussed due to the wide variance in models and methodology that may be used.

The three examples presented here are not intended to be an exhaustive illustration of any of these approaches, but rather are presented to solidify the principles discussed thus far. By understanding each of these examples, the reader will be able to identify the critical steps in the practice of pairs trading and apply these methods to his or her own portfolio. Each example provides a thorough exploration of its given approach and addresses common issues that face a portfolio manager when executing this type of strategy.

Following these examples, the possible effects of using options are explored from both an overlay and a substitution perspective. These approaches can yield very different results that are situation specific. The reader must be familiar with all the preceding material in order to be able to adequately place each of these cases into perspective. While the discussion of options is not exhaustive, it highlights some of the advantages and pitfalls commonly associated with options trading within a pair structure.

THE FUNDAMENTAL TRADE

The two companies being considered in this trade are Bed, Bath & Beyond (BBBY) and Linens n' Things (LIN). These companies make an appropriate pair because they are not only in the same sector and industry, but they follow similar business plans; both stores focus on the specialized home goods market. For the purpose of this example, it will be assumed that the pairing has met with the fundamental manager's pair criteria, which may include such metrics as relative P/E, relative industry ranking, growth expectations, as well as a variety of others; a vastly simplified comparison will be presented. Generally, a fundamental manager will determine that of the two companies being considered, one company is positioned to outperform the other over the expected duration of the trade, usually several months. While different managers use different criteria, the common element necessary to select a trade is a belief that one stock is a better value than the other based on fundamental criteria.

Consider the following set of conditions for these stocks on May 1:

- BBBY has reported earnings in line with expectations.
- BBBY predicts earnings growth will continue in line with expectations.
- LIN has missed earnings expectations.
- LIN has cut earnings outlook and warned on future earnings.
- BBBY has a P/E of 22.4.
- LIN has a P/E of 23.4.

While this is a simplified picture of these two stocks, the rationale for executing this pair can be explored. On a straight P/E comparison, there is not a strong argument for BBBY over LIN. Each company is positioned similarly relative to the industry, and a simple value argument is not available. The manager is not simply concerned with current positions, however, and when the relative P/E values are considered from a forward-looking perspective, BBBY becomes a better value. LIN expects its earning to decrease (or grow at a slower than predicted rate). Given this assumption, if P/E ratios are held constant, BBBY will outperform LIN in the coming months. The manager may further expect that a negative price reaction to the bad news issued by LIN will affect the trade. The market will likely discount the price of LIN at a faster pace than is warranted by pure P/E considerations, or, conversely, reward BBBY, which has presented no such earnings warning.

The Execution

The chart in Figure 17.1 represents the trailing 12-month price ratio of the two stocks leading up to the initiation of the trade, with BBBY being considered as the long candidate and LIN as the short candidate. While the pair has not performed well, there are no clear technical signals that a price reversal is imminent. The manager is basing his trading decision on the fundamental analysis performed rather than technical indicators or charting patterns. He believes that BBBY is a stronger company with a more favorable outlook and that this fact will ultimately be reflected in the two prices of the respective stocks.

On May 3, BBBY is trading at $37.11 at the open and LIN is trading at $32.42. The manager is running a $400,000 portfolio and has decided to allocate 5 percent of his portfolio to this trade ($20,000 per side). The resulting calculations yield a purchase of 540 shares of BBBY (538.9 shares rounded up) and a short sale of 620 shares of LIN (616.9 shares of LIN rounded up). It should be noted that some portfolio managers will always choose to round share amounts down so as to produce a slightly more conservative result relative to the targeted trade exposure. The execution of this trade results in roughly $20,000 of exposure to each side of the trade and an entry ratio of 1.114. The profit objective is set at 14 percent,

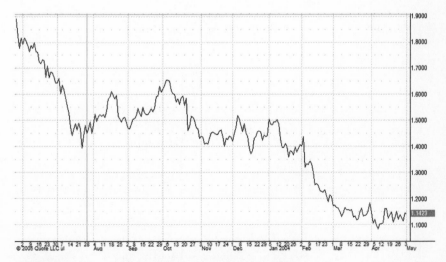

FIGURE 17.1   Trailing 12-Month Price Ratio of BBBY and LIN

which yields a closing ratio of 1.305 or better, and a stop-loss of 7 percent, which yields a closing ratio of 1.065. This trade is assigned a duration limit of five and a half months.

The trade is executed by placing the short order first and waiting for it to be filled prior to placing the buy order. This practice is a function of the uptick rule and protects against the possibility that after buying the long side of the trade, the stock on the short side falls without the manager participating in the move. Should a stock that a manager wishes to short fall significantly before the trade is opened, the manager may wish to cancel the order (close the trade if it has been filled at an unfavorable price) and seek another trading opportunity. This most commonly occurs when a trade is placed before the open and the stock opens gap-down with no participation by the manager. There are a sufficiently high number of potentially attractive trades available, such that a trade should never be chased if it cannot be opened at or near the anticipated ratio. Once the short side of the trade has been opened, the manager can place the buy order, thus completing the execution process.

Managing The Trade

After a trade has been opened, it is the manager's responsibility to monitor the trade, making updated adjustments to both profit objective and stop-loss levels, and to his opinion of the effect of extrinsic factors. Figure 17.2 shows the chart of the trade on June 1, one month after the trade was

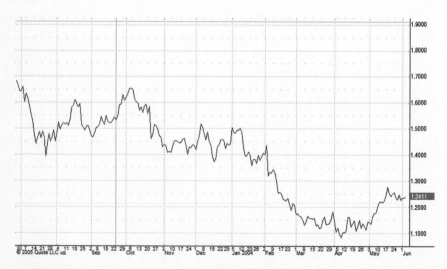

FIGURE 17.2   BBBY/LIN Pairs Trade after One Month

opened. While the trade did not reach its profit objective, there is graphical evidence that the trade may have peaked; the price action has been
sideways for several days, with a slight downward trend. The manager
must now decide how to manage the trade. He may wish to close the trade
and protect the profit that has been earned to date, or he may wish to trust
his original assessment and allow the trade to run, hoping that the profit
objective is attainable. The third, and most appropriate, option is that the
trader may wish to raise the stop-loss level. This action allows the manager to protect a portion of the profit, while still allowing for the possibility that the trade may move to the profit objective. The use of a trailing
stop-loss can be an effective risk management tool, but it requires that the
manager be skillful in setting the level. If the stop is set too high, the trade
may be closed prematurely; if the stop is too low, the manager may lose
more of the previously earned profit than necessary. For the sake of this
example, assume that the stop level is raised to 1.18.

The chart in Figure 17.3 depicts the price action of the pair an additional two months later. As can be seen from the chart, the trade has
achieved and passed its original profit objective. In most cases, the manager, immediately upon the achievement of the profit objective, would
have closed the trade. In this case, however, assume that as the manager
raised the level of his trailing stop-loss, he also raised the level of the profit
objective. This practice can be dangerous and should be considered quite
aggressive, but is not always without merit. If a manager finds his trade in
the midst of a strong price trend, particularly one driven by fundamental

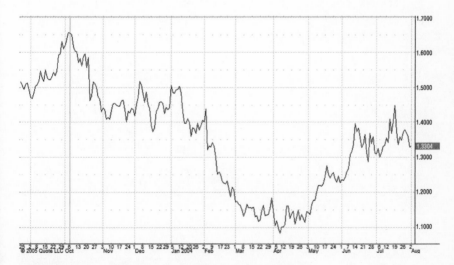

FIGURE 17.3 BBBY/LIN Pairs Trade after Three Months

information, riding the trend until such time as clear evidence of a reversal is present is a profitable approach. The chart in Figure 17.3 suggests that the trend has been interrupted, but there is no clear sign it has reversed. A manager adopting this approach runs the risk that a reversal may occur quite quickly and erode a significant amount of his profits; when using this approach, strict adherence to stop-losses is critical.

The additional risk that should be considered before adopting such an approach is opportunity risk. While the trade appears to be in the midst of a strong price trend, every day that the trade is consolidating (moving sideways) or reversing represents a missed opportunity. This trade has produced the expected profit, and the funds backing the trade could be utilized to execute new trades with similar profit expectations. While this trade may continue to rise, the probability that any additional rise will outpace the rise in a newly analyzed trade is modest. While there are many cases in which the right decision is to leave a profitable trade alone, as will be demonstrated, in the majority of cases the lost opportunity will outweigh the additional performance.

The chart in Figure 17.4 confirms that the manager was right to remain in the trade and participate in the movement of a strong and steady price trend. This chart depicts the trade on October 18 at which time the price ratio is 1.78 (an increase of 56 percent from the opening ratio of the trade). At this point the trade should be closed regardless of the price trend. When the trade was opened, it was assigned a duration limit of five and half months. While it may be acceptable to violate price objectives or

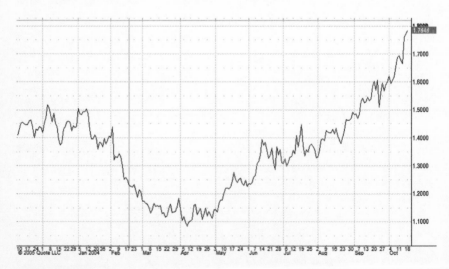

FIGURE 17.4   BBBY/LIN Pairs Trade after Five and a Half Months

to ignore duration limits in certain cases, both should not be breached simultaneously. This trade is well beyond its targeted profit objective and should, therefore, be closed at its duration limit.

Exiting the Trade

In order to exit a trade, a manager may use simple market orders to close each leg of the pair. The simple rules to be remembered in managing and exiting a trade are that a profit objective should be observed intraday, while a stop should be considered only at the close. In this example, if at any time the pair trades at or above 1.305 (the original profit objective) the trade should be closed. If, however, the pair trades below 1.065 on an intraday basis, but rises above that level prior to the close, the trade need not be closed. If the pair trades below 1.065 and is likely to close there, the trade should be considered stopped-out and closed at the end of the trading day.

THE TECHNICAL TRADE

The two companies being considered in this trade are Linear Technology (LLTC) and KLA-Tencor (KLAC). These companies make an appropriate pair because they are in the same sector and industry, although, this is of less importance in a purely technical trade. When technicals are the only factors being considered, a manager may choose to make pairings that cross both industry and sector lines. However, some managers, even pure technical analysts, may wish to limit candidate pairs to those in the same sector or industry because they will share similar characteristics that make a trade more predictable. It is important to note that because a technical trader believes that all pertinent information about a stock or a pair is contained in the price action, relative industry position, current news, and other fundamental metrics are not deemed important. A technical manager believes that through the identification of chart patterns and the study of technical or statistical indicators, he has sufficient data to determine whether a trade should be included in his portfolio. For the purpose of this example, the specific method by which the pair was identified will not be considered.

The chart in Figure 17.5 depicts the price action of the ratio between the two stocks being considered in this trade; LLTC is the long candidate (the numerator) and KLAC is the short candidate (the denominator). The graph illustrates that over the nine months leading to the potential trade date, the pair has traded within an identifiable range. The extremes of

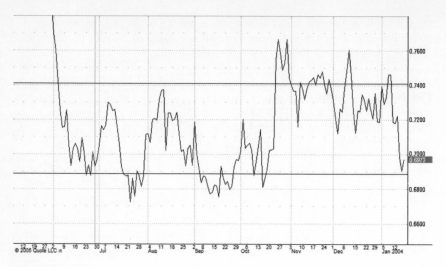

FIGURE 17.6 Price Ratio of LLTC and KLAC

this range, or points just beyond them, represent likely reversal points for the pair and, thus, appropriate entry points. The trade objective is to capture the movement of the pair from one of these entry points back to the average price relationship (mean reversion). The importance of following this discipline, rather than attempting to capture the move from one extreme of the range to the other, can be seen by considering the price action from late October to late December. During this period, the pair moved from the upper extreme of the range back to the average several times without passing through to the lower extreme. A disciplined trader could have profited from this price action several times during this two-month period, while a more aggressive trader would likely have realized little or no profit.

In order to help confirm the chart pattern evidence, a technical trader will consider a variety of technical indicators. The chart in Figure 17.6 depicts the identical price action of the pair as in Figure 17.5, but adds two technical indicators for consideration: the 10-day moving average and the 14-day relative strength index (RSI). The specific indicators used depend on the preferences of the manager, as do the specific periods; a 10- and 14-day indicator are used in this example because the manager has identified an approximate five-week trade duration from the fluctuations observed in the chart. Given the expected duration of the trade, the use of indicators with a slightly shorter time span is appropriate. The moving average serves to demonstrate to the manager that the price ratio of this pair has, in fact, pulled significantly below its average. Recall that moving average

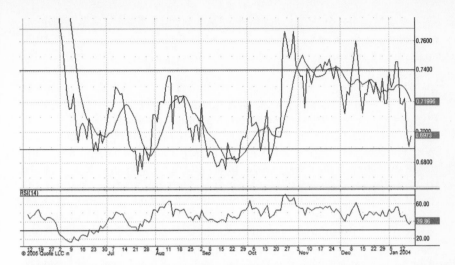

FIGURE 17.6 Price Ratio, Moving Average, and RSI for LLTC/KLAC

indicators serve as a proxy for the relative average price of the pair under consideration. A pair below its moving average will likely rise to its average as that average falls to meet it; a reading below the moving average is a confirmation indicator for mean reversion.

The other indicator that the manager considers is the RSI. This is an overbought/oversold indicator that tells the manager that the price action may be more positive or negative than is supported by the expected equilibrium in the market. If a pair is oversold, as is the case with LLTC/KLAC, this is a bullish sign that suggests the price ratio will rise. The converse is also true on the overbought side of the range for RSI. In the case of this trade, RSI is near an extreme, but, similar to the price action, has shown a small reversal at the end of the observed period. This can often indicate the reversal that a manager seeks for ideal entry into a pair. A price reversal supported by a reversal in RSI can often indicate that the mean reversion process has begun and entry into the pair is appropriate.

The Execution

Having analyzed the trade and determined it to be a good candidate for his portfolio, the manager must now execute the trade. Working with the same $400,000 dollar portfolio and 5 percent allocation as in the previous example, the manager initiates this as a dollar-neutral trade by purchasing 470 shares of LLTC (rounded down from 470.9 shares) and selling short 320 shares of KLAC (rounded down from 325.2 shares) using opening prices on January 16; the opening ratio is 0.691. There is no difference in execution between a fundamental or technical pairs trade; in either case, the short side of the trade should be completed prior to initiating the long side.

This trade has been given a profit objective of 0.72 and a stop-loss level of 0.66; the expected trade duration is five weeks. The profit objective is set at or near the average historical price relationship (AHPR), with special attention paid to the current level of the moving average. If the moving average is significantly below the AHPR, the manager may set the profit objective below the AHPR because this represents a downward trend in the average price. Likewise, if the moving average is above the AHPR, the profit objective may be set slightly higher. The stop-loss level should be set sufficiently far below the lower extreme of the price ratio range to allow for minor fluctuation outside of that range. The worst situation a trader faces is when his stop-loss triggers the close of a trade just prior to a positive price reversal. The technical pairs manager needs to provide adequate leeway to allow for some increased divergence without taking unnecessary risk.

Managing the Trade

After a trade has been opened, it is the manager's responsibility to monitor the trade, making updated adjustments to both profit objective and stop-loss levels, and to his opinion of the effect of technical factors. Figure 17.7 shows the chart of the trade on January 28, 12 days after the trade

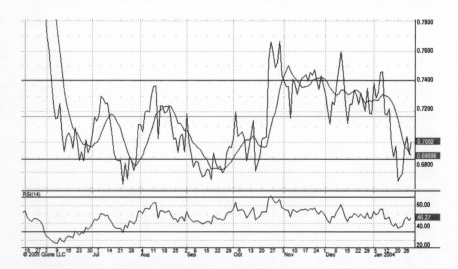

FIGURE 17.7   LLTC/KLAC Pairs Trade after 12 Days

was opened. The trade dipped outside of the historical range but recovered before it reached the stop-loss level. Of greater concern to the manager are the facts that the price ratio is now slightly above the moving average and the RSI reading is somewhat neutral. The trade has realized a slight profit and presents a less attractive picture than when it was opened. A conservative manager may wish to close the trade and look for another opportunity, while more aggressive managers will maintain that the trade is still within its acceptable range and wait.

The chart in Figure 17.8 represents that price action of the pair on February 13. As can be seen from the graph, the pair has moved through its profit objective all the way to the upper extreme of the range. This is another case in which the trade would likely have been closed prior to this move's completion, unless the manager chose to use a trailing stop. If a trailing stop was used in this case, the trade should be closed at this point for multiple reasons. The simplest of these reasons is that the trade has reached the end of its expected duration. As was explained in the previous example, while it is acceptable to violate the profit objective or stop-loss and the trade duration parameters, both should not be violated at the same time.

Aside from the fact that the trade has reached its expected duration, it should be closed as a result of both price action and technical indicator readings. On the 13th, the trade has reached the upper extreme of its trading range and should not be expected to experience any additional increases. Furthermore, the trade is now far outpacing its moving average

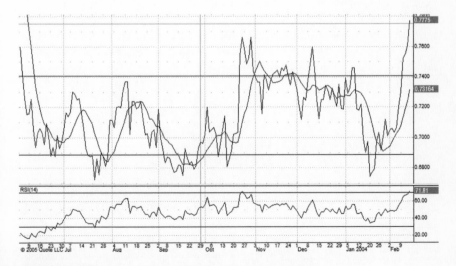

FIGURE 17.8   LLTC/KLAC Pairs Trade after Four Weeks

and has an extreme overbought RSI reading of over 70. Either of these factors would be sufficient to warrant the closing of this trade, but the combination of the two makes it necessary. The reason technical indicators are used is to give support to a manager's belief about the future price action of a pair. With a greater number of indicators that support his belief, in the absence of contradicting indicators, the manager may proceed with greater confidence. Technical indicators are used in combination for precisely this reason.

Exiting the Trade

As in the previous example, a manager may use simple market orders to close each leg of the pair; a profit objective should be observed intraday, while a stop should be considered only at the close. In the current example, this would indicate that if at any time the pair trades at or above 0.72 (the original profit objective) the trade should be closed. If the pair trades below 0.66 on an intraday basis but rises above that level prior to the close, the trade need not be closed. If, however, the pair trades below 0.66 and is likely to close there, the trade should be considered stopped-out and closed at the end of the trading day.

Technical trades differ from fundamental trades in a number of ways that affect how various levels are set and how the trade is exited. Technical trades tend to be shorter in duration and are wholly dependent on price action; therefore the stop-loss levels, particularly trailing stops, tend to be tighter than with fundamental trades. The shorter duration tends to lead to a lower profit objective because the trade simply does not have time to move as far; stop-losses are therefore adjusted accordingly to keep the risk/reward relationship properly intact. Additionally, because a technical trader is basing all of his decisions on price action, tighter stops help to protect against a steady decline caused by real, yet unknown, fundamental factors.

THE BLENDED APPROACH TRADE: APPLICATION OF THE UNIFIED THEORY

This example will most closely mirror the approach favored in the rest of this book and will be the foundation upon which future examples will build. The two companies being considered in this trade are JB Hunt (JBHT), on the long side, and Yellow Roadway (YELL), on the short side. Each of these companies is in the transportation sector and in the trucking industry; they make an appropriate pair because they will likely be similarly affected by market conditions and extrinsic factors. For the purpose of this example, it will be assumed that the manager has matched these two stocks based on a predetermined model or screening function, and that the pair meets his criteria. Having identified an acceptable candidate pair, the manager will subject it to both a fundamental and a technical screen.

The first step is to consider the pair as a simple output of whatever methodology is used to identify candidate pairs. The chart in Figure 17.9 shows this pair on April 4, the potential trade date of the pair. Upon initial observation, the pair appears acceptable; it trades within a relatively defined range, shows appropriate fluctuation within that range, is at or near one extreme of the range, and does not appear to be caught in a significant trend. This basic chart observation allows the manager to determine whether the pair warrants additional investigation. It is not uncommon to identify pairs that meet generally defined screening criteria but fail a simple chart study. In some cases the range is not clearly defined, while in others the chart reveals a clear trend that appears unlikely to reverse. Only after the pair has passed this cursory observation should a thorough analysis be conducted.

The second step, prior to the performance of the two overlays, is to add basic technical indicators to the chart and determine whether the pair still appears promising. While this may seem redundant, observing the pair without these indicators allows the manager to consider the pair free of the possible influence provided when the indicators are added. The addition of

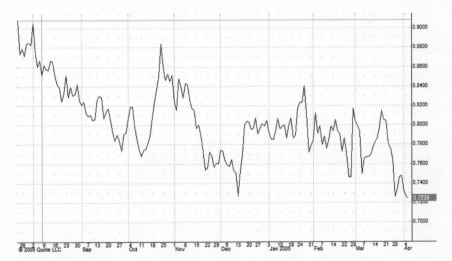

FIGURE 17.9 Candidate Pair for Blended Approach Trade: JBHT/YELL

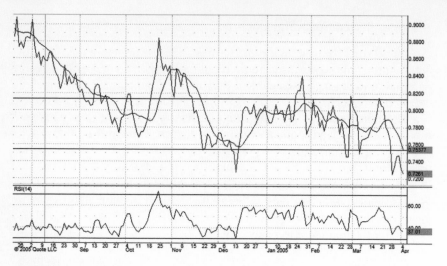

FIGURE 17.10   JBHT/YELL with Range Trend Lines, Moving Average, and RSI

technical indicators may then serve as confirmation or contradiction of the manager's original position. Figure 17.10 shows the chart of the pair with the addition of range trend lines, the 10-day moving average, and the 14-day RSI readings. In this case, the manager's opinion is confirmed. While the pair is trading below the definable range, there is a recent support level that adds conviction to the manager's position. Furthermore, the pair is trading near an extreme RSI reading and well below the near-term moving average. This combination of factors serves as confirmation that the model output and the cursory investigation have yielded an appropriate candidate pair that warrants further detailed analysis.

The Fundamental Overlay

In order to perform the fundamental overlay, the manager must be aware of his expected trade duration. In this case, based on the historical price action, the expected trade duration is set at four weeks. This is an important consideration because it defines the scope of the fundamental investigation. The manager is not concerned with potential fundamental events that are not scheduled to occur during this time period; announcements that occur beyond the anticipated duration are unlikely to have an effect on the trade. Recall that the purpose of the overlay is determine if any conditions are present that would preclude the manager from placing the trade.

For the purpose of this example, consider the following set of information collected from various sources as well as the information included in Table 17.1:

- February 28: Yellow Roadway to acquire USF Corporation for $1.47 billion (Associated Press).
- March 28: Yellow was upgraded by JP Morgan (Briefing.com).
- March 21: *Fortune* magazine names JB Hunt to Most Admired Companies list (*Business Wire*).
- JBHT has been consistently beating earnings.

This information is readily available and, while by no means exhaustive, provides sufficient data to make the needed observations. The first observation that can be made from the information provided is that YELL was recently upgraded by a major investment house. This is usually a bullish sign for a stock, and the manager is considering YELL for the short side of the trade. Additionally, YELL is in the midst of an expected merger, another factor that can cause price shocks in a given stock. Finally, on a pure P/E basis, JBHT is relatively expensive when compared with YELL. This combination of factors may be sufficient for some managers to reject

TABLE 17.1 Technical Overlay Information for Proposed JBHT/YELL Pairs Trade

TICKER		JBHT	YELL
Current price		43.69	59.69
EPS (trailing 12-month)		1.75	3.73
Estimated consensus EPS (current)		2.58	4.56
Estimated consensus EPS (next year)		2.91	5.06
One year ago EPS		2.16	4.09
Price/earnings ratio		24.69	15.87
PEG ratio		1.13	1.08
52-week high		50.05	64.04
52-week low		28.62	54.32
% difference from 52-week high		−13.8	−7.2
% difference from 52-week low		50.8	9.41
	1 month change	−4.14	−0.42
	% 1 month change	−8.75	−0.7
	3 month change	−0.94	−2.72
	% 3 month change	−2.13	−4.38
Beta		1.4	0.55
Dividend		0.48	NA
Dividend yield %		1.10	NA
Market capitalization (billions)		3.51	2.89
Average daily volume (millions)		0.81	1.59

this pair. The fundamental news on the short candidate is strong, one stock in the pair is involved in a potentially volatile merger, and the fundamental news on the long candidate is neutral. At this point the decision on whether to proceed with the pair is a matter of judgment, although it is likely influenced by the importance the manager puts on fundamental information. Technically minded managers may conclude that these facts are not sufficient to reject the trade, while fundamentally driven managers may take a different view. For the purpose of demonstration in this example, the pair will be considered to have passed inspection on the fundamental overlay.

The Technical Overlay

In order to perform the technical overlay, each stock must be considered independently. Figure 17.11 is the chart of JBHT for the period leading up to the potential trade date. From the technical perspective, this stock appears to be a very solid long candidate. It has recently experienced a notable pullback, which appears to be a correction in a significant uptrend. RSI readings are near extreme oversold levels and are at a recent low for this particular stock. The price action of the stock is below the near-term moving average and pressure is upward. Overall, the chart suggests that, while a reversal is possible, JBHT has both upward potential and bullish pressure. There is no technical data to suggest that this stock must be avoided as a long candidate.

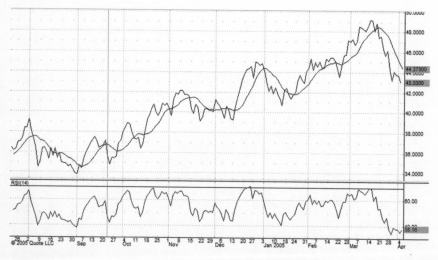

FIGURE 17.11 JBHT Price Action, Moving Average, and RSI

The chart of YELL is displayed in Figure 17.12. This chart presents a somewhat neutral picture, trading at the near-term moving average and in the middle of the RSI range. The general trend is upward, but the lower-high and lower-low price action suggests a reversal. While it is difficult to get a good technical read on this stock from either the chart pattern or the technical indicators, the purpose of the overlay is to determine whether any factors are present that would eliminate the trade. While not of particular use, a fully neutral reading on the technical overlay is not sufficient to eliminate the trade from consideration. There is no technical data that suggests that this stock must be eliminated as a short candidate.

The manager must now view the results of the overlays within the context of the overall situation. While neither overlay presented a sufficient reason to reject this pair, he must decide whether the combination of the overlays, when considered in juxtaposition to his initial analysis, provides reason to reject the pair. This process is highly subjective and involves the use of experience and judgment. The manager is seeking to discover if the whole of his analysis is greater than the sum of its parts. If the manager is uncomfortable with the trade at any level, it should be rejected. In this case, it will be assumed that the manager did not find sufficient cause to reject the trade and is prepared to move to execution.

The Execution

Having analyzed the trade and deemed it a good candidate for his portfolio, the manager must now execute the trade. Working with the same

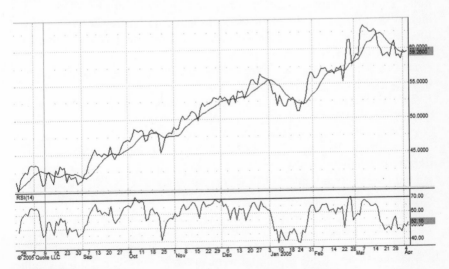

FIGURE 17.12 YELL Price Action, Moving Average, and RSI

$400,000 dollar portfolio and 5 percent allocation as in the prior examples, the manager initiates this as a dollar-neutral trade by purchasing 460 shares of JBHT (rounded up from 457.7 shares) and selling short 340 shares of YELL (rounded up from 335.1 shares), using closing prices on April 3; the opening ratio is 0.732. Again, the short side of the trade should be completed prior to initiating the long side.

This trade has been given a profit objective of 0.78 and a stop-loss level of 0.70; the expected trade duration is four weeks. As with the previous trade, the profit objective is set at or near the average historical price relationship (AHPR), with special attention paid to the current level of the moving average. If the moving average is significantly below the AHPR, the manager may set the profit objective below the AHPR because this represents a downward trend in the average price. Likewise, if the moving average is above the AHPR, the profit objective may be set slightly higher. The stop-loss level should be set sufficiently far below the lower extreme of the price ratio range to allow for minor fluctuation outside of that range. Because this pair is already trading somewhat outside of its historical range, the stop-loss should be set more tightly than it would otherwise. This level will need to be carefully monitored because if the pair continues to decline, it may signify the onset of a new range and be difficult to predict.

Managing the Trade

After a trade has been opened, the manager must continue to monitor it, making updated adjustments to both profit objective and stop-loss levels, and to his opinion of the effect of technical factors. Figure 17.13 shows the chart of the trade on April 11, one week after the trade was opened. The trade has well surpassed its profit objective and would have been closed by some managers. Those using a trailing stop approach will note that the pair is trading well above its moving average and that, while the RSI reading is not yet at the extreme high end of the range, it has risen dramatically since the trade was opened.

Further investigation into the price action of this pair will reveal that the success of the pair is largely fundamental. On April 7, USF Corporation, the company to be acquired by YELL, announced lower than expected earnings and guided lower for the upcoming quarter. This had a doubly negative effect on the price of YELL because not only did it call into question the valuation agreed to in the merger, the prudence of management was also called into question. What should be noted in this example is that despite the fact that the technical argument most integrally led to the execution of this trade, the fundamental effects were more significant. In such cases, there should be an increased sensitivity on the part of

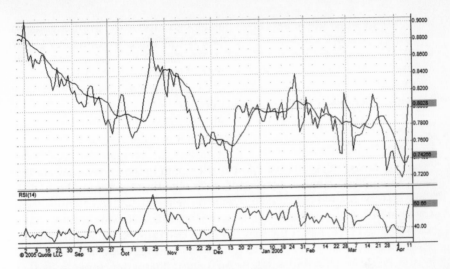

FIGURE 17.13 JBHT/YELL Trade after One Week

the manager to the drivers of the price action. While YELL may continue to decline, with very favorable results for the pair, fundamental price shocks may reverse equally quickly and profits should be protected.

The chart in Figure 17.14 confirms that the manager was right to remain in the trade and participate in a movement of a strong and steady price trend. This chart pictures the trade on April 18, at which time the

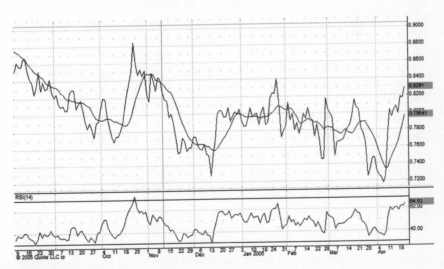

FIGURE 17.14 JBHT/YELL Trade after Two Weeks—a Good Exit Point

price ratio is 0.829 (an increase of 13.26 percent from the opening ratio of the trade). At this point the trade should be closed regardless of the price trend. While the pair has continued to rise, the price action has slowed and reached certain key resistance levels. The trade duration has not expired, but with an aggressive profit in place, the result of unexpected fundamental volatility, safety should outweigh greed.

Exiting the Trade

Again, a manager may use simple market orders to close each leg of the pair, remembering that a profit objective should be observed intraday, while a stop should be considered only at the close. In this example, if at any time the pair trades at or above 0.78 (the original profit objective) the trade should be closed. If the pair trades below 0.70 on an intraday basis, but rises above that level prior to the close, the trade need not be closed. If, however, the pair trades below 0.70 and is likely to close there, the trade should be considered stopped-out and closed at the end of the trading day.

USING OPTIONS

In order to provide the reader with some additional insights into the use of options, the most recent example, the trade of JB Hunt versus Yellow Roadway, will be considered using both an options overlay and a simple substitution approach. The objective of each strategy is different and thus leads to opposite results. This distinction is very clear when analyzed looking back in time, but at the moment of execution there are strong arguments for either approach. It is important to note that neither position is more legitimate than the other, but given the resulting price action, one approach is more profitable.

The Overlay

A manager familiar with options theory, when analyzing this trade, may have chosen to include an options overlay. The fact that YELL was in the midst of a corporate merger introduces a risk factor that can be hedged to protect against the possibility of a significant surge in the price of the stock. In order to create the overlay hedge, the manager will buy calls of YELL. There will be a cost associated with this approach, but if the stocks runs up, the losses that would result from being on the short side will be hedged with an offsetting gain in the options. It is important for the manager to keep in mind that the purpose of an options overlay is to protect a trade, not to enhance its profitability. While in some cases the net effect of this approach may be a greater profit than with an un-hedged trade, if the original analysis is correct, the overlay will be a drag on performance.

The equity trade previously described involves the purchase of 460 shares of JBHT and the short sale of 340 shares of YELL. In order to hedge the short side of the trade, the manager will purchase four May $60 calls on YELL. It is at the discretion of the manager to approximate the appropriate number of options contracts (either three or four contracts in this case), but because of the low relative cost, most managers will err on the side of too many contracts rather than too few. After execution, the manager will hold the following positions for this pair:

Long 460 shares of JBHT

Short 340 shares of YELL

Long 4 May $60 calls YELL

The manager could choose to use May $55 calls rather than calls at the 60 strike price, depending on the level of caution desired. The May $55 calls are already trading ITM, so the resulting change in the price of these options for every $1 of change in the price of the stock will be closer to $1 (delta near 1) than for the May $60 calls. The ITM options will be significantly more expensive, however, and the manager may not wish to bear the additional cost. It most cases, the OTM options are a more appropriate choice because the overlay is designed to protect against a significant loss. In an ideal situation, the options will not be a factor in the underlying trade and will simply serve as an insurance policy; in this case, the cheaper options have less of a negative impact on performance.

As noted earlier, the corporate merger did not cause a rise in the price of YELL, but rather served as the catalyst for its decline. The options overlay turned out to be an unnecessary precaution, but one that was not unreasonable for a careful manager. The chart in Figure 17.15 shows the price action of the YELL May $60 calls from the day of execution through the day the trade was exited. From the graph, it can be determined that the initial cash outlay required to purchase the options was $700 ($1.75 × 100 × 4 contracts). When the trade was closed on April 18, the options were trading at $0.15. The net loss that resulted from the use of this strategy was $640 (($1.75 − $0.15) × 100 × 4), or approximately 25 percent of the gain that would have resulted if no overlay was used. The options are not sold until the trade is closed because in situations like this one, sharp reversals may require the use of the hedge later in the duration. In cases

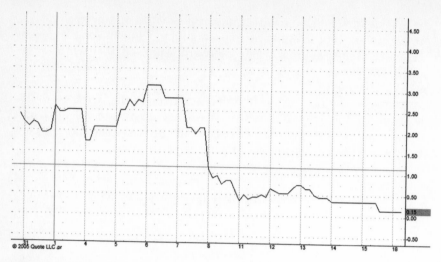

FIGURE 17.15 Price Action of YELL May $60 Calls

involving earnings reports, the hedge may be closed shortly after the announcement because no further price action is likely.

Several conclusions may be drawn from this example that give solid insight into the use of this approach. The scenario just described represents the worst-case outcome for this strategy if it is assumed that the trade is not stagnant. Other possible outcomes include a run-up by YELL that would be hedged in this case and protect against losses, and a run-up by JBHT with little movement by YELL. In the latter case, the price of the options would change very little and be closed for a modest loss. While it is up to the individual manager's discretion to determine if the potential drag on performance is sufficiently offset by the protection afforded by the overlay, over time, the performance drag in situations like the one in this example will be at least offset by the protection that is received. When an identifiable risk factor is present that may be hedged, the prudent manager will hedge, even at the expense of some performance.

Options Substitution

Rather than using an options overlay as described above, an options-savvy manager may wish to use a simple substitution to create a pairs trade. Staying with the same example base trade, an option substitution would involves buying calls on JBHT and buying puts on YELL to create the desired pair exposure. Recall that this trade involved the purchase of 460 shares of JBHT and the short sale of 340 shares of YELL. To create

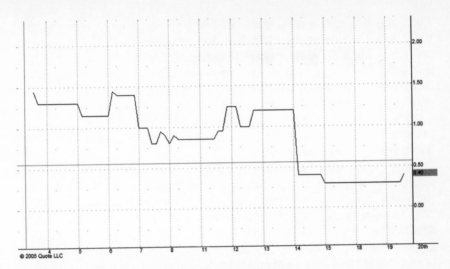

FIGURE 17.16 Price Action of JBHT May $45 Calls

the options version of the trade, the manager buys five JBHT May $45 calls and buys four YELL May $60 puts. These options are selected because the manager believes they combine the most aggressive mix of exposure and affordability.

The charts in Figures 17.16 and 17.17 show the price action of these two contracts over the duration of the trade. At execution on April 4, the

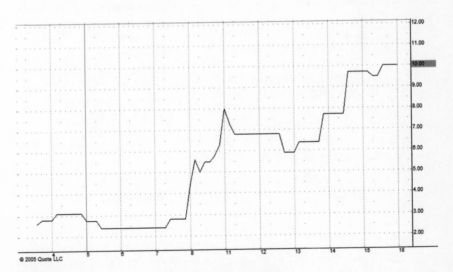

FIGURE 17.17 Price Action of YELL May $60 Puts

JBHT May $45 calls were trading at $1.30 for a net debit of $650 ($1.30 × 100 × 5 contracts) and the YELL May $60 puts were trading at $2.80 for a net debit of $1,120 ($2.80 × 100 × 4 contracts). The net investment in this pair is $1,770. The manager's net exposure to the market is immediately limited to the premium paid for the combination of options; this represents 8.85 percent of the cost of one leg on the trade using equities, or 4.425 percent if the equity trade is fully paid. The maximum loss in the trade is now limited to under 5 percent if options are used, compared to limitless risk in the equity trade.

If the trade were held until April 18, the closing date in the equity example, the net profit can be calculated from the graphs. JBHT May $45 calls were trading at $0.40 for a loss of $0.90 per contract or $450. YELL May $60 puts were trading at $10.00 for a gain of $7.20 per contract or $2,880. The net profit on the trade is $2,430 or 37.29 percent; this a much larger percent gain and only a slightly smaller dollar gain than would have been achieved in a pure equity pairs trade. Furthermore, the option substitution provided a level of downside protection not available in the equity trade, adding to its appeal. This is obviously a bit of an extreme case because so much of the performance of the trade was driven by a significant move in YELL rather than a combination of the two. This example does, however, demonstrate the potential rewards that can be associated with the use of options.

CONCLUSION

In this chapter, three equity trades and two options have been presented to the reader in an attempt to solidify the theory discussed in this book. It is the author's hope that these examples have provided sufficient substance to allow the would-be pairs trader to transition from theory to practice. By applying the methods described in these pages, a trader or manager may begin the process of both developing his distinctive style and building the foundation on which to execute a successful portfolio. While these examples are but a glimpse of the various complexities that may be added to the unified theory, they should afford the reader a place to begin.

Epilogue

It is the sincere desire of this author to provide the reader with sufficient tools to successfully begin managing his own pairs portfolio. This work has been an attempt to combine the critical substance of the author's knowledge and experience into a medium that would be useful to seasoned professionals as well as novice practitioners. Pairs trading is simultaneously a simple, elegant approach to portfolio management and a complex, intertwined matrix of pieces of other disciplines. The reader is encouraged to use these pages as a reference tool when pursuing this strategy and to avail himself of the vast resources available beyond this book.

Screen shots and simplified explanations of the various software packages available have not been included. Instead, the reader is encouraged to use those programs to which he has access and with which he is comfortable. Pairs trading, like any serious field, is always changing as new products come to market to aid the manager and focus his efforts. It is important to recognize that the dynamics of a changing system must be recognized in time to effectively integrate them into one's broader understanding.

One web site that the author does recommend to readers is Pair Trader.com. This web site provides visitors with a vase array of resources that can aid in the successful implementation of a pairs strategy. Having recently merged with PairsTrading.com, the other industry-leading site dedicated to this discipline, PairTrader.com offers services ranging from pairs trading newsletters and software to full-blown training, supervision, and a proprietary trading desk. While clearly not for everyone, this site provides useful tools that can benefit anyone who has read this book.

About the Author

Douglas S. Ehrman is a hedge fund manager and a leading authority on pairs trading. He is one of the founders and the CEO of Alph America Asset Management LLC in Chicago. He also served as the CEO of AlphAmerica Financial, Inc., the company that operated PairsTrading.com. Mr. Ehrman's research is now featured through Pair Trader.com with enhanced infrastructure and additional trading tools.

Mr. Ehrman holds several securities licenses and held several positions with prominent investment firms prior to launching his own enterprise. He has been a featured speaker at several investment conferences, is the editor of a daily research newsletter, and has been a guest on the CNN Financial Network to discuss pairs trading and market-neutral strategies.

Mr. Ehrman graduated cum laude from Lake Forest College with special honors in both economics and philosophy in 1998.

Index

An Invitation

If you are looking for a trading career or business, and need capital or professional mentoring, contact PairCo Capital Holdings, LLC (PCH).

PCH sponsors traders, providing them with sufficient capital to trade pairs and related strategies. Sponsored traders benefit from automated programs, tools, data and resources provided through www.pairtrader.com. This valuable information is available the investing public for a small monthly charge.

Mentoring courses have benefited many people around the world whether new to trading, young or old. There are different formats available to accommodate traders in a variety of situations. Some of the topics addressed in mentoring and workshops are:

- Mechanics of Pair Trading
- Risk Arbitrage
- Money Management & Optimized Capital Allocation
- A Business Plan for Each Pair
- Union of Technical Analysis & Fundamentals
- Opening Orders with Pairs
- 3-way, 4-way, & 6-way combinations
- Basket Trading
- Tape Reading & Enveloping
- Automating Pair & Related Strategies
- Value Pair Investing
- Spreads for Relative Strength Trading

For information regarding courses, website subscriptions, programs, or sponsorship, contact info@pairtrader.com

Save $200!

on a
PairCo Full Mentoring Course or Automated Program*
and
Receive Two *Free* Months of www.pairtrader.com

*$200 off any programs listed at $750 and above.